ORGANIZATION MATTERS

Agency Problems in Health and Education in Latin America

William D. Savedoff

Editor

Distributed by The Johns Hopkins University Press
for the Inter-American Development Bank

Washington, D.C.
1998

Cataloging-in-Publication data provided by the
Inter-American Development Bank
Felipe Herrera Library

Organization Matters: agency problems in health and education in Latin America/
William D. Savedoff, editor.

   p. cm
   Includes bibliographical references.
   ISBN: 1886938199

   1.Human services—Latin America. 2.Education—Latin America. 3.Education and
state—Latin America. 4.Public health administration—Latin America. 5.Medical
policy—Latin America. 6.Latin America—Social policy. I.Savedoff, William D.
II.Inter-American Development Bank.

361.61 O85—dc21   98-74216

ORGANIZATION MATTERS

Agency Problems in Health and Education in Latin America

Produced by the IDB Publications Section
Distributed by The Johns Hopkins University Press
2715 North Charles Street
Baltimore, Maryland 21218-4319

The views and opinions expressed in this publication are those of the authors and do not
necessarily reflect the official position of the Inter-American Development Bank.

Contents

The Latin American Research Network

The Inter-American Development Bank created the Latin American Research Network in 1991 in order to strengthen policy formulation and contribute to the institutional reform agenda in Latin America. Through a competitive bidding process, the network provides grant funding to leading Latin American research centers to conduct studies on economic and social issues selected by the Bank in consultation with the region's development community. All of the studies are comparative, which allows the Bank to build its knowledge base and draw on lessons from experiences in macroeconomic and financial policy, modernization of the state, regulation, poverty and income distribution, social services and employment. The individual country studies are available as Working Papers in the IDB Bookstore (e-mail: idb-books@iadb.org). For more information about the Latin American Research Network, visit the Bank on the internet at www.iadb.org/oce.

Acknowledgments

The studies presented in this book were financed by the Latin American Research Network Program of the Inter-American Development Bank. Ricardo Hausmann provided the initial insights and impulse for the project by drafting the terms of reference, collaborating on the design of the proposals, and participating in discussions on the various projects. His continuing guidance and input have been greatly appreciated. Claudio de Moura Castro and Juan Luis Londoño served on the selection panel, participated in the seminars, and reviewed many of the studies. Special thanks to Claudia Piras for her review of the proposals, support in the seminars, and insightful and timely comments. Helpful comments and suggestions were also received from Ruthanne Deutsch, Anne-Marie Smith, Daniel Maceira, Philip Musgrove and many others who took part in the seminars and workshops. Norelis Betancourt, Cristina Echavarren, and Graciela Thomen managed critical phases of the project, while Leticia Cuevas provided valuable assistance.

The authors of the country studies also wish to thank the following people for their assistance: Josefina Bruni-Celli, Adriana Cassoni, Anabel Castillo, Manuel Cocco, Rosana Fernández, Ramón Flores, Eduardo García Michel, Rosa Amelia González, Carlos Grau, Gerardo la Forgia, Osvaldo Larrañaga, José Luis Londoño, Veronica Loyola, Katie Makhlouf and Patricia Márquez.

Foreword

After a decade of reforms, Latin Americans are still dissatisfied with the payoffs—whether measured by economic growth or income distribution. Yet it has become apparent that the fault does not lie with the economic reforms themselves. In fact, the removal of protection and the achievements of price stability have laid bare a number of other features that are restraining growth and harming social conditions. One is the poor performance of social service systems in the region. Without rapid progress in education, training, health and social security, Latin America is likely to continue to lag behind other regions in both growth and equity.

This book takes a bold step toward understanding social service systems by demonstrating that the critical differences in performance are related to the way responsibilities are delegated to different agents and how these agents are held accountable. The studies bypass the debate over decentralization and privatization. Instead, they explore the more fundamental questions of organization that hold the key to more propitious behavior by governments, service providers and citizens.

This book also represents the first in a new series of Latin American Research Network studies administered by the Office of the Chief Economist of the Inter-American Development Bank. The goal of the series is to produce top-quality applied research into policy questions important to Latin America, strengthen the capacity of the region's applied policy research, and complement the Bank's other activities to promote economic and social development in the region. In this latter regard, the book crystallizes elements of the policy dialogue between the Bank and its member countries, and builds on other Bank studies, including the special section, "Making Social Services Work", of the 1996 Report on *Economic and Social Progress in Latin America.*

Ricardo Hausmann
Chief Economist
Inter-American Development Bank

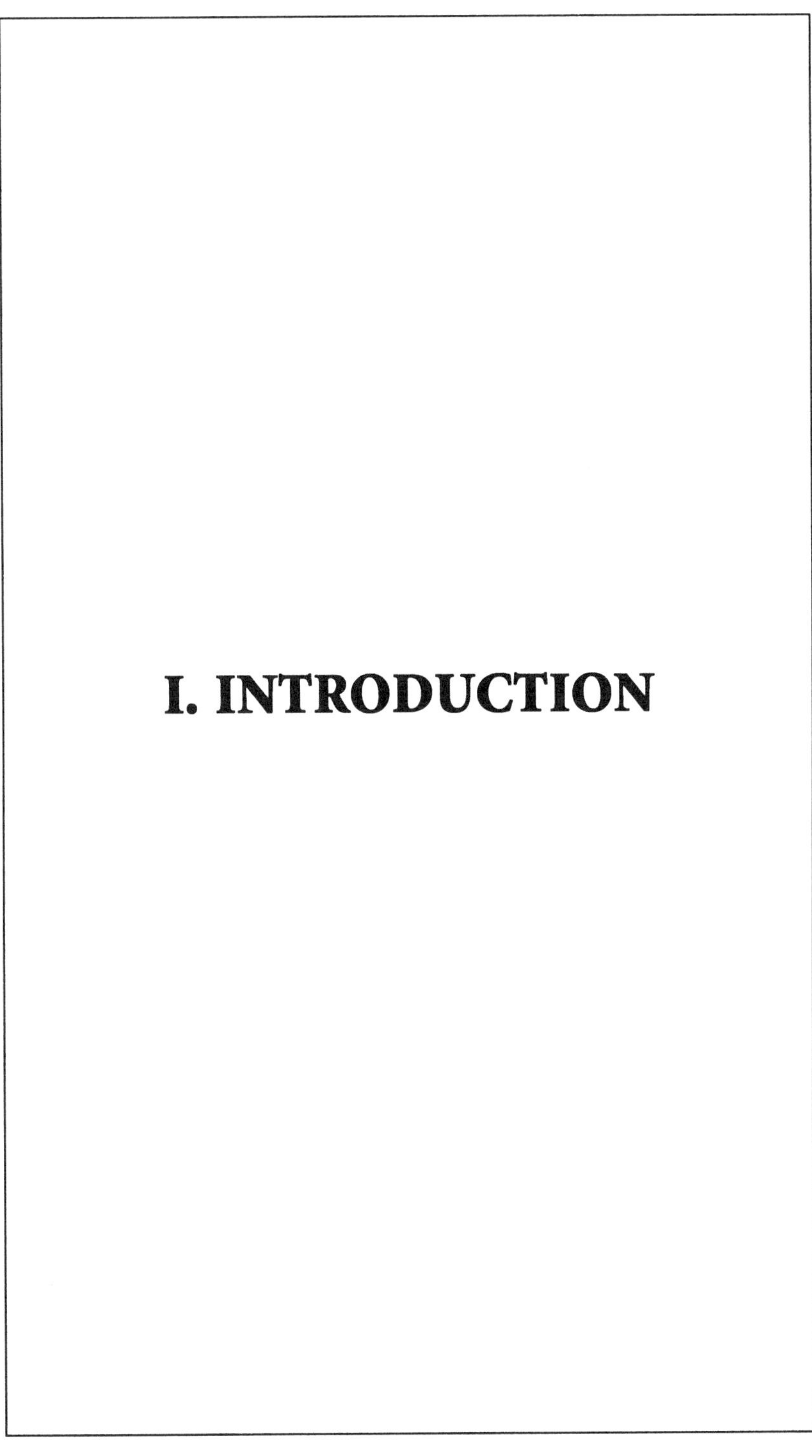

I. INTRODUCTION

CHAPTER 1

Social Services Viewed Through New Lenses

William D. Savedoff[1]

Health and education systems in Latin America have made dramatic strides in increasing literacy and reducing mortality and morbidity over the last thirty years. Nevertheless, the region expends large amounts of resources in these services, occupies a large share of its skilled human resources, and fails to perform as would be expected given its level of income.[2] The diagnoses of inefficiency and inequity are ubiquitous and the recommendations are generally quite clear: the systems need to be open to pedagogical and medical innovation, provide sufficient complementary inputs, and maintain facilities. In the case of education, teachers need improved formal and in-service training, better working conditions, and adequate leadership and support. In health, care needs to be shifted toward preventive medicine, and access to care needs to be increased.

Knowing all this, however, fails to explain why the region systematically lacks in-service training, books or maintenance. Attributing these failures to weak bureaucracies or political interference are facile explanations that confuse symptoms with causes. Instead, analysis of the organization of social service systems in terms of the delegation of functions and the system's mechanisms for coordinating individual decisions can lead to practical recommendations that address fundamental flaws. Such recommendations can have an impact in the short run, by reorienting the incentives that motivate service providers, consumers, and policymakers. They can also af-

---

[1] Senior Research Economist, Office of the Chief Economist, Inter-American Development Bank.

[2] See Inter-American Development Bank (1996) and Londoño (1996b).

fect the long run by establishing dynamics that strengthen groups and individuals with the greatest interest in positive performance.

The essays in this book grew out of a recognition of these issues as they have come to be debated in Latin America, and they seek to apply a framework that is relatively new to the fields of education and health in the region. This first chapter proposes a method of analysis that relies upon theories of the firm and of agency. In the subsequent chapters, authors have chosen at least two education or health systems to compare within a particular country. The comparisons demonstrate the ways that differences in organization affect performance, creating incentives and accountability mechanisms that impact on education and health conditions.

Missteps Along the Way

The assembly line in factory production has long been the classic example of how organization can affect performance, from Adam Smith's rendering of the division of labor in a pin-making shop, to the Ford assembly plants of the early 20th century. However, another classic story has emerged in explaining how General Motors surpassed Ford in mid-century.[3] Whereas Ford continued to produce homogeneous products within a highly hierarchical management structure, General Motors experimented with creating different divisions that could design different cars, interact with other divisions horizontally for a wide range of activities, and be compared one to another regarding their performance. This innovation in organization helped General Motors solve several problems simultaneously. Not only was it easier to monitor the performance of smaller production groups with independent output measures, but it became possible to measure a division's performance by comparing it to other divisions (since all were equally influenced by outside factors not "visible" to higher management). Secondly, the new organization forced divisions to face clear incentives regarding the timing and use of inputs. Third, the divisions had greater flexibility and could take advantage of decentralized information to make adjustments to the mix of inputs, and to the allocation of resources among different functions. Finally, the divisions themselves had a direct interest to innovate, seeking new market

---

[3] See Milgrom and Roberts (1992).

niches, developing new products and features, finding more cost-effective materials, and improving internal efficiency. Thus, General Motors was better able to respond to changing markets, reward innovation, and use decentralized information more effectively.

The education and health systems which emerged in Latin America in the middle of this century can be compared to the Ford model of service production. The aim was to create a homogeneous service for all citizens. And although an assembly line was the farthest thing from a model for education and health, the administrative structure to direct and manage these social services followed a similar logic: central management planned and directed the provision of services, allocated resources and distributed inputs.

Of course, unlike the automobile industry, education and health systems gave their services away for free. This left them with no competitive pressures to fight for clients, and no incentives to adapt or expand their output. Also, the public systems were so dominant in their sectors that they had monopsony power in employing teachers, doctors, nurses and other specialized personnel. Once employees unionized to confront this monopsony power, the resulting bilateral negotiations stiffened and restricted employment management practices. Furthermore, the package of pay and benefits was modified to respond to budgetary and administrative requirements, often keeping pay low but providing generous "off budget" benefits such as pensions and early retirement. This distortion in the payment package made it difficult to respond to changes in the labor market, as well as to attract and motivate high employee performance. Guaranteed public financing in these systems meant that the providers did not have to market their services, which insulated them from consumers. Meanwhile, the rigid employment contracts insulated providers from external accountability to the government.

The limitations of this model in Latin America have been explored and debated in numerous studies. However, the recommendations emerging from these debates have revolved around two incomplete and generally misleading concepts: decentralization and privatization. With rising dissatisfaction from centralized service systems, it was perhaps natural that the opposite would be considered an avenue for improvement. Theoretical support for decentralization came from literature which noted that public services can be provided more effectively when they are organized to serve groups with relatively homogeneous preferences. Research emphasized the lower costs of collecting and processing information for smaller areas or organizations. Further support came from the contention that local public officials would be more accountable for decisions affecting local conditions than national officials, who respond to a wider constituency. There seemed to be many potential gains from decentralized distribution of management, decisionmaking, and accountability.

However, equally strong critiques have been made of decentralization because it poses problems related to economies of scale, scope, equity and persistent political manipulation at different levels. First, the units of service production have to be large enough to capture certain scale economies. For example, it is not clear that most municipalities are in any position to run a health insurance scheme because that generally requires covering at least 100,000 people to be economically efficient. Second, the literature recognizes that services should be organized in large enough units to internalize externalities. Management of sewerage systems, for example, has to be organized in a way that addresses the impact of effluents from one community on another. Third, decentralized systems have the potential to be inequitable. Redistribution from one community to another is more difficult when financing and provision of services is self-contained within financially homogeneous communities. Finally, the advantages of local accountability may be offset by opportunities for local corruption. Local accountability clearly depends upon the strength of the political process and the distribution of power within a particular area. Decentralization does not necessarily resolve such problems.

Even if decentralization were an appropriate response to the problems of providing social services, its actual implementation in the last decade has had its share of problems. In many countries, decentralization as a political program has often been used to hide a continuance of centralized administration behind a screen of decentralized organizational charts. In some cases, the policy of decentralization has resulted in the creation of new administrative regions, justifying employing more bureaucratic staff. Furthermore, where decentralization has actually occurred, it has been unbalanced in the sense that functions or resources were delegated to lower levels of government without a fully articulated system to support, coordinate and moderate the actions of these many agents. Many articles have discussed the problems of decentralization in its "pure" form and the kinds of arrangements and assignments of functions that would best address the goals of public policy. But the policy debate, which has been fairly simplistic, has now responded with discussions of the need for "recentralization"—a particularly puzzling term since the focus ought to be on what functions are best discharged by whom, rather than letting the pendulum swing once more. Policy analysis needs a fuller appreciation of what makes a social service system function than the decentralization debate has been able to offer.

The other dichotomy that has clouded debate over the last decade has been the privatization of social services. Again, in seeking a new approach, the contrast with public systems led people to the private sector for solutions. This was also motivated by a recognition of certain gains from the private sector: incentives to reduce costs, increase output, and induce innovation. Private provision of services is supposed to reduce costs because it places an agent in a direct position to profit from providing service at a lower cost. This is in direct contrast to public services, where any innovation that reduces costs simply reduces pressure on a government agency budget, i.e., no one in particular gets a large benefit. Private provision also holds the promise for expanding output of services because, again, the owners profit any time they can provide services to another person for whom the marginal payment exceeds the marginal cost of provision. By contrast, public managers do not necessarily receive extra budget for serving more clients, and certainly do not benefit in terms of their personal remuneration. Finally, a competitive private sector fosters innovation. Public bureaucracies find it difficult to take risks on new ways of providing services. If they make changes that fail, there are nationwide implications. Small private firms, however, can take risks that generate information and new technology without jeopardizing the system as a whole.

When using their broadest strokes, advocates of privatization paint a picture that fails to recognize its limitations. First, private firms respond directly to effective demand, not to broadly stated social or community goals. Therefore, privatizing social services still entails public financing and subsidies. Second, market efficiency requires that consumers be well-informed and able to exercise their option among providers. But the quality of different education and health providers is not necessarily apparent, and switching from one service to another may be costly. Third, the risk of private providers failing for financial reasons is more problematic for social services than for normal consumer products because of long-term commitments in education or insurance commitments in health.

The debates and analyses surrounding privatization have also been misleading and incomplete. They have been misleading because they focus on private or public ownership as the critical factor when in fact many public systems also have competitive pressures and incentives for efficiency. In other words, many of the advantages ascribed to private provision do not necessarily require private ownership. General Motors solved many of the problems faced by public service systems—imperfect monitoring, weak incentives and little innovation—by creating "internal" markets between its divisions, while retaining full ownership. In the same way, many social service systems have introduced changes that mimic the private sector without eliminating public "ownership." Countries as diverse as Sweden, France and the United States have modified social services using performance budgeting, competition and efficiency pricing to reap the rewards of these "market" mechanisms within wholly publicly-owned and operated systems.

The debates around privatization have also been incomplete because they have not sufficiently addressed the contextual issues that can make a privately operated system serve the public interest.[4] It is widely agreed that private provision of social services requires regulation, but the character and content of that regulation is still poorly understood. Such regulation would have to address traditional regulatory issues such as anti-trust enforcement, minimum service or disclosure standards, and limits on adverse selection in insurance, as well as new areas such as the redistributive impact of a highly decentralized process.

The debates over decentralization and privatization have created many missteps along the way toward better health and education systems. Nevertheless, they have yielded valuable analyses and motivated several experiments in the region that go beyond simplistic levels of discussion. In these cases, they addressed issues essential to social service provision: the problems of agency and regulation.

New Lenses: Theories of the Firm and Agency

Once the diversions created by the debate over decentralization and privatization are set aside, a more complete framework can be used to analyze and

---

[4] Studies that give more nuanced perspectives include van der Gaag (1995) and Zuckerman and de Kadt (1997).

make recommendations for social service systems. A useful framework is provided by the extensive literature on industrial organization and its various branches. As in the comparison of General Motors and Ford, many studies have illuminated the principles underlying effective forms of organizing public and private firms. These include issues related to delegation, transaction costs, and the relative efficiency of hierarchical and horizontal arrangements. Other studies have focused on how to improve the social outcomes of the interaction of firms within the market, addressing questions of monopoly power, information and regulation.

The organization of firms has evolved significantly from their characterization by simple production function, as is found in neoclassical texts, toward models that view firms as a nexus of implicit or explicit contracts. This view does not necessarily supplant the neoclassical model, for its main areas of inquiry relate to allocation and market efficiency. It is, however, essential to investigate such important social and economic questions regarding the size of firms, mobilization of financing, sources of innovation, and externalities of the workplace. The literature has analyzed the firm as an institutional arrangement that reduces transaction costs, establishes a nexus of contracts, generates and economizes information, or results from cooperative games.[5] A common aspect of all these models is that they open the "black box" of the firm and analyze behavior of agents within it in relation to one another and the external environment. A number of particular relationships have received extensive analysis, such as the implicit contracts between employers and employees and the potential divergence between the actions of managers and the interests of shareholders.[6]

Another part of the industrial organization literature has focused on the interaction between firms and whether this interaction is socially optimal. The classic problem in this literature is its dealings with natural monopolies, leading to prescriptions for efficient regulation of a single firm. The literature demonstrates how the introduction of competition can improve social welfare, either by forcing potential producers to bid for a franchise (in cases with ever decreasing average costs) or by enforcing anti-trust provi-

---

[5] See Williamson (1971, 1985); Jenson and Meckling (1976); and Aoki (1984).

[6] For implicit contracts between employers and employees see Azariadis (1975); for manager-shareholder issues, see Lambert and Larcker (1985); for a textbook treatment of these issues see Milgrom and Roberts (1992).

sions to maintain a competitive market (in cases where scale economies are modest relative to the market).[7]

Applying the insights from this literature to social services has shown that there are two related ways that organization affects performance. The first is related to the theory of the firm and in particular the concept of *agency*—how society delegates functions in its social service systems. The second is related to the literature on regulation and focuses on the distributional implications of different forms of organization, along with the policies to address them.

Agency in Social Services

With any kind of division of labor comes the delegation of certain responsibilities. Economists have demonstrated that under common conditions, any time one person (denoted the *principal*) delegates a function to another (denoted the *agent*), certain problems emerge.

In its simplest form, the outcome of delegating responsibility to an agent will be inefficient whenever (i) there is a divergence between the objectives of the principal and the agent, and (ii) the principal and agent have different information about events (asymmetric information).[8] Consider the example of a principal who wants to hire an agent to produce goods. The principal's objective may be to maximize output, but the agent may want to minimize effort, i.e., a difference in objectives. If on top of this, the principal cannot directly observe the agent's effort in production (i.e., asymmetric information), it becomes difficult to know whether output is being maximized.[9] If the principal offers the agent a fixed payment for time spent on the job, the agent has very little incentive to put in any more effort than is required to avoid being "caught" shirking. If at the other extreme, the principal offers to pay the agent on the basis of output alone, the agent has a large incentive to expand output, but only by assuming the risk for condi-

---

[7] See Laffont and Tirole (1993).

[8] Models can also be developed where the information asymmetry is generated or compounded by uncertainty. However, uncertainty is not sufficient as long as the principal can observe that the agent is fully applying the contracted level of effort.

[9] For greater discussion of the principal-agent problem, see Milgrom and Roberts (1992) and Spremann (1989).

tions outside the agent's control that may affect output (e.g., material inputs not arriving on time, weather). The simple principal-agent problem can be compounded by the introduction of multiple principals.[10] In such cases, a particular principal is not only trying to hire an agent, but has to worry about the impact of other principals on the agent's behavior. This is an issue for the government when it hires people to staff its regulatory agencies who can be influenced by the regulated industry when it implicitly offers future employment possibilities.[11] It occurs in the health care sector when doctors are paid by insurers but chosen by patients.[12] In fact, social service systems are highly complex and involve multiple principal-agent relationships: voters and government officials, political leaders and bureaucrats, ministries and staff members, managers and doctors, school principals and teachers, parents and schools, hospitals and medical staff, and doctors and patients, to name just a few.

In social service systems, societies have developed a range of structures, with varying degrees of incentives and accountability to solve these problems. But difficulties remain. The most obvious solution is for the principal to simply order the agent to do exactly what needs to be done. Although never fully realized in practice, this approach is implicit in many of the centralized health and education ministries of Latin America and the Caribbean. However, this option is limited in several ways (as frequently discovered by many organizations). First, the principal may not have all the information he or she needs to make proper decisions. Hence, resources for repairing hospital roofs or distributing books may not arrive at the right place when they are needed. Second, the principal may not be able to observe the agent's actions. It is very costly to monitor geographically dispersed agents to be certain they are complying with the principal's orders. Third, the principal may not be able to attribute the outcomes to the actions of agents. The resulting test scores of students reflect more than just the effort of their teachers, just as a patient's health is affected by other conditions beyond the intervention of medical personnel.

Consequently, any division of responsibilities necessarily involves giving discretion to the agent. But if the principal is clever, he or she can orga-

---

[10] See Stiglitz (1985).

[11] See Spiller (1990).

[12] See Ellis and McGuire (1993).

nize the system—with incentives and accountability—in ways that encourage the agent to do things that are more in line with the principal's own objectives.

One example is to *reward outputs rather than inputs*. Measuring some form of output and linking it to an agent's pay or status creates an incentive for greater productivity. The Chilean education system establishes that public funds will go to schools largely on the basis of student attendance. The more students attend, the more resources are allocated. Consequently, schools have an incentive to attract and retain students. They are held accountable to the degree that parents pay attention to school test scores and reputation, choosing among schools on the basis of their perception of performance. In the health sector, numerous studies demonstrate that doctors who are paid a fee for each service they perform are much more "productive," in the sense that they provide more services than doctors who are on fixed salaries. Medical providers who receive payments for the number of clients they serve also have an incentive to seek out new patients. Such an incentive scheme has been used effectively in Colombia to expand health service coverage for poorer citizens.

The principal can also *increase the accountability* of the agent. This requires several related actions: delegating authority to the agent, generating information about the agent's outputs (or activities), and giving oversight to an interested party. A recent education program in the Brazilian state of Minas Gerais demonstrates all three of these features. Primary schools have been given financial autonomy over their nonpayroll budgets. This means they can allocate resources according to their knowledge of local conditions and priorities; for example, deciding whether it is more important to paint the classrooms or buy new maps. Alongside this increased autonomy, the state has also established standardized examinations to measure and compare school performance over time (adjusted for socioeconomic conditions and other factors). Since it is too costly for the state education department to review these test results and monitor school performance on a daily basis, the state also established community councils (*colegiados*). The councils are composed of parents, teachers and community representatives, and have the authority to audit school spending, set the local budget, and deal with some personnel issues. The creation of the *colegiado* is a more efficient solution to the state's difficulty in monitoring performance, since the community has its own direct interest in schools that function well.

Another important instrument to increase accountability is *contests between providers.* Organizations as different as the Chilean education system, General Motors and the Swedish health system have all introduced contests of one form or another between different service providing units. Sometimes these contests take the more limited form of publishing information about relative performance, in other cases they involve competition between divisions or service providers to attract clients. Such contests are useful because they can help generate information, encourage innovation, and reward good performance.

One of the key advantages of systems with contests between providers is their capacity to generate information. Agents that are more autonomous and accountable can justifiably be compared to one another. The school or hospital in such a situation can no longer plead ignorance of its budget or of the kinds and number of services it provides. Instead, the providers have a direct interest in collecting, organizing and providing information that demonstrates their worth. That way, they can argue for continued support from their constituency. They also have a clearly defined responsibility to provide the services for which they receive their budgets and salaries.

Second, greater pluralism means that service providers—managers, teachers, and doctors—can have both the capacity and interest to innovate and experiment. Because they have authority to make decisions and adaptations, they have the capacity to introduce changes that may make their own work easier or more productive. And because they are subject to evaluation and comparison with other providers, the implicit rivalry can generate an interest in learning from groups that have solved similar problems or discovered more effective methods. By monitoring such variations, public policymakers can also detect and disseminate better ways of teaching or improving health.

Third, contests can be particularly effective when used to reward or sanction performance. Systems that are fully public, with no consumer choice, can still use contests to highlight which schools or medical plans have achieved targets or performed better than their peers. When such contests are tied to budget discussions, they can set the stage for negotiating performance improvements and evaluating managers and teams.

Public systems that include explicit mechanisms for exercising consumer choice, such as the Chilean education system or the Colombian health plan, make even stronger use of the "rewards and sanctions" side of contests.

When consumers can choose among providers, feedback regarding performance comes directly from the registration or exit of students and patients. The payment mechanism assures that the ones who attract more clients are rewarded, and those who lose clients are penalized. Furthermore, this kind of responsiveness encourages dimensions of service quality (such as "service with a smile") that are impossible to legislate or monitor bureaucratically.

The advantages of pluralistic systems that include contests are best realized under certain conditions related to information and collusion. Information is extremely important to an effective use of contests. The information upon which contests are judged should be as reliable and as closely linked to desired outcomes as possible. When this is achieved, providers' incentives are more clearly aligned with the social aims of providing these services. In the event that consumer choice is involved, consumers need clear and relevant information. Sometimes this requires imposing structure on the services provided, such as limiting the range of health plan options or requiring disclosure of standardized information. The other factor, collusion among providers, can clearly undermine contests. Particularly in systems with choice and limited direct regulation, some kind of anti-trust surveillance is important to assure that the social gains from contests are achieved.

The problem of efficient delegation is much more fundamental to social services systems than what is suggested in general discussions of privatization or decentralization. Using agency theory, it is possible to be more systematic and thorough in evaluating the alternative ways of better structuring social services. Such an approach highlights the critical roles that can be played by improving the linkage between resource allocation and payments to outputs. It suggests the importance of structuring social services to increase the autonomy of service providers, information about their activities, and oversight by interested parties. It makes possible a more sophisticated view of competition than is usually developed in the literature on privatization, since contests and competition can be used within the public as well as private spheres.

Distributional Implications of Organization

Equity is an important consideration in social services. However, equity has been poorly served by systems that tend to concentrate resources in richer and urban areas rather than respond to needs and demand for services independent of income and political clout. Delegating more responsibilities to social service providers and introducing pluralism or even competition might be advantageous to higher income groups and those with greater capacity and access to the political system. On the other hand, many of the allocation mechanisms (such as capitation—paying for each student served or for each citizen affiliated with a health plan) actually do more to equalize the distribution of resources among citizens than other more traditional approaches. In this way, the structure of payments discussed above can have a strong egalitarian impact on social services.

Other payment systems can lead to inequalities when consumers are given greater choice and are allowed to complement public funding with their own resources. The Chilean health system allows individuals to choose among private and public health plans, and the better quality private plans serve clients whose insurance premiums are high enough to cover such services. Lower-income people are effectively excluded. The recent Colombian health reform addresses this problem by creating a "solidarity fund" to channel a portion of the obligatory payments from those with higher incomes to cross-subsidize the lower-income people. As in the case of contests, any system will be more equitable to the degree that all potential clients have access to information about different services, the capacity to evaluate it, and the means to act on their decision.

Problems of *adverse selection* deserve special attention in social services because students and patients are not all the same. Some cost more to serve than others. Unless some adjustment is made for these variations, institutions in more pluralistic systems will either be discouraged from providing services or will find ways to discriminate among their clients. This "adverse selection" can occur when schools that are under pressure to show high test scores discourage slower learners from applying, or when health insurance plans exclude older clients who are at higher risk of illness. These difficulties can be addressed by various means. In education, additional compensatory funding for disabled students can overcome the financial disincentive to attract and teach them. The same can be done for schools serving lower-income families by adjusting for the risk of higher costs. In health, pre-establishing groups (such as by geographic area or employer) who choose medical plans collectively can also diminish the negative impact of adverse selection. This partly resolves the problem by pooling high-risk with low-risk individuals.

Addressing distributional implications is important regardless of whether the system is centralized or decentralized. While the traditional centralized systems are theoretically capable of being redistributive, in practice the lack of transparency and the political pressures on the systems lead to significant failures. By contrast, the inequities of resource allocation become readily apparent in systems that give service providers greater autonomy. This generates information that can be used in the design of better allocation rules.

The rest of this chapter discusses the six case studies in education and health that utilize this approach. By comparing education and health systems within the same country, these studies have been able to isolate the impact of organization on performance from international differences. They have shown that schools in Venezuela, Brazil and Chile that had greater autonomy and accountability tended to perform better, even after controlling for the socioeconomic background of their students. The health providers in the Dominican Republic, Chile and Uruguay that were more autonomous and faced competition systematically attracted new clients while controlling costs. In the studies on health, distributional issues also come to the fore because of the potential for adverse selection and the impact of flight by higher-income groups from the public systems.

Studies in Education

The case studies on education present comparable approaches to measuring the impact of particular measures affecting managerial discretion, supervision, accountability and performance. In Chile and Venezuela, the existence of schools which are publicly-funded but managed by non-governmental institutions made it possible to demonstrate, in some detail, the advantages of greater autonomy for schools in allocating resources, managing personnel, and being accountable to sponsors or clients. In Brazil, a statistical analysis comparing the public school systems of different states that introduced innovations in school level management, election of school directors, and parent-teacher councils showed the degree to which such changes had an impact on student test scores, attendance and repetition.

Although the studies in this book emphasize and evaluate organizational impact on educational performance, other studies have addressed the question somewhat indirectly by looking primarily at the difference between private and public schools. For the United States, studies include Chubb and Moe (1990), Manski (1992), Hanushek (1994), Hoenack (1994), and Hoxby (1996). In Latin America, numerous studies have found that private schools perform better than public schools even after controlling for selection and socioeconomic factors, including Valdés (1997), Saavedra (1996), and Cox and Jiménez (1987). Recent studies by van der Gaag (1995) and Zuckerman and de Kadt (1997) confirm these differences and ask questions related to the sources of the private sector advantages. In some of these studies, the emphasis on the private-public distinction has distracted attention to some degree from the organizational features that can make either private or public schools function better. The case studies in the education chapters demonstrate how, even within public sector schools, incentive structures make a difference.

Chapter 2 compares several kinds of schools in *Chile* that receive similar amounts of funding but are organized differently, face different incentives, and vary significantly in terms of student test scores. The Chilean system is unique in Latin America because it allocates resources to schools on the basis of the number of students who attend and it allows nongovernmental schools to compete for students and public funds. Better than any other case, the Chilean education system confounds the traditional distinction between private and public schooling. To be sure, some 8.5 percent of students still attend traditional private schools financed exclusively through tuition and serving only higher-income groups, Chile has a large and growing number of schools that are managed privately but financed from taxes. These publicly-funded private schools, accessible to students from a wide range of socioeconomic backgrounds, operate with amounts of money similar to that of the municipal schools but have higher test scores, even after controlling for the socioeconomic background of students and selection effects.

The advantage in test scores (71 percent for privately-operated and only 64 percent for municipal schools) is partly a result of more motivated or capable students seeking the private schools. But even after controlling for these factors, a test score advantage remains, ranging from more than 13 points for Catholic schools to about 3 points for the private nonreligious schools. From interviews with teachers and directors, it appears that better test scores were associated with the greater autonomy and clearer incentives in the nonmunicipal schools.

Directors' incentives differ because a nongovernment school is run by its sponsor and its director within a clear and unforgiving budget constraint. In fact, a recent study documents that nongovernment schools operate with less funding on average than municipal schools.[13] By contrast, municipal schools are run by the city government, which complements shortfalls with its own resources. This soft budget constraint gives the school few rewards for improved performance and no sanctions for poor performance.

Directors can be extremely important to schools for providing leadership, selecting and managing personnel, making budget decisions and setting priorities. Carrying out this role depends in turn upon their knowledge, scope of action, mechanisms for obtaining resources, and accountability. Directors in the municipal schools have very little notion of how much their schools cost to run, whereas directors in the nongovernmental schools are more informed of the broad outlines of their budget and collaborate on the preparation of budgets with their superiors. The degree of autonomy in the nongovernmental schools makes it possible for more innovation to occur: changing schedules, teaching methods, textbooks or content to respond better to students. In the nongovernmental schools, directors also have greater scope of action in terms of selecting, disciplining and rewarding teachers. The selection of good teachers is judged to be one of the most important functions and capacities of a director in these nongovernmental schools. By contrast, directors in municipal schools have little input into the selection and management of teachers, whose contracts are rigidly influenced by the national *Estatuto de Docentes*.

Human resource management differs in other significant ways as well. The teachers in the municipal school system who are covered by the *Estatuto de Docentes* enjoy strong job guarantees, protecting even their right to teach in a particular school, and have no links from pay or stability to performance. In interviews, they recognized that the nongovernment schools do a better job of teaching and attributed it to better infrastructure, more demands on teachers, and the ability to select students. They felt that the municipal schools had better benefits, job stability, and were less demanding. By contrast, teachers in the nongovernment schools are ruled by the national labor regime, which gives them fewer job guarantees. Nonetheless,

---

[13] Larrañaga (1997): 19-62.

the teachers in these schools who were interviewed felt they have job stability, but that it depends on their performance rather than a union contract.

Some of the consequences of these differences are seen in better collaboration between sponsors and directors in privately-run schools than between public school directors and the municipalities that oversee them. Even within the municipal schools, those administered directly by the municipal government (DAEM) do not perform as well as those managed by a public corporation *(corporaciones)*. More innovation is seen in the private schools, which also subsidize more in-service training.

The study recognizes that public schools do have to fulfill obligations from which the private sector is exempt, including special education and schooling for more disadvantaged children. But the fact remains that the constraints under which the municipal schools operate in terms of management and budget create incentive problems. They are restricted in the ways they can manage personnel and they face soft budget constraints. By breaking the sample into many categories—not just private versus public but also between religious and nonreligious schools and between DAEMs and *corporaciones*—the study shows that institutional arrangements make a difference where it counts: in student learning.

Chapter 3 comes to similar conclusions about the organization of schools by focusing on the public sector in *Brazil*. Using the evidence afforded by state initiatives to implement three innovations over the last 10 years, and a database of test scores which have only become available since the late 1980s, Barros and Mendonça show systematically that organization can affect student performance. Nevertheless, since innovations tend to have been introduced in states with other positive factors related to family background and teacher quality, it is difficult to attribute the differences to organizational innovations alone.

Brazil's municipalities are formally responsible for primary education; however, in most cases, networks of state schools cover more students than do those of the municipalities. With the political "opening" of the 1980s, people demanded greater avenues for democratic participation and local involvement in schools. As a result, many states began to create parent-teacher councils *(colegiados)* in order to govern schools, allow school directors to be elected by the community, and give schools greater financial autonomy. Although these innovations were originally introduced as ends in themselves—to increase democratic participation after years of military rule—they were later supported for their expected impact on school performance.

Financial autonomy gives the school the power to act on its local knowledge of what is most important. There is a potential tradeoff between the efficiency gained by using this local information to make a better allocation of school funds and the loss of scale economies which are possible with central purchasing and planning. Nevertheless, the experiments with financial autonomy in Brazil are fairly limited; spending authority at the school still excludes teachers' salaries and investments, focusing almost exclusively on maintenance, teaching materials and general consumable materials.

The parent-teacher councils create a new forum for monitoring, judging and holding schools accountable. And this is done by a very interested party in the community—parents. Parental involvement is expected to support decisions focused more on improving school performance, although parents may be least informed as to the best pedagogical methods, curricula or teaching materials. Teachers, on the other hand, may be better informed but have a vested interest in improving their pay and working conditions, which can be at odds with the best interest of students or taxpayers. In cases where financial resources are transferred to the school, the councils may play a very important role in auditing school expenditures to minimize misallocation and corruption.

The election of school directors is also a way of increasing accountability. In theory, a well-informed central office might select the best candidates for school principals; however, in practice state-level politicians treat appointments to the position of director as spoils. Selection of school directors by community representatives may be more effective for several reasons. The community may better evaluate the local needs and particular characteristics of candidates. The community has a strong direct interest in choosing the best candidate. And, the election of directors insulates these appointments to some degree from state-level political interference. To incorporate technical criteria which the community may not be able to judge, the state of Minas Gerais uses an interesting mixture of these two mechanisms. Candidates are put through a series of state examinations and only the top three qualified candidates are placed before the community for discussion and vote.

Looking at the data as a panel, including 20 states that introduced these innovations at different times during a 10-year period, confirms that these innovations may have improved school performance. On average, states that transferred financial resources to schools, elected school directors and created parent-teacher councils had better school attendance, lower repetition rates, fewer delayed students, and better test scores. However, the states that adopted these innovations were also, on average, more likely to have higher incomes and better quality teachers. After controlling for these observed factors and for unobserved factors using a fixed-effects model, the results are not as statistically clear. Once these controls are introduced, the election of school directors fails to show a significant impact on student performance. However, even after controlling for these other factors, transferring financial resources and creating parent-teacher councils has a measurable impact on improving school attendance and reducing the share of students who are behind in their studies.

In *Venezuela*, schools with greater autonomy, clear budgets and more flexible contracting arrangements clearly performed better. Chapter 4 describes three kinds of schools—those run by the Ministry of Education, by the state of Mérida, and by a religious organization called *Fe y Alegría*. The three systems are comparable in the amount of resources that they spend. Although *Fe y Alegría* selects the students who attend their schools, the organization's commitment to educating children from poor families means that the students come from similar socioeconomic backgrounds to those in the state and national schools that were studied. However, the schools differ in the way they are organized and managed. By analyzing these differences, the chapter shows that centralized management, strong unions and overspecified contracts are associated with less efficient spending, ineffective supervision and lower morale. For example, the *Fe y Alegría* schools spend about 12 percent of their budget on teaching materials, maintenance and items other than teachers' salaries, while the state and national schools spent 5 percent and 1 percent, respectively, on these important nonsalary expenditures. Also, the employment contracts in the *Fe y Alegría* schools are only two pages long, leaving the teachers and school directors who supervise them sufficient room to develop trust and interpret the various obligations and rights in their particular context. By contrast, teachers hired in national and state schools have extremely detailed collective contracts that make it very difficult to apply effective personnel management to specific cases.

This clear impact of organization on intermediate factors in the operation of schools seems to have had an impact on student learning as well.

Students in the *Fe y Alegría* schools performed significantly better than those in the other schools on reading, writing and mathematics examinations. Meanwhile, the state schools, which were less centralized and more flexibly managed than the national schools, performed better in some areas but not in others. The authors note that the state schools had only been operating for five years, and so the benefits of the alternative form of management may not have fully materialized, particularly since they performed much better than the national schools in terms of the intermediate indicators of school quality.

The Venezuelan case holds other important lessons. Parental involvement was formally introduced into the school system in the 1970s, but had little impact as a consequence of the limited autonomy of the schools. Local communities have little incentive to organize, mobilize resources or debate issues over which they have no control. The heavy centralization of the Ministry of Education barred anyone from effectively voicing their opinions on how the system should operate or improve, unless they were organized nationally. And in Venezuela, the only national organizations with an interest in the school system were the teachers' unions and the political parties.

The Venezuelan case also shows how perverse the incentives for middle managers can be in a centralized system. Since the paychecks for all 300,000 teachers in the system are issued from the central offices in Caracas, a school director who wants to discount a certain amount from a particular teacher's salary because of absenteeism has to travel to the ministry's regional office. This is so costly for school directors in distant areas that even the possibility of a financial penalty for absenteeism is extremely remote.

The contrast between the Ministry of Education and the *Fe y Alegría* schools is also instructional. Both systems are "centralized" in that they have well-defined hierarchies, and centralized financing. Nevertheless, the *Fe y Alegría* system has clearly divided functions at each level with significant delegation of functions. The central offices focus on strategic planning and financing, while regional offices provide advice and assistance to the schools. The schools themselves are the basic unit of management activity. The school director has to develop a budget, select teachers, and provide school leadership, all with wide discretion. In exchange, the director is held accountable for acting within the guidelines provided by the central and regional offices. In this sense, the differences between the two systems are not so much a result of being "centralized" or "decentralized" but rather a consequence of dividing functions efficiently among the different levels and delegating significant responsibilities to the schools.[14]

In all these cases, student test scores were higher in schools that had greater control over the use of their budgets, and teachers were selected and evaluated on the basis of their performance. Interestingly, the absence of job guarantees did not result in lower performance or a perception of greater insecurity. In the survey, teachers expressed much greater satisfaction in the *Fe y Alegría* schools, with the state schools and the national schools ranked successively lower.

Studies in Health

The three case studies in the health sector also demonstrate the impact of organization on performance, or more specifically, the impact of payment mechanisms, consumer choice, adverse selection and regulation upon the efficiency, quality and cost of the different systems. Systems provide higher quality and more efficient medical care when consumers have greater choice and when the systems are more competitive. Prepaid insurance plans that contract with doctors and medical facilities do a better job of raising utilization rates and satisfying clients than do centralized systems with doctors on fixed salaries. In each study, the public sector role as a regulator was criticized as deficient. In Chile and the Dominican Republic, this criticism focused on the absence of quality monitoring and mechanisms to assure financial solidarity. In Uruguay, the government's frequent, erratic and rigid regulation of the private prepaid systems is an important source of large inefficiencies in health care.

The literature on health services is quite rich in studies on the impact of organization on performance, but much of it is theoretical.[15] The empirical studies have focused on segments of health services such as pharmaceuticals, hospital management, and payment mechanisms. In Latin America, discussion of health reforms in many countries has generated new studies,

---

[14] For a more detailed discussion of setting aside the centralized-decentralized dichotomy and analyzing a variety of functions within social service systems, see Inter-American Development Bank (1996).

[15] See Arrow (1963); Newhouse (1978); Evans, in van der Gaag and Perlman (1981)); Enthoven (1988); and Ellis and McGuire (1993).

beginning with Chile and more recently on Colombia and Mexico.[16] The evidence is quite clear that policymakers need to think hard about the best ways to structure their health systems if progress is going to be made in improving health conditions.

Chapter 5 studies the **Dominican Republic**, comparing the *Instituto Dominicano de Seguros Sociales (IDSS)* to a growing and diverse group of *Igualas* that are private prepaid medical insurance plans. The differences in organization demonstrate how the absence of incentives linked to performance in the IDSS system leads to high costs and poor services, compared to the more effective incentive structure of the *Igualas.*

The IDSS is managed centrally, financed by an obligatory 12 percent payroll tax, and covers a little less than 7 percent of the population, a group made up of formal sector employees. Managers from the maximum authority down to the directors of hospitals are appointed centrally and are generally removed with each election cycle. Political criteria take precedence in the management of the IDSS over concerns for health care and efficiency. Consequently, hospitals are maintained in provinces with too few potential patients, and utilization rates, at about 50 percent, are among the lowest in the region. The short horizon for political decisions leads to the hiring of new personnel in the face of strikes. Since the new personnel cannot be dismissed later, staffing expands excessively. It has reached some 48 doctors and 55 general nurses per 10,000 affiliates; by comparison, Mexico's social security system had 8.7 doctors per 10,000 affiliates in 1993.

Because care is free for everyone affiliated with social security, there is no incentive to seek attention in primary care centers. Nor do doctors or managers have any interest in controlling the use of costly hospital care, since higher use provides arguments for more budgets. As a result, the hospitals are overburdened with simple high-cost consultations that could be more efficiently provided elsewhere in the system.

Furthermore, doctors are paid fixed salaries by IDSS, but also maintain private practices. Since their IDSS salaries are fixed and guaranteed, the doctors have a clear interest in recommending that patients see them at their private office, where they attend to the patients for a fee. Productivity for doctors, then, is very low. In 1994, the average doctor attended only 4 pa-

---

[16] On Chile, see Miranda (1991) and Chapter 6; on Colombia, see Londoño de la Cuesta (1996a); on Mexico, see Fundación Mexicana para la Salud (1995).

tients per day, and the average dentist only 1.2. The effectiveness of these visits is also extremely low. Each consultation in the IDSS system required an average of 4.3 additional visits, while in the Public Health Ministry that figure was 0.8 and in the private sector 0.5.

The poor quality of service perceived by clients is demonstrated by the fact that fewer than one-half of those who are affiliated actually make use of the IDSS services. They prefer to pay additional fees to private doctors or clinics; to pay additional premiums to private insurers; or to consult the Ministry of Health system rather than the IDSS system.

The *Igualas* also cover a little more than 7 percent of the population (also predominantly formal sector employees), but represent a strong contrast to the IDSS. They are very decentralized and must seek out paying clients in order to thrive. The organizational structure of the *Igualas* varies. Some negotiate contracts with a wide range of doctors and medical facilities, while others directly contract their own doctors and maintain their own facilities. The most common structure is owned and managed by doctors, maintains a contract for services with a single hospital, and pays the doctors by a prenegotiated fee per service.

This combination gives doctors an incentive to be productive—the more services provided the higher their income—yet remain conscious of costs. As a result, there are 2,248 initial consultations per 1,000 affiliates per year in the *Igualas* compared to only 837 per 1,000 in the IDSS. However, the doctors do have an interest in minimizing costs, insofar as they are shareholders and their main purpose in establishing the *Iguala* is to channel patients their way. The average hospital stay is less than 3 days for the *Igualas*, while it is 6.8 days in the IDSS. Costs per consultation in *Igualas* are roughly half that of IDSS consultations, and hospital treatments are more than a third cheaper.

Part of the efficiency demonstrated by the *Igualas* derives from their ability to exclude particularly high-risk patients—such as those over 65 years of age or those infected with HIV. Most of the costliest procedures are also excluded from coverage. Nevertheless, the utilization rates are much higher than those of the IDSS; and the fact that the *Igualas* are growing rapidly indicates popular preference for their services. Adjusting for both these factors, then, confirms the relative efficiency and better quality of health care provided under the *Igualas*.

Like the IDSS and other health care providers in the Dominican Republic, however, the *Igualas* lack proper oversight and monitoring. This makes it possible for some to deny care, although a bad reputation can eventually affect their ability to attract and retain clients. What is most remarkable is the lack of competition among the *Igualas*. Contracts are negotiated between personnel managers of firms, on behalf of the employees, and the *Igualas*. As a result, the process is not transparent. There is evidence that the *Igualas* have arranged tacit collusion by agreeing not to "raid" clients from their competitors.

Chapter 6 compares the three main kinds of health service providers in *Chile;* the Public Health Ministry and two kinds of private insurers called *Institutos de Atención Prepago de Salud (ISAPREs)*. As a result of the health reform in the early 1980s, Chileans who pay a tax of 7 percent of their wages were given the option of having those funds applied to a private health insurance plan or to the public system under the *Fondo Nacional de Salud (FONASA)* which acts as a public insurer. As a result, it is possible to compare changes in the quality of care and services under different organizational structures and incentives. The organizational structure also has implications for global efficiency and equity as a result of its dualism, since some people have access to ISAPREs and others do not as a function of income and location.

The public health system is structured in ways which would be expected to lead to low efficiency. Doctors and other medical personnel are paid fixed salaries, largely unrelated to their work effort and performance.[17] Who gets what services is largely determined by government decisions regarding which facilities to expand, staff and maintain. The system is financed by taxpayers and users through their copayments, and it faces competition for its higher-income and lower-risk clients from the expanding ISAPREs. Although the system suffered a sharp decline in funding during the 1980s, the post-military governments have increased funding significantly. Public sector spending rose from $28 per capita in 1987 to over $60 per capita in 1995 at a time when the number of public sector beneficiaries dropped by 10 percent. Surveys continue to demonstrate that users of public services are less satisfied than those of the private services.

The ISAPREs are private, generally for-profit companies that develop and sell health plans to individuals or groups. Because all formal sector em-

---

[17] Since 1990, Chile has begun to experiment with prospective payments to doctors in municipal health centers based on the number of users who become affiliated. To date, there have been no evaluations of that experience

ployees are obligated to contribute 7 percent of their salaries into a health plan, the amount of money this contribution represents varies from person to person according to their income. For example, a client who earns only $1,000 per month is obligated to contribute $70 per month, while a client with twice the salary contributes $140 per month. To attract both clients while remaining profitable, the ISAPREs have offered a variety of plans with different prices to accommodate these different contribution levels. The plans differ in terms of the number of options available to users as well as the levels of deductibles and copayments. Some ISAPREs are "closed" in the sense that they are attached to a particular company and exclusively cover the employees of that firm. Others are "open," that is, anyone can apply and affiliate.

The ISAPREs have much more sophisticated contracting for physicians and hospital stays than the public system. Most of them reimburse health providers on the basis of the services provided. However, some ISAPREs have created integrated plans and are developing cost management through prospective payments and prenegotiated fees.

The open ISAPREs are subject to much greater competitive pressures than the closed ones because of the way they attract business. The two kinds of ISAPREs also vary significantly in terms of who determines the cost and character of the health plans. These decisions generally emerge from the process of collective bargaining in the closed ISAPREs, with the firms paying a substantial amount into the health plans over and above the contribution from employees. The plans offered by open ISAPREs and chosen by individuals are the outcome of market competition and pressures, since there is little evidence of collusion or oligopoly profits. In fact, the concentration ratios for ISAPREs declined over the past decade as more ISAPREs entered the market and enrollments rose.

There is dramatic evidence to indicate the superior performance of the open ISAPREs. The share of the population affiliated with ISAPREs rose from under 418,000 in 1985 to more than 3.5 million in 1994. Despite population growth, this increase has even reduced the number of people served by the public sector, which declined from almost 10 million to 9 million over the same period. The closed ISAPREs grew about 50 percent over this period, with approximately 190,000 affiliates in 1994. The expansion of the open ISAPREs has been attained by attracting users with services that are perceived to be better quality and by expanding the range of plans to attract successively lower income groups. Over the same time period that the costs per beneficiary in open ISAPREs rose 14 percent, they rose by over 80 percent in the closed ISAPREs and 200 percent in the public sector. Administrative costs were also driven down by competition—a 35 percent decline for the open ISAPREs compared to a 200 percent increase in the closed ISAPREs. The impact of incentives and competition on the cost-efficiency and quality of the open ISAPREs is strong and positive relative to the other two systems.

At the global level, the country's health system has developed in a dualistic direction. Those who have sufficient income can purchase their way into the ISAPREs, while others are left with only FONASA as an option. Therefore, access to particular kinds of care and options is greater for those with higher incomes. The structure also ensures that the highest risk population is covered by the public sector, which is the insurer of last resort for many of the costliest procedures.

The development of the Chilean health system shows that decentralized institutions that must compete for clients can respond very effectively under a system of obligatory contributions. The ISAPREs controlled costs while providing services that attracted large inflows of clients. They also generated a variety of service packages to respond to the differing levels of contributions, thereby allowing them to reach successively lower income groups. The Chilean system also demonstrates the importance of considering the global impact of the regulatory scheme with regard to adverse selection, equity and distribution of risk.

Chapter 7 analyzes the *Institutos de Asistencia Médica Colectiva (IAMCs)* in *Uruguay* that provide services to some 50 percent of the population. The chapter shows that the structure of ownership and payment mechanisms can have important effects on the efficiency of services. The IAMCs originated in the 19th century as *mutualistas,* established primarily as self-help associations serving particular occupations or ethnic groups. Over time they evolved, with the original occupational or ethnic criteria diminishing in importance, so that today the *mutualistas* act as consumer cooperatives for medical services and are selected by individuals for many different reasons. Parallel to the *mutualistas,* other IAMCs have developed that are owned or controlled by doctors. These IAMCs are of two varieties: nonunion cooperatives and union-associated cooperatives. Of the latter, the largest is the *Centro de Asistencia del Sindicato de Médicos del Uruguay (CASMU)*, operated by the medical union of Montevideo. These four types of IAMCs—*mutualistas,* nonunion cooperatives, union-associated cooperatives, and CASMU—represent different forms of ownership and utilize different payment schemes, and therefore face different incentives as to how they serve their clients.

In contrast to the Chilean ISAPREs and the Dominican *Igualas*, the IAMCs are heavily regulated by the government. The IAMCs are restricted both as to what services they must provide and what prices they can charge. These regulations leave little room for discretion. Furthermore, the rapidity and facility with which the government changes the rules introduces uncertainties that affect the ability of the IAMCs to plan. Since the early 1980s, regulations have changed regarding ceilings on premiums (except for two relatively brief periods in the 1980s and 1990s); restrictions on changing IAMCs (in some periods, liberalized and promoted in others); and minimum size (introduced over 1983–86). Directors cannot be paid and technical directors (doctors) have final authority.

Other regulations of longer standing that affect the IAMCs include requirements that they provide comprehensive coverage and that "promoters" cannot be legally hired to advertise and attract new clients.

What is notable is that of the various regulations, the ones related to quality of care are very poorly enforced. As a consequence, regulations that seek to protect consumers and increase their ability to select among IAMCs have had the perverse consequence of making it more difficult to judge the differences among IAMCs. Since they are unable to openly differentiate their packages and adjust their prices, the IAMCs necessarily make adjustments in the quality and effective coverage of their services. These adjustments, however, are not transparent and consumers remain uninformed of the real differences between plans.

By conducting an econometric analysis of the movement of people into and out of different IAMCs over time, and taking advantage of the small periods when prices and copayments were liberalized, it is possible to see a number of price effects. For example, the experiment with liberalizing copayment schedules in the 1990s demonstrated strong price responsiveness in Montevideo and much less in the interior, perhaps an indication of differences in competitiveness in this period.

Chapter 7 also shows how ownership affects service efficiency by influencing the cost structure. Since the law prohibits IAMCs from distributing profits to their owners, the medical cooperatives have higher shares of salary expenses, maximizing the income going to the owners, who are the doctors themselves. The nonunion cooperatives also had the highest share of subcontracted services, reserving more income from the IAMC for doctors' salaries. There was little impact on investment of the different structures because IAMCs are able to apply to the Ministry of Health for "extra premiums" to cover authorized investments. The extra premiums take the investment decision outside the current budget, in which medication and equipment compete for funding against personnel and nonmedical services.

As in education, the fixed salaries paid to doctors in many of the IAMCs are associated with lower output or absenteeism. However, unlike the case studies in education, this chapter has direct evidence of how doctors' response to payments are directly linked to output, i.e., the number of consultations or services rendered. The evidence demonstrates strongly how much more work is done by doctors who receive some additional compensation from attending patients than by those for whom work is rewarded by a fixed monthly payment.

Summary

In sum, organization makes a difference. Delegation of functions, mechanisms for resource allocation, existence of competition, output measures, and monitoring entities all affect the incentives for service providers and the degree to which they are held accountable for performance. The new lenses provided by Theories of the Firm are tested in these studies, and demonstrate that addressing incentive problems through better organization can improve performance. By allocating resources on the basis of outputs rather than inputs, providers receive a net benefit from serving more clients and reducing unit costs, as shown by the rapid and efficient expansion of health services in the *Igualas* in the Dominican Republic and ISAPREs in Chile. Accountability for the services "purchased" in these systems can be improved by delegating authority to service providers, generating information about their performance, and giving oversight to an interested party. The organizational innovations introduced into the state schools of Brazil are clear examples of increasing accountability in this fashion, with positive results. The *Fe y Alegría* schools of Venezuela also share some of these advantages. The introduction of contests that encourage efficient production, generate information and reinforce the incentive effect of resource allocation mechanisms can be seen in the Chilean education system, although the incentives in the municipal schools are attenuated by their softer budget constraints.

The new lenses also provide a clearer focus on the distributional implications of different forms of organization. Selection problems are clearly apparent in the health systems of Chile and the Dominican Republic, although the more recent reform in Colombia has found ways to address this issue. The Chilean education reform demonstrates how allocating resources on the basis of the number of students can equalize spending and lay the groundwork for more transparent and effectively targeted compensatory programs.

Focusing on the organization of health and education systems in Latin America should help accelerate improvements in educational levels and health conditions. Such progress is necessary for the region to meet the challenges of the global economy and to redress its inequitable distribution of income and opportunities. These studies and future studies as well can form the empirical foundation for this endeavor by identifying the policies that will significantly change incentives and accountability, with the goal of improving the access, quality and efficiency of health and education.

Bibliography

Arrow, Kenneth. 1963. Uncertainty and the Welfare Economics of Medical Care. *American Economic Review* 53(5).

Azariadis, C. 1975. Implicit Contracts and Underemployment Equilibria. *Journal of Political Economy* 79: 294-313.

Aoki, Masahiko. 1984. *The Cooperative Game Theory of the Firm.* London: Oxford University Press.

Chubb, John E., and Terry M. Moe. 1990. *Politics, Markets, and America's Schools.* Washington, D.C.: Brookings Institution.

Cox, Donald, and Emmanuel Jiménez. 1991. The Relative Effectiveness of Private and Public Schools: Evidence from Two Developing Countries. *Journal of Development Economics* 34: 99-121.

Cremer, J., A. Estache, and P. Seabright. 1996. The Decentralization of Public Services: What Can We Learn from the Theory of the Firm. *Revue d'Economie Politique* 106(1) Jan-Feb: 37-60.

Enthoven, A. 1988. *Theory and Practice of Managed Competition in Health Care Finance.* Lectures in Economics Series, No. 9. New York: Elsevier Science, 1988.

Ellis, R., and T. McGuire. 1993. Supply-Side and Demand-Side Cost Sharing in Health Care. *Journal of Economic Perspectives,* 7(4) Fall: 135-51.

Evans, R. G. 1981. Incomplete Vertical Integration: The Distinctive Structure of the Health Care Industry. In *Health, Economics, and Health Economics,* eds. J. van der Gaag and M. Perlman. North-Holland Publishing Company.

Fundación Mexicana para la Salud. 1995. *Economía y salud: propuestas para el avance del sistema de salud en México.*

Gaynor, Martin. 1994. *Issues in the Industrial Organization of the Market for Physician Services.* Working Paper No. 4695, April, National Bureau of Economic Research, Cambridge, MA.

Goudriaan, René, and Hans de Groot. 1993. State Regulation and University Behavior. *Journal of Economic Behavior and Organization* 20(3) April: 309-18.

de Groot, Hans. 1988. Decentralization Decisions in Bureaucracies as a Principal-Agent Problem. *Journal of Public Economics* 36(3) August: 323-37.

Hanushek, Eric. 1994. *Making Schools Work: Improving Performance and Controlling Costs.* Washington, D.C.: Brookings Institution.

Hoenack, Stephen. 1994. Economics, Organizations, and Learning: Research Directions for the Economics of Education. *Economics of Education Review* 13(2) June: 147-62.

Hoxby, Caroline. 1996. How Teachers' Unions Affect Education Production. *Quarterly Journal of Economics* 111(3) August: 671-718.

Inter-American Development Bank. 1996. Making Social Services Work. In *Economic and Social Progress in Latin America, 1996 Report.* Baltimore: Johns Hopkins University Press.

Jensen, Michael, and William Meckling. 1976. Theory of the Firm: Managerial Behavior, Agency, Costs and Capital Structure. *Journal of Financial Economics.*

Laffont, Jean-Jacques, and Jean Tirole. 1993. *A Theory of Incentives in Procurement and Regulation.* Cambridge, MA and London: The MIT Press.

Lambert, R.A., and D. F. Larcker. 1985. Executive Compensation, Corporate Decision-Making, and Shareholder Wealth: A Review of the Evidence. *Midland Corporate Finance Journal* 2(4): 6-22.

Larrañaga, O. 1997. Chile: A Hybrid Approach. In *The Public-Private Mix in Social Services: Health Care and Education in Chile, Costa Rica, and Venezuela,* eds. E. Zuckerman and E. de Kadt. Washington, D.C.: Inter-American Development Bank.

Londoño de la Cuesta, Juan Luis.1996a. Managed Competition in the Tropics: Health Reform in Colombia. Paper presented at the International Health Economics Association, Vancouver, May.

————. 1996b. *Is There a Health Gap in Latin America?* LATD Working Paper, World Bank, Washington, D.C.

Manski, Charles. 1992. Educational Choice (Vouchers) and Social Mobility. *Economics of Education Review* 11(4) December: 351-69.

Milgrom, Paul, and John Roberts. 1992. *Economics, Organization and Management.* Englewood Cliffs, NJ: Prentice Hall.

Miranda, Ernesto. 1991. Descentralización y privatización del sistema de salud chileno. *Estudios Públicos* 39. Centro de Estudios Públicos, Santiago.

Newhouse, J. 1978. *The Economics of Medical Care.* Addison Wesley Publishing Company.

Saavedra, Jaime. 1996. Public and Private Education: Their Relative Impact on Earnings: Evidence from Peruvian Survey Data. GRADE, Lima, Peru. October. Mimeo.

Spiller, Pablo. 1990. Politicians, Interest Groups, and Regulators: A Multiple-Principals Agency Theory of Regulation, or "Let Them be Bribed." *Journal of Law and Economics* 33(1) April: 65-101.

Spremann, Klaus. 1989. Agent and Principal. In *Agency Theory, Information and Incentives,* eds. Günter Bamberg and Klaus Spremann. New York: Springer.

Stiglitz, J. E. 1985. Credit Markets and the Control of Capital. *Journal of Money, Credit, and Banking* 17: 133-52.

Valdés, Eduardo Aldana. 1997. La medición del logro educativo en Colombia. *Formas y Reformas de la Educación* (3)1. PREAL.

Williamson, Oliver. 1971. The Vertical Integration of Production: Market Failure Considerations. *American Economic Review.*

————. 1985. *The Economic Institutions of Capitalism.* New York: The Free Press.

Zuckerman, Elaine, and Emanuel de Kadt, eds. 1997. *The Public-Private Mix in Social Services: Health Care and Education in Chile, Costa Rica, and Venezuela.* Washington, D.C.: Inter-American Development Bank.

II. EDUCATION

CHAPTER 2

Differences in Schools and Student Performance in Chile

Cristián Aedo[1]

Education in Chile is provided through a mixed system in which the public and private sectors participate in both producing and financing activities. Education financed by the public sector is decentralized and operates through private and municipal producers.

Most of the resources belonging to the primary and secondary school system are concentrated at the primary level. Primary education is provided through municipal schools, privately-run schools with vouchers, and paid private schools. The latter are financed through tuition fees, whereas municipal schools and private voucher schools are usually tuition free and are basically supported by fiscal transfers. Such funding is provided through an educational voucher or a per-student subsidy, which must cover the institutions' operational and capital costs. This mechanism is intended to promote competition among both public and private schools that receive government funds. By making schools' income depend on the number of students they serve, this mechanism encourages the schools to attract and retain students. The aim is to promote greater efficiency and quality in educational services.

In 1993, the municipal sector accounted for 57 percent of the country's school-age population, private voucher schools 34.1 percent, and private tuition schools the remaining 8.5 percent.

---

[1] Cristián Aedo is Director of the Post-graduate Program for Economics, ILADE/Georgetown University, Santiago, Chile.

This chapter analyzes the structure of the municipal school subsystems and private education under public funding in order to explain the differences in the internal and external efficiency of both types of learning institutions. Both subsystems provide services under relatively similar conditions: both derive their funding chiefly from educational grants, are usually tuition-free, are targeted toward children from low or moderately low-income families, and are located in similar settings. Despite these similarities, both systems differ in the cost per student and in the quality of the education they deliver. This is due to the different incentives and restrictions that apply to the respective institutions.

This chapter places special emphasis on identifying how various factors generate different incentives that determine the quality and cost of the services rendered. These factors include the legal and institutional environment, organizational context, type of ownership, financial autonomy, constitutional commitments, institutional supervision and control, and the resolution of the input market monitoring.

The next section presents the structure and operation of the school system in Chile and discusses various aspects of coverage, educational quality, external efficiency, funding, types of schools, and institutional features. This is followed by econometric estimates of the chief determinants of the quality of education provided by the schools, after controlling for the possible presence of selection on the part of learning institutions and families. Empirical evidence is then presented from interviews with public and primary school teachers and principals in order to identify the chief incentives and restrictions that apply to them.

Structure and Financing of the School System

Chile's educational system extensively uses a voucher or per-student subsidy for all students in order to finance the educational costs of a large percentage of the population. This system resulted from the educational decentralization that began in 1980; it directly links the income received by schools eligible for public funding to the students' decision to attend. Parents are free to send their children to any subsidized public or private school,[2]

---

[2] Besides the subsidized municipal and private schools, there are also paid private schools that chiefly target middle- and high-income groups.

and the government grants the subsidies for student attendance directly and on a monthly basis. Schools must therefore compete in order to attract and retain students.

The central administration maintains legal jurisdiction over various issues affecting the performance of subsidized institutions. These include designing the academic curriculum, determining the number of hours and days spent in the classroom, establishing criteria for evaluating student performance and promoting students, yearly testing of basic learning skills, and assuming responsibility for financing subsidized schools and providing them with technical support. The Ministry of Education (MINEDUC) is responsible through the Provincial Departments (DEPROV) for supervising student attendance and giving schools technical support.

The role of subsidized schools was basically reduced to institutional management and to pedagogic and disciplinary issues, within the framework of the guidelines established by MINEDUC. It is worth noting that private voucher schools have greater flexibility than municipal schools insofar as hiring employees and fixing salaries is concerned, since they are not subject to the special labor laws that favor teachers in municipal schools.

School System Coverage

In 1993, 91.5 percent of the country's school-age children were enrolled in municipal and private schools. That figure includes 57.4 percent within the municipal sector and 34.1 percent within the private, subsidized sector. The remaining 8.5 percent of the student population is served by paid private schools. The subsidized sector (municipal and private) is practically the only one that offers special education. In the metropolitan region, which has more than a third of the country's school-age population, these proportions are different. As seen in Table 2.1, the municipal sector has a smaller fraction, particularly as compared to the private sector under subsidy. The latter serves 47.4 percent of all children attending school, whereas the municipal schools serve 40.2 percent. Paid private schools serve 12.4 percent of the population.

This situation can be mostly explained in terms of supply. In parts of the country where a substantial proportion of the population is rural, the private sector is less interested in establishing schools because populations are smaller and more scattered and socioeconomic conditions poorer.

Table 2.1. Enrollment by Type of School and Educational Level, 1993

Type of school	Educational level	National total		Metropolitan area	
		Number	%	Number	%
Total	Total	3,007,628	100.0	1,139,418	100.0
	Preschool	256,348	100.0	106,227	100.0
	Special	32,419	100.0	16,201	100.0
	Primary	2,066,046	100.0	762,849	100.0
	Secondary	652,815	100.0	254,141	100.0
Municipal	Total	1,725,620	57.4	458,312	40.2
	Preschool	134,370	52.4	43,994	41.4
	Special	16,763	51.7	5,797	35.8
	Primary	1,239,941	60.0	324,559	42.5
	Secondary	334,546	51.2	83,962	33.0
Subsidized Private	Total	973,515	32.4	514,249	45.1
	Preschool	86,315	33.7	44,018	41.4
	Special	15,535	47.9	10,295	63.5
	Primary	69,200	32.4	350,254	45.9
	Secondary	202,465	31.0	109,682	43.2
Paid Private	Total	256,700	8.5	141,021	12.4
	Preschool	35,596	13.9	18,148	17.1
	Special	121	0.4	109	0.7
	Primary	155,824	7.5	86,955	11.4
	Secondary	65,159	10.0	35,809	14.1
Corporation[1]	Total	51,793	1.7	25,836	2.3
	Preschool	67	0.0	67	0.1
	Special	0	0.0	0	0.0
	Primary	1,081	0.1	1,081	0.1
	Secondary	50,645	7.8	24,688	9.7

Source: Statistical records, MINEDUC, 1993.

[1] Corporations are nonprofit, private legal entities that run secondary-level technical and professional schools.

Levels of coverage at the primary and secondary levels are substantially different. By 1993, primary education had almost complete coverage (98.3 percent), while at the high school level the figure was 75.1 percent. Figure 1 shows changes in coverage by primary and secondary school coverage from 1970 to 1993. There was a significant increase in coverage at the

FIGURE 2.1. Educational Coverage, 1970–93

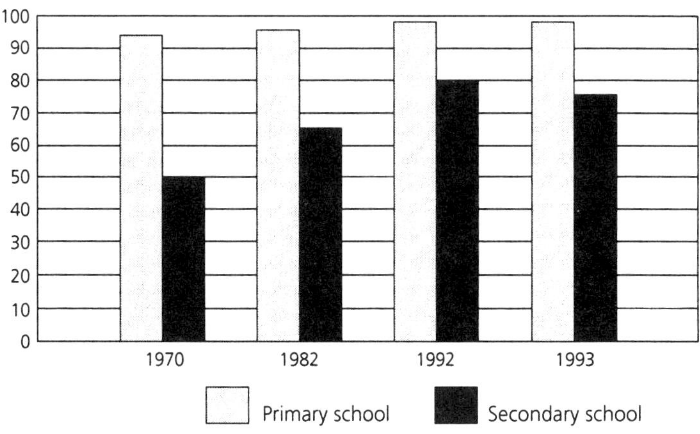

high school level during those years, although the extrapolation for 1993 suggests a slight decrease.[3]

Table 2.2 shows the substantial growth in enrollment experienced by subsidized private schools during the 1980s. In municipal schools, enrollment dropped at the start of the decade, while the municipal sector faced registration losses during the early 1980s, followed by a small recovery toward the end of the decade and the early nineties. Despite this drop in enrollment, the number of institutions run by the municipal governments did not fluctuate substantially, with the result that an important percentage of schools began to have excess capacity.

Quality of Education

The Chilean system is based on the notion that all parties involved should make informed and autonomous decisions. With this in mind, the central level evaluates schools through the System for Measuring the Quality of Education (*Sistema de Medición de la Calidad de la Educación*, SIMCE).

---

[3] This may be due to the fact that figures for 1970, 1972 and 1992 come from census data, whereas the 1993 figures are extrapolations.

Table 2.2. Changes in Enrollment: Number of Children by Type of School, 1981–93

			Type of School				
Year	Total	National	National/ Municipal	Municipal	Subsidized private	Paid private	Corporation
1981	2,841,726		2,215,973		430,232	195,521	
1982	2,819,139	425,518		1,695,038	553,600	144,983	
1983	2,869,435	369,189		1,672,593	643,868	183,785	
1984	2,886,552	341,994		1,626,968	758,842	158,748	
1985	2,963,410	331,110		1,605,185	832,455	194,660	
1986	2,967,864	316,594		1,555,059	913,925	182,286	
1987	2,962,755			1,797,953	910,968	196,200	57,634
1988	2,989,032			1,781,413	939,445	209,758	58,416
1989	2,976,011			1,745,598	954,642	217,737	58,034
1990	2,963,139			1,717,222	960,460	228,205	57,252
1991	2,938,720			1,698,842	949,038	234,442	56,398
1992	2,983,383			1,721,375	963,061	245,858	53,362
1993	3,007,628			1,725,620	973,515	256,700	51,793

Source: Statistical records, MINEDUC, 1993.

Note: Enrollment is for April 30 of each year. Enrollment figures for fiscal and municipal schools in 1981 have been added together because the greatest number of schools changed over to the municipal sector in that year.

Box 2.1. System for Measuring the Quality of Education (SIMCE)

The fundamental objective of SIMCE is to gather information on student performance by testing fourth and eighth-grade students in Spanish, mathematics, natural sciences, history and geography. The tests for Spanish and mathematics are structured progressively. This makes it possible to evaluate, for each grade, the extent to which goals are attained (fourth-grade objectives include those for the first and second subcycles, while eighth-grade objectives include those for the fourth, sixth and eighth grades). Tests for the natural sciences, history and geography measure the objectives of the first primary school cycle (first to fourth grades at the primary level) and of the second primary school cycle (fifth to eighth grades at the primary level).

Tests are given in all schools in the country by an examiner from outside the institution. In the case of the natural sciences, history and geography, a sample of schools is drawn and notified early, through DEPROV, of the dates when the tests will be given.

Table 2.3. SIMCE Fourth Grade Scores, 1994

Type of school	Spanish	Mathematics	Average
Municipal	63.44	65.41	64.42
Subsidized	69.93	71.39	70.66
Paid private	83.69	86.44	85.07
National average	**72.35**	**74.41**	

Source: Espínola (1985).

The results of the SIMCE Spanish and mathematics tests show lower scores for municipal schools and private voucher schools than for paid private schools. They also indicate that municipal schools get lower scores than private voucher schools (Table 2.3). Other factors besides the different types of schools may explain the differences in school performance. These include the selection of students by the majority of private schools, both subsidized and tuition-funded; demand, as determined by the students' socioeconomic level; and the extent to which a given setting is rural.

The average performance on these tests has improved gradually since 1988. According to some (Matte and Sancho, 1992), this suggests a systematic improvement in the quality of education. However, one must consider two factors that cast doubt on such a conclusion: first of all, teachers are probably "preparing students for the test;" secondly, a conflict of interests arises when MINEDUC gives a test (SIMCE) that somehow evaluates its own work.

Public officials have, in turn, used this indicator, along with others, to select schools for special programs. For example, direct attention is being paid to the 10 percent of schools facing the most serious problems, through the special program for 900 schools (P-900). Under this program, resources and technical orientation are concentrated on the poorest, most isolated schools that score worst on the SIMCE test. Other measures being taken to improve the quality of education in the publicly-funded sector include the Program for Improving the Quality of Education (MECE), with support from the World Bank, which aims to improve primary and high school level teaching by increasing school resources, particularly for better infrastructure and educational materials. Teacher participation in school development projects is also encouraged.

External Efficiency of the School System

The retention rates in Table 2.4 can be used to evaluate the efficiency of the school system. As shown, there have been substantial improvements in these rates, especially at the primary school level.

When retention rates are examined by cohort and type of school, they show lower figures for the municipal sector and subsidized private schools than for the paid private sector (77.26 and 78.81 percent, respectively, versus 92.3 percent). On the other hand, students enrolled in municipal schools take longer, on the average, to finish their primary education than those enrolled in the private subsidized sector, the difference being more significant than in the case of the paid private sector, as shown in Table 2.5. In the subsidized sector, only seven of every 10 children of a cohort entering primary school manage to finish their studies in less than 11 years, with an average of 10 years to complete the eighth grade. This shows the inefficiency of the subsidized school sector, considering the fact that it could aim for results similar to those obtained by the nonsubsidized private sector.

Table 2.4. Retention Rates by Educational Level, 1981–93

Years	Primary school				Secondary school			
	Total	Passed (%)	Failed (%)	Dropouts (%)	Total	Passed (%)	Failed (%)	Dropouts (%)
1981	2,188,187	83.32	8.12	8.06	533,895	78.97	12.68	8.35
1982	2,129,104	89.43	7.86	2.71	575,969	82.94	10.85	6.22
1983	2,096,693	88.71	6.92	3.05	605,712	82.82	10.50	6.69
1984	2,055,485	88.31	8.47	3.22	630,625	81.82	10.88	7.30
1985	2,049,512	89.11	7.81	3.08	651,201	80.81	11.36	7.83
1986	2,039,719	90.41	6.70	2.89	664,315	81.71	10.64	7.65
1987	2,013,948	91.19	6.08	2.73	677,293	84.18	88.90	6.92
1988	1,997,061	90.47	7.00	2.53	722,773	82.54	10.29	7.17
1989	1,998,044	88.91	8.39	2.70	748,606	78.59	13.07	8.34
1990	1,984,288	89.91	7.80	2.29	720,230	80.27	12.35	7.37
1991	2,005,708	90.59	7.37	2.04	694,602	80.95	12.29	6.76
1992	2,030,007	90.83	7.24	1.92	671,360	81.41	12.23	6.36
1993	2,060,699	91.24	6.90	1.86	657,896	81.28	11.96	6.77

Source: Statistical records, MINEDUC, 1993.

Table 2.5. Internal Efficiency by School Type for a Specific Primary Cohort, 1983–93

Type of school	On-time completion (%)	Total completion (%)	Retention rate (8th grade)	Years before completion	Excess cost (%)
Total	41.00	71.33	78.43	10.09	26.12
Municipal	38.55	70.29	77.26	10.27	28.39
Subsidized private	44.44	71.73	78.81	9.93	24.08
Nonsubsidized private	66.81	83.76	92.30	8.83	10.42

Source: Statistical records, MINEDUC, 1993.
Note: The figures for total completion are based on no more than three repetitions per cohort. The cohort refers to the group of students that entered the first year of primary school and took a minimum of eight years and a maximum of 11 to complete that level of education. On-time completion refers to students who complete the primary level without repeating any grade.

Efficiency problems within the publicly-funded sector generate excessive expenditures for the state than might otherwise be used to improve the quality of education. Official estimates suggest that in 1993 the municipal sector was responsible for the highest excess costs within the system (around $98 million), followed by the private voucher sector ($44 million). This implies total excess expenditures of $141 million in the publicly-funded sector.

Structure of School System Financing

Municipal and private voucher schools are funded on the basis of a subsidy per student. The value of the subsidy is expressed as a factor of the educational subsidy unit (*Unidad de Subvención Educacional*, USE) and depends on the educational level (preschool, primary, special differentiated, adult primary, secondary-level science and humanities or technical and professional studies, and adult high school) and on whether the learning institution offers internships or special programs (Table 2.6). The basic voucher is also adjusted upward and by zone.[4]

---

[4] Special assignments per zone consist of a percentage increment over the value of the voucher, which is granted to learning institutions in remote areas or where the cost of living justifies a supplement. The rural subsidy is given to schools located at least five km from the city limits or from a similar learning institution, and with a total enrollment of 85 students or less.

Table 2.6. Amount of Subsidy (Educational Subsidy Units)

Type of schooling	USE[1] Index
Preschool	0.936
Primary	
1st to 6th grades	1.030
7th and 8th grades	1.140
Special differentiated primary	3.090
Adult primary	0.700
Secondary:	
Science and humanities	1.282
Technical/professional in agriculture and maritime	2.029
Technical/professional in industry	1.524
Technical/professional in commerce and technology	1.339
Adult Secondary	0.816

[1] The value of the USE in April 1995 was $14.70 per student per month.

The subsidy is paid monthly to the school's sponsor according to the average student enrollment in the three-month period prior to payment. Only vouchers given for internships are paid on the basis of actual attendance.

In the municipal sector, the subsidy is generally just enough to cover personnel costs in the various institutions. For this reason, most municipal districts experience a deficit. These deficits are funded through municipal transfers, which are financed with local resources or with transfers from the central level. The reasons for these deficits are unclear, but may have to do with administrative problems at the municipal level (Espínola, 1995) or with an inadequate subsidy in real terms.[5]

Beginning in mid-1993, two new sources of funding became available to the publicly-funded school sector: shared funding[6] and tax exemptions for donations for educational purposes. In the shared funding modality, parents or guardians contribute a moderate complementary sum to the

[5] The amount of the subsidy declined 32 percent in real terms from 1981 to 1991 and only recovered its actual 1981 value sometime around 1992 (Infante and Schiefelbein, 1992).

[6] Shared funding was a possibility as early as 1990. However, the system did not function due to weak financial incentives and insufficient political will to actually implement it.

voucher so that the school can have more resources with which to improve education quality. Depending on the tuition charged at each school grade, there is a less than proportional reduction in the education voucher. Subsidized private schools can voluntarily choose this modality, both for the primary and secondary school levels. In the municipal sector, the choice of this modality depends on approval by the authorities and can only be applied to secondary schools.

Statistics show that shared funding has been widely accepted within the voucher sector. In fact, around one-third of such establishments—representing around 50 percent of the sector's enrollment—had decided to switch to the new system by 1994, with about 73 percent of all institutions charging less than $7.50 a month (tax exempt bracket). Response has been rather timid in the municipal sector, where only 36 institutions have switched.

Another funding option, though less than permanent, is through donations for educational purposes to municipal schools and private voucher schools. According to Ordinance No. 19.247, donating companies can obtain a tax discount or credit for the payment of the first category tax, or the equivalent of 50 percent of the donation. These credits cannot be more than 2 percent of the donating company's earnings or more than 14.000 UTM (one UTM is approximately equal to $52). Furthermore, the portion that is not used for credits can be viewed as a company expenditure. It is hoped that this measure will increase those resources destined for investment in infrastructure and human capital, and that both measures will increase the financial resources for a significant share of all learning institutions. If this increase is accompanied by an improvement in the quality of educational services, it follows that these measures will represent an important achievement in terms of making options available within the school system that give a good portion of the population access to a better quality education.

Types of Schools

Within the educational sector there are three main types of institutions: municipal, subsidized private, and paid private schools. However, within the subsidized sector, whether it be municipal or private, one can also discern important differences.

Municipal schools can be classified according to the management model adopted by the municipality. There are two different modalities:

(i) creation within the municipality of Departments for the Administration of Municipal Education *(Departamentos de Administración de la Educación Municipal, DAEM)*, and ii) Municipal Corporations *(Corporaciones Municipales)*, which are independent entities linked to the municipality through the mayor and the Municipal Finance Department *(Departamento de Finanzas Municipales)*.

The role of the DAEM is limited to managing municipal learning institutions, which primarily involves providing the human, financial and material resources necessary for the adequate operation of schools; overseeing adherence to technical and pedagogical standards and to the Ministry of Education's programs; and promoting the training of teaching and non-teaching staff. Even though the head of the DAEM should be a teacher with a professorship granted by the state, in practice the role of the chief is mainly administrative. DAEM employees are municipal workers; thus, their remuneration is fixed in accordance with the corresponding laws and is subject to a single salary scale.

The other management option for municipal education is that of the Municipal Corporations, which were instituted as corporate bodies in charge of managing schools, primary health care clinics, homes for minors, and multipurpose centers. The Municipal Corporation is a nonprofit, private legal entity with its own legal staff. It is run according to its own statutes and managed by a directing body of four people and presided over by the mayor. Direct management of the corporation is the responsibility of the secretary general. In order to hold this position it is not necessary to be a teacher, like the head of the DAEM, and in a good many of the existing corporations the position is held by a manager. The corporation's staff does not belong to the municipality and is hired through a private work contract, which allows for remuneration to be determined in accordance with the corporation's criteria. This is contrary to what occurs in the DAEM, most of whose employees are municipal workers. Furthermore, staff can be fired without the need for a summary report, as in the case of municipal workers. The corporation has no legal ties with the municipality, save for its relationship with the Finance Department for the payment of subsidies, and with the mayor, owing to his being president of the corporation's directing council. This situation neither allows the municipality to supervise or control the corporation's activities nor to incorporate them into community planning.

Most municipalities chose the DAEM modality because it was easier and less costly in the short term, since it required hiring just enough staff members for its implementation.[7] By contrast, creating a corporation called for more substantial resources and for recruiting personnel outside the municipality. The creation of new corporations was banned in March 1988, when it was declared unconstitutional for municipalities to transfer public duties to legally private institutions.

Subsidized private schools are marked by great heterogeneity. There are religious schools that may be dependent on the Catholic church (archbishoprics, religious congregations, parishes) or other religious groups (Adventist, Evangelical, etc.). In general, these institutions administer more than two schools. There are also both for-profit and nonprofit lay schools. The former operate like business enterprises, generating profits distributed among proprietors. Most subsidized private schools belong in this category. Nonprofit institutions include schools whose funding comes from private foundations and corporations. In both for-profit and nonprofit schools, those in charge may be responsible for more than one learning institution.

Legal and Institutional Aspects

A number of legal and institutional restrictions chiefly affect the municipal school sector, particularly the teachers' statute and constitutional restrictions.

In July 1991, Ordinance No. 19.070—the Professional Statute for Teaching Professionals (*Estatuto de los Profesionales de la Educación*)—was enacted to set professional standards for teachers employed by the municipal sector. The ordinance introduced a number of rigid rules within the municipal school system that affected both its financial management and the quality of teaching.

The ordinance practically guarantees teachers job security and prohibits dismissals and teacher reassignments to other municipal schools within the community. This often results in a teaching staff in excess of the needs of the learning institution.

Table 2.7 shows the reduction in the student/teacher ratio within the municipal sector, which went from 25.6 in 1987 to 20.7 in 1993. It also shows

---

[7] The DAEM can contract employees, subject to the regulations of the Labor Code.

Table 2.7. Changes in the Student/teacher Ratio by Sector

Year	Municipal sector	Subsidized private sector
1987	25.6	27.2
1989	22.1	26.2
1991	20.7	25.8
1993	20.7	26.7

Source: Compendio de Información, MINEDUC, 1993.

how this contrasts with the subsidized private sector, which has succeeded in adapting its teaching staff to the number of students enrolled.

Teachers in the subsidized private sector are governed by the norms set forth under the general Labor Code with regard to matters pertaining to all issues not addressed under the Teachers' Statute. Thus, salaries are fixed by individual and collective negotiation, with agreement on a minimum weekly or monthly sum.

In September 1995, a series of modifications to the Teachers' Statute were introduced to improve the system's flexibility. It is hoped that these modifications will solve some of the financial problems faced by the municipal school sector and improve the quality of the education provided by these institutions.

With regard to constitutional restrictions, the Chilean constitution makes it an obligatory responsibility of the states to provide basic education to whoever seeks it. Since the decentralization process, this responsibility has been transferred to the municipalities. Thus, in actual practice the municipalities as a whole cannot select their students. In many cases this forces municipal schools to accept poor students or students with learning disabilities or behavioral problems, while subsidized private schools do not face this restriction.

Econometric Estimates of Education Quality

This section attempts to explain the main factors determining the quality of primary education. In deriving these econometric estimates, special attention has been paid to measuring the impact of different types of schools on the quality of education. The estimates given have been controlled for selection bias.

The data used were constructed by combining and adapting official information provided by various departments of the Ministry of Education. For every school, the data contain the results of the SIMCE test for different grades and for Spanish and mathematics; the amount spent by families on education; parents' educational level; type of school (municipal, subsidized private, or paid private); type of education (child or adult) and geographical code; number of basic education courses offered by each school; number of students enrolled in each of the courses (initial enrollment); teaching staff and level of accreditation; number of students that passed, failed or repeated the same grade; and the deprivation index, which identifies the average presence of nutritional deficiencies in children attending a particular school.

An effort was made to construct a number of variables in connection with the managerial model adopted by the schools, namely their ability to choose the students; degree of autonomy enjoyed by the principal; type of personnel management and salary determination; administrative model; sources of funding; degree of parental involvement; and mechanisms for evaluating teacher performance. These variables are not available in existing data bases and thus have to be constructed for each school, either by directly consulting them or through contacting different institutions that are familiar with the schools.

Consulting the schools directly was ruled out for several reasons. In some cases the answer was obvious and straightforward, given the regulatory framework (as in the case of sources of funding or of the ways salaries are determined in municipal schools). In other cases, schools would answer that they either did or did not fulfill a certain condition, making it impossible to determine the accuracy of the information without knowing the school in greater detail (take, for example, its degree of autonomy, choice of students, profit or nonprofit status, and degree of parental involvement). In still other cases, the variable turned out to be multi-dimensional, which made it impossible to construct a single indicator that allowed for comparisons between schools (the case for general management and personnel management models).

Ultimately, the path pursued was to try to construct some of these variables by drawing on the knowledge of different organizations about the various schools, including MINEDUC, the different municipalities, the National Corporation of Private Schools (*Corporación Nacional de Establecimientos Privados*, CONACEP), the Vicarage for Education (*Vicaría de la*

Educación), and the Federation of Secondary Schools (*Federación de Colegios Secundarios*). This allowed us to construct variables, case by case, for the more than 800 schools included in the sample. The variables indicate whether the school is religious or nonreligious; for-profit or nonprofit; or a member of a given group of schools. As for the remaining variables, it was impossible to obtain quantitative or qualitative variables that could be used for the econometric analysis.

This sample was supplemented with demographic and socioeconomic information for a sample of children from the Santiago metropolitan area who are receiving a normal education, obtained from the 1992 Social and Economic Profile Survey (*Encuesta de Caracterización Socioeconómica,* CASEN 1992).[8]

The econometric model seeks to determine the indirect impact of different variables on the quality of education. For this purpose, a school's performance on the SIMCE test is used as a *proxy* for the average quality of education offered in that institution. The dependent variable, which is the 1994 SIMCE score, represents the average results in fourth-grade Spanish and mathematics during 1994. The fourth-grade SIMCE was chosen because it measures skills that lay the groundwork for student learning in later stages of their educational development.

As explanatory variables we use a number of dummy variables corresponding to the types of schools; variables representing the students' social and economic background; indicators of the institutions' external efficiency; and variables representing the approximate amount of resources the institutions make available to students to support their learning. The explanatory variables employed are a dummy variable that takes on the value 1 if the school is religious and the value 0 if it is not; a dummy variable that takes on the value 1 if the school is private and subsidized and its holder runs several schools, and 0 if it is not; a dummy variable that takes on the value 1 if the school is municipal and is managed by a corporation and the value 0 if it is not; a dummy variable that takes on the value 1 if the school is nonreligious and the value 0 if it is religious; a dummy variable that takes on the value 1 if the school is classified as belonging to the lowest social and

---

[8] See Aedo (1997) for a more detailed discussion of the descriptive statistics derived from this sample, and the CASEN survey of 1992.

economic stratum and the value 0 if it is not; a dummy variable that takes on the value 1 if the school is classified as belonging to the middle social and economic stratum and the value 0 if it is not; dummy variables measuring the average monthly expenditure on education in a particular institution (supplies, transportation, tuition costs, PTA fee, etc.), classified as low (less than $11), low-middle (between $11 and $28), and middle (between $28 and $53);[9] dummy variables measuring parents' average educational level for a given school, classified as low (more than half have not finished primary school), low-middle (more than half have finished primary school or have not finished secondary school), middle (more than half have completed high school or have not completed college);[10] the school's deprivation index; the number of students per teacher; and the number of students per administrative staff.

Table 2.8 shows the main econometric results. In all the estimates, which are summarized in Table A of the Annex, the variables representing a school's profit or nonprofit status, its status as a subsidized, private lay institution, and the ratio of students to teachers and administrative staff are not significant at the 10 percent level, and they were thus excluded from the analysis.

The results presented here show first that religious schools offer a better education, and second, that private schools that belong to an institution that runs several schools offer a better education than schools whose sponsor has only one. This is an important result which is probably linked to the experience accumulated and passed on to schools by their sponsors.

Third, schools dependent on municipalities that chose the corporation management model deliver better education than schools dependent on municipalities that chose the DAEM management model. These results are compatible with anecdotal reports suggesting municipal corporations are more efficiently managed than those belonging to the DAEM.

Fourth, as expected, schools classified as low-income show poorer performance, on the average, than schools classified as high-income. This probably has to do with the greater difficulties faced by schools for financially underprivileged children in terms of teaching and motivation. In other words, more affluent families have greater resources (education, time and money)

---

[9] The omitted category corresponds to high expenditure (greater than $53).
[10] The omitted category corresponds to high educational level (more than half have completed college).

Table 2.8. Estimates of Factors Determining Quality

	Parameter	t value
Constant	76.88	68.83
Religious school	5.84	6.27
Grouped schools	2.31	2.80
Municipal corporation	1.96	3.64
Poorest social bracket	−3.66	−3.31
Deprivation index	−0.19	−13.05
Low expenditure on education	4.14	3.75
Low parental education	−5.56	−1.87
Low-medium parental education	−6.81	−5.00
Medium parental education	−2.45	−2.13

Note: Number of observations = 866; R^2 = 0.43; Adjusted R^2 = 0.43; Log likelihood = −2908.77; Durbin Watson = 1.83; *F* value = 74.39.

to devote to their children's education, and this fosters better academic performance. One more factor to be borne in mind is the peer effect, which suggests that on the whole, schools with "better" students offer a better average education. This is further supported by the fact that, according to the estimated parameter for the deprivation index variable, schools whose students have a greater average nutritional deficit show a poorer performance on the SIMCE test.

Fifth, the dummy variable representing low spending on education had a positive coefficient. This result is difficult to interpret unless we recall that the great majority of institutions in this category are municipal schools. Thus, it is believed this result may be related to special programs run by the Ministry of Education in these schools.

Sixth, the dummy variables representing low, low-middle and middle educational levels had negative coefficients. This indicates that schools whose students have parents with better education (the dummy variable excluded from the analysis) perform better on the SIMCE test.

If one considers the fact that each type of school could have been chosen by families at random, the estimate reported here is suitable. However, anecdotal evidence suggests that there is a process of nonrandom assignments in the various institutions, and that it stems from demand (families) as well as supply (institutions). This suggests the need to correct the quality estimates for the possible presence of selection bias when deriving quality estimates.

To this end the following methodology was deemed appropriate: three types of schools were considered for the analysis (municipal schools, lay private schools and religious private schools); a multinominal logit model was used to derive an equation combining selection factors related to supply and demand; and these estimates served as a basis for constructing, for each school in the sample, a variable measuring selection bias, and for each of the subsamples under study a controlled version of the educational quality model was estimated.

The selection equation for different types of schools was estimated on the basis of individual data taken from the 1992 CASEN survey. The variables used were the amount spent by the institutions[11] and parents' educational level. The choice of these variables for the regression was made because they are linked to each home's socioeconomic level and because they are available for each of the learning institutions included in the sample.[12] Results of estimates suggest that the greater the amount spent and the higher the parents' educational level, the greater the likelihood that the choice will be a private subsidized education, whether in a nonreligious or religious school.

A variable for selection bias is derived from these estimates, and a quality model, adjusted for selection bias, is estimated for each subsample. The main results are indicated in Table 2.9.[13]

The results are qualitatively similar to those reported in Table 2.8. Most important is the fact that the variable for selection bias is statistically significant, save in the case of religious private schools. The pattern of signs observed suggests that there is a positive selection bias in favor of subsidized private schools, whether they be religious or nonreligious, and a negative bias against municipal schools. This suggests that, whether on account of factors linked to supply or demand, a child attending a subsidized private school would get a better than average education, and that a child attending a municipal school would get an education worse than the average.

---

[11] This includes supplies, materials, uniforms, books, tuition costs and PTA fees.

[12] Other socioeconomic variables, such as income, age, family structure, and age of family members, etc., are not available for learning institutions.

[13] Tables B, C, and D of the Annex show selected regressions for these subsamples.

Table 2.9. Estimates of Factors Determining Quality

	Municipal	Nonreligious	Religious
Constant	72.4	82.0	89.0
	(–14.8)	(–48.8)	(–33.5)
Religious schools			
Group of schools	2.5		
	(–2.2)		
Municipal corporation	1.7		
	(–2.8)		
Socioeconomic bracket	–7.9		
	(–1.7)		
Intermediate socioeconomic bracket	–10.6		
	(–2.2)		
Deprivation index	–0.2	–0.3	–0.2
	(–9.2)	(–9.2)	(–5.7)
Selection bias	–11.2	5.8	4.1
	(–6.1)	(–3.8)	(–2.2)
Number of observations	510	276	80
R^2	0.31	0.37	0.49
Adjusted R^2	0.30	0.36	0.48
Log likelihood	–1685	–954	–262
Durbin Watson	1.8	1.8	2.1
F value	45.4	52.5	37.2

Analysis of the Factors Involved in School Administration

This section contains the main results of interviews with the various actors involved in providing an education, with the aim of seeking their opinions on the incentives and restrictions they face. Structured interviews were held with teachers and principals. This was done with focus groups with private and municipal schoolteachers. Administrative personnel from various learning institutions were personally interviewed and queried according to a structured questionnaire.

Teachers

Three focus groups were held with teachers from municipal and subsidized private schools. During these meetings special emphasis was placed on the teachers' self-perceived role and on the differences perceived between municipal and subsidized private schools.

The role of teachers. In general terms, teachers perceive themselves as having an important professional role, both in the eyes of their students and for society as a whole. Teachers tend to compare their activities with those of physicians or psychologists, since they can diagnose, counsel, offer solutions and give therapy. In general, teachers feel responsible for children's comprehensive education, and quite often they even feel they assume the role of surrogate parents.

Despite the great importance with which teachers view their role, the confidence society bestows on them as educators, and the college-level education required of them, teachers feel society does not readily acknowledge their importance and does not value them as highly as other professionals, even in economic terms.

In general, teachers tend to acknowledge they fall short of fulfilling their self-assigned role to the fullest. This is often due to factors unrelated to the individual, such as infrastructural problems in the different institutions, teachers' financial difficulties (low salaries), and problems stemming from the quality of the students.

Teachers feel highly frustrated, and this leads them to perceive themselves as inferior to other professionals. In light of this diagnosis, one wonders if it is possible to improve the quality of education when an actor so critical to its attainment shows such levels of frustration.

Differences between various types of learning institutions. Teachers who participated in the focus groups are clearly aware of the existence of three types of learning institutions: paid private schools charging tuition, subsidized private schools, and municipal schools. Even though only the last two types of schools were spontaneously discussed in the group sessions, teachers pointed out that paid private schools offered the best employment option, owing to their infrastructure, salaries and general atmosphere.

Teachers tend to perceive subsidized private schools as superior for a number of reasons. These include better infrastructure, stricter demands on teachers (both by the institutions themselves and by the parents), and better choice of students. Municipal schools, on the other hand, tend to be perceived as offering greater job stability, which implies greater benefits and less demands on teachers. It is notable that teachers in subsidized private schools also claim to have great job stability, but that such stability depends on the professional quality of the teachers. Given the competition between institutions, the latter need good teachers in order to successfully compete within the market.

According to teachers, one factor distinguishing different types of schools is the greater involvement of parents in subsidized private institutions. In general, it is claimed that municipal institutions have a more heterogeneous student body because of their less rigorous academic demands, since they have to accept students of all kinds.

Contrary to the researcher's expectations, there was no distinct awareness of salary discrepancies between both systems. Nevertheless, everyone agrees that teachers are underpaid.

Nor was any clear-cut difference noted between the two systems in terms of teaching materials, the application of new learning methodologies, opportunities for planning and evaluating student activities, academic meetings and continuing education. Teachers claim to have support in these areas.

In terms of relationships within the workplace, teachers in municipal and subsidized private schools both perceived a more horizontal relationship between the principal and teachers in the municipal schools. However, they felt in some cases this relationship led to a loss of efficiency because the principal's authority was lost.

These differences were not considered essential and teachers invariably referred to paid private schools as being the ideal. In this sense, it would seem that both municipal and subsidized private schools constitute a lower division in which most teachers have to perform their duties.

School Principals

School principals were given structured interviews based on a questionnaire designed for this purpose. Twenty principals from municipal and subsidized private schools within the metropolitan Santiago area were personally interviewed in their respective schools.

Institutional relations. Municipal schools as well as subsidized private schools are linked to MINEDUC through the Provincial Department (*Departamento Provincial*, DEPROV). DEPROV supervises technical, pedagogical and managerial aspects. It is generally felt that the technical support received from the central level through DEPROV is insufficient, since it is limited to overseeing the implementation of MINEDUC's academic curricula and there is no major technical or pedagogical input. It is believed that DEPROV lacks adequately trained staff and suffers high turnover.

Insofar as the principals' degree of autonomy is concerned, most municipal schools, whether they belong to corporations or are managed by DAEM, want greater flexibility in contracting teachers. With some exceptions, teachers are chosen and designated by the secretary general or the director of DAEM. Only occasionally is the school principal's opinion taken into account when teachers are hired.

In subsidized private schools, the principal displayed greater autonomy in human resource management. Overall, the principals felt they should have more autonomy with respect to directions from their central offices, such as those relating to the school calendar. They also wanted greater freedom to create special academic curricula and programs more in tune with the needs of the school.

A view of the school's educational situation. Most of the schools that were visited perform well on the SIMCE test, and the majority of the students attending such schools come from middle- and lower-middle-class families.

The principals of the municipal schools expressed different viewpoints with regard to how their schools compared to those of the subsidized private sector. Some feel the essential difference lies in the choice of students; that is, they feel subsidized private schools are able to select their students and thus the human factor is better, enjoys greater family support, and has parents who belong to a higher social class. On the other hand, all of the subsidized private school principals interviewed agreed that the main difference between municipal schools and their own lay in the higher quality of the teachers and their commitment to the school, which bestowed the school with the ability to offer a comprehensive, better education. Other differences were also pointed out, among them better infrastructure, greater job flexibility for teachers, greater teacher motivation, and greater managerial autonomy, both in administrative and financial terms.

Relations with teachers. All municipal school principals interviewed stated that teachers were encouraged to participate in continuing education classes. Many such classes must be paid for by the teacher, although funding can be obtained through projects, the Ministry of Education, and the corporation or DAEM. In religious and nonreligious subsidized private schools, training is also encouraged. The head office usually covers between 50 percent and 100 percent of the cost of the continuing education class.

Insofar as teachers' autonomy is concerned, practically all the school principals interviewed stated that teachers are free to establish their own goals and teaching methods under the supervision of the technical and pedagogical units.

Organizational system. In municipal schools, the hiring, firing and promotion of staff members are the responsibility of the corporation or DAEM. In most schools the principal can eventually make recommendations; however, the corporation or DAEM is the one that ultimately decides. With few exceptions, the principal searches for the teacher and recommends to the corporation that he or she be hired. Salaries are established according to the guidelines set forth in the Teachers' Statute, while years of service (in biennia), continuing education classes, and level of responsibility are the factors taken into account. According to most principals, a teacher's salary ranges from $300 to $450 a month.

In subsidized religious and nonreligious private schools, there is no single rule with regard to the hiring or firing of school staff. In some cases this is a task shared by the principal and the head office; in others, the school principal or chief of personnel is solely responsible. Salaries are established by the head office according to the Teachers' Statute and supplemented with certain incentive payments for performance or, in the case of some religious schools, according to criteria established by the Federation of Private Educational Institutions (*Federación de Instituciones de Educación Particular,* FIDE). The salary scale depends chiefly on educational background and experience.

In the area of financial resource management, municipal schools lack large sums of money and have only petty cash. The principal is not familiar with the school budget, which he does not manage, or with the amount and structure of inputs and outputs. Everything having to do with budget management is done centrally through the DAEM or the corporation. In nonreligious, subsidized private schools, the principal does not manage the budget, but is at least familiar with the main expenses of the institution. The head office controls and manages resources according to the needs of the school, with greater participation by the principal. In religious subsidized schools, the principal controls and manages resources with occasional support from the school's management team.

Most subsidized religious and nonreligious private schools have shared funding. This allows them to make infrastructural improvements, raise teachers' salaries, and acquire better educational materials than those provided by MINEDUC.

With regard to choice of students, there are some differences between municipal schools and subsidized private schools. In most municipal schools, students are selected primarily when there is high demand for the school relative to a limited number of vacancies. Some schools bar students who have to repeat a grade, and the majority require a minimum grade point average. In nonreligious, subsidized private schools, only half the principals interviewed stated that there are certain prerequisites for students who are admitted (a minimum grade point average and an interview with the parents). The others do not select students, since the number of vacancies is not fully covered. For their part, all religious schools visited choose students chiefly on the basis of an interview with the parents.

Administration. In looking at the factors that negatively influenced the results obtained by the schools, principals of municipal schools singled out the lack of family support as most important. This was attributed to parents working and spending most of the time outside the home, or to students coming from atypical households. Ranking next in importance was the excessive number of medical absences on the part of teachers, which create havoc and delay academic activities. Also mentioned were enforcement of the Teachers' Statute and the lack of teaching materials, given the fact that those provided by MINEDUC are not sufficient, and poor participation on the part of authorities. Less frequently cited were certain factors related to the inability to choose students, inadequate teaching methods, low teachers' salaries, and the lack of adequate infrastructure, as in the case of libraries and study centers.

For principals of subsidized private schools, the strongest negative factors cited were a lack of family support and the teacher's tenuous institutional commitment. Also mentioned were excessive medical leaves, parents' low cultural and socioeconomic background, and poor teacher training.

According to municipal school principals, the positive factors influencing school results were the commitment and motivation of the teaching staff. Following in importance were student participation in school activities; parental cooperation with the institution, especially through the Parents' Center; school-sponsored activities; good teacher relations, and having a well-trained teaching staff. In the case of nonreligious, subsidized private schools, most directors pointed to a good organizational climate as being the factor that most strongly contributes to good school performance. Other factors mentioned were the work environment, the permanent presence of the sponsor in the school, financial incentives for teachers, student participation, implementation of educational projects in the school, and good relations between teachers. In the case of religious, subsidized private schools, teachers' commitment and dedication were cited as essential to obtaining good results. In addition, school discipline and good relations between teachers and management were also mentioned.

Insofar as teacher performance is concerned, municipal school principals stated periodic evaluations were performed. Even though the results of these evaluations do not necessarily translate into "rewards" (salary raises) or "punishments" (being fired), certain privileges are granted, such as leaves, better treatment, or tickets for particular events. In other cases a letter of recognition is issued. On the other hand, when a teacher has performed poorly, communication with him or her is limited to discussing ways to correct mistakes.

In the case of the subsidized nonreligious or religious private schools, all have a system for evaluating teacher performance, even though only one "rewards" a teacher through financial incentives (a bonus for good performance and salary raises according to achievements). In other cases, teachers are acknowledged for their special merits in public events, and special concessions are granted from time to time. If performance has been poor, private conversations are held with the teachers, who are asked to correct their mistakes. If this fails to occur, contracts are not renewed. This point marks the difference between these schools and municipal schools, where the teacher cannot be fired for poor performance.

Conclusions

The most important factor to recognize is that, in theory, schools experiencing a drop in enrollment, and thus in income, should either close or merge. Although this occurs in the subsidized private sector, in the municipal sector, officials view this as politically costly, and thus it is common to see municipalities make direct financial transfers to schools in order to cover their deficits. Therefore municipal schools receive, in addition to the income derived from subsidies, voluntary or involuntary municipal contributions, while subsidized private schools have to finance all their expenses, including capital costs, solely with the income derived from subsidies, or accept private contributions. For this reason, it is widely accepted that municipal schools in general face softer budgetary constraints than subsidized private schools, which not only affects institutional efficiency, but also the level of competition between them.

The central level also imposes a number of regulations on the subsidized educational sector in matters linked to infrastructure, curricular content, salary structure, and experience-based remuneration, all of which directly affect the potential educational innovations that would be generated by competition among learning institutions. However, punishment for lack of compliance has a different impact on the various sectors: in the subsidized private sector it means substantial financial penalties, while in the municipal sector it translates into a greater municipal deficit in education, along with greater pressure on the central government for municipal transfers to cover the deficit. In other words, sanctions are softer for municipal schools, and this, in turn, affects efficiency.

Insofar as the organizational system is concerned, clear-cut differences were noted between municipal and subsidized private schools. First, in subsidized private schools the owner (sponsor) and the principal work together directly and permanently in the school's affairs. In municipal corporations, on the other hand, no direct team effort was noted between the principal and the sponsor. Instead, a different degree of delegation of authority was noted, depending on the individual in charge of the corporation. Thus, the issue of school ownership serves as an incentive to more direct involvement by the sponsor in the management of learning institutions.

Second, in subsidized private schools staff is hired jointly by the sponsor and the school principal. In the case of municipal schools in general, teachers are hired by the corporation or DAEM, and only now and then is the principal asked for an opinion. Thus, in subsidized private schools, principals exercise greater control of human resources.

Third, salary scales established by subsidized private schools are generally arrived at through collective negotiation and on the basis of the Teachers' Statute. In some cases, individual agreements are reached, especially when the teacher is held to be highly efficient. The criteria for determining a teacher's salary depend on experience, training and performance. In general, part of the income derived from shared funding is spent on improving salaries. This may take the form of an increase equally distributed among all teachers or be based on individual performance.

On the other hand, municipal sector salaries are established in accordance with the Teachers' Statute, while criteria for determining salary scales are inflexible and depend on experience, training and level of responsibility. The type of educational performance has no influence on the salary earned.

Fourth, in municipal schools the school budget is managed by the municipal holder, while the principal usually knows nothing about the size or distribution of the budget to different items. In subsidized private schools, the principal is at least familiar with the main elements of the school's sources of income and expenditure. This allows for greater flexibility in managing the budget, which encourages greater inventiveness on the part of the principal and teachers.

In addition, the lack of incentives within the municipal school system and the difficulty in controlling the school principal's managerial practices and eventually rewarding or sanctioning them lead to inefficient institutional management. The performance of municipal schools depends primarily on the individual managing the school rather than on a management model. Even worse, in many instances when a principal's work has been found lacking, the harshest punishment amounts to a transfer to a smaller school, since the Teachers' Statute prohibits firing, unless a serious infraction has been committed. This type of situation is unimaginable in the subsidized private sector.

Thus, the municipal system faces a number of work restrictions that add to the inefficiency of the system. Teachers' job stability, which is guaranteed by their work statute, in most cases leads to overstaffing and to keeping individuals in posts that are unsuitable for them. The system does not "reward" or "punish" a teacher's performance. This leads to less dedication and neglect of work, as noted especially in the excessive medical leave petitioned by teachers.

The final factor that bears on the effort to achieve greater managerial efficiency is assigning resources on the basis of the results. Sponsors of subsidized private schools, which depend exclusively on subsidies and on shared funding, have an interest in exerting themselves to obtain good results in order to attract students and maintain high student attendance. If owners of municipal schools do not cover their expenses with the income from the subsidy, they receive municipal transfers, which often are ultimately financed by the central level (MINEDUC or the Ministry of Domestic Affairs). Thus, municipal schools work under a soft budget that fails to generate the proper incentives.

Even though the Chilean educational system is based on competition between institutions, in practice service providers often display a low level of effort, both in making use of market elements to meet their competition (such as publicity, for example) and in making a sustained effort to increase student enrollment. The two main reasons for this are, first, that there is a "cultural" factor that acts on educational service providers, the vast majority of whom have been trained in an academic tradition that seldom encourages competitive behavior; and second, the progressive deterioration of the Educational Subsidy Unit has not only kept for-profit schools from entering the market, but it has also forced some of them to leave the market. This has led to a predominance of schools with a less competitive tradition, such as municipal schools, congregational schools and nonprofit schools.

Nevertheless, and particularly in the municipal schools that were visited, school principals were conscious of the need to aggressively seek out students. However, they often lack the appropriate background to be able to plan in a professional manner the more commercial aspects of their institutions.

The results suggest that the crucial issue does not lie in whether a school is public or private, but in other attributes having to do with educational expertise of its staff. This is shown by the fact that better results were obtained by schools under institutional or corporate leadership, such as Catholic schools and schools whose sponsors were in charge of several institutions.

This points to possible economies of scale in the administration of such institutions, which creates opportunities for improving efficiency through the specialization of different agents in various activities. Thus, certain decisions to purchase equipment or to manage particular items (such as the training of teachers and the content of curriculum) can be made by the owner or sponsor in support of the schools, whereas other decisions having to do with pedagogical aspects, personnel management or spending on certain items can be delegated to the school principal. Such division of functions makes not only for greater efficiency within the units, but also for establishing performance comparisons between schools and disseminating successful methodologies among them.

Bibliography

Aedo, C. 1997. *Organización industrial de la prestación de servicios sociales.* Serie de documentos de trabajo, R-302, IDB/OCE, Washington, D.C.

Aedo, C., and O. Larrañaga. 1993. Políticas sociales II: el caso chileno. *Revista de Análisis Económico* 8(2) November, ILADES/Georgetown University: 149–78.

Cox, D., and E. Jiménez. 1991. The Relative Effectiveness of Private and Public Schools: Evidence from Two Developing Countries. *Journal of Development Economics* 34: 99–124.

Espínola, V., and A. Guzmán. 1995. Transformaciones en los procesos de gestión educativa en el marco de la descentralización: el caso de Chile. Santiago, CIDE. Mimeo.

ILADES/Georgetown University. 1990. Estatuto Docente. Informe TASC, No. 7, Santiago.

________. 1991. Estado de avance de proyectos. Ley de pesca y estatuto docente. Informe TASC, No. 17, Santiago.

________. 1994. Estado de avance de proyectos. Ley de pesca y estatuto docente. Informe TASC, No. 17, Santiago.

Infante, M., and E. Schiefelbein. 1992. Asignación de recursos para la educación básica y media: el caso de Chile. Santiago. Mimeo.

Larrañaga, O. 1994. *Descentralización en educación y salud en Chile.* Santiago: Programa de Postgrado en Economía, ILADES/Georgetown University.

Manski, C., and D. Wise. 1983. *College Choice in America.* Boston: Harvard University Press.

Ministerio de Educación. 1994. *Orientaciones básicas, objetivos y componentes del Programa MECE.* Santiago: MINEDUC.

Ministerio da Educação. 1995. *Relatório do Sistema Nacional de Avaliação da Educação Básica.* Brasília: Instituto Nacional de Estudos e Pesquisas Educacionais.

Montt, P., and P. Serra. 1994. *La descentralización educativa en Chile: el traspaso de la educación a los municipios.* ILPES Working document No. 3, Santiago.

Ruíz Fernández, Julio. 1994. *Municipios y servicios sociales: la experiencia chilena.* ILPES, Working document No. 2, Santiago.

Schiefelbein, E. 1988. Siete estrategias para elevar la calidad y eficiencia del sistema de educación. Boletín Proyecto Principal de Educación en América Latina 16, UNESCO, Santiago.

SIMCE. 1994. *Folleto técnico: directivos y docentes.* Santiago: Ministerio de Educación.

————. 1995. *Folleto técnico 1995: directivos y docentes, educación básica.* Santiago: Ministerio de Educación.

UNESCO. 1994. *Medición de la calidad de la educación: instrumentos.* Volume II, OREALC, Santiago.

UNICEF/Fundación ANDES. 1994. *Aportes de la empresa privada al mejoramiento de la educación en Chile.* Santiago: Fundación Andes/ UNICEF.

Varun, G. 1994. *Hay diferencias entre padres de alumnos en colegios municipales y particulares?* Serie de Investigación I-81, Programa de Posgrado en Economía, ILADES/Georgetown University, Santiago.

Annex

Table A. Results for the Entire Sample, Dependent Variable, SIMCE, 1994

	MODEL 1	MODEL 2	MODEL 3	MODEL 4	MODEL 5
CONSTANT	78.925	78.749	78.804	76.882	78.762
t value	23.869	37.443	37.190	68.830	37.421
Religious	5.332	5.824	6.083	5.839	5.957
t value	4.808	6.249	6.496	6.265	6.416
Private	2.269	2.264	2.307	2.310	2.272
t value	2.622	2.743	2.774	2.802	2.751
Nonreligious	0.426				
t value	0.246				
For profit	−0.897				
t value	−0.532				
Corporation	1.746	1.940	2.005	1.961	1.902
t value	2.735	3.601	3.696	3.642	3.530
Teacher-student ratio	0.010				
t value	0.664				
Deprivation Index	−0.192	−0.192	−0.200	−0.192	−0.195
t value	−12.921	−13.049	−13.656	−13.053	−13.313
Lower class	−8.747	−6.060	−3.252	−3.658	−7.650
t value	−2.748	−2.381	−1.328	−3.309	−3.336
Middle class	−4.983	−2.435	−2.611	−3.889	
t value	−1.684	−1.048	−1.115	−1.851	
Low expenditures	7.679	4.114	4.138	3.789	
t value	2.066	3.728	3.750	3.476	
Middle-low expenditures	3.50				
t value	0.999				
Middle expenditures	0.070				
t value	0.021				
Low schooling	−6.025	−4.993	−3.287	−5.559	
t value	−1.935	−1.655	−1.094	−1.872	
Low-medium schooling	−7.319	−6.245	−4.556	−6.813	−4.175
t value	−4.431	−4.256	−3.240	−4.997	−6.138
Medium schooling	−2.928	−1.874	−1.342	−2.445	
t value	−1.986	−1.475	−1.055	−2.132	
No. of observations	866	866	866	866	866
R^2-BAR	0.431	0.433	0.425	0.433	0.432
F value	44.763	67.070	71.894	74.392	83.265

Table B. Results for the Subsample of Municipal Schools, Dependent Variable, SIMCE, 1994

	MODEL 1	MODEL 2
Constant	72.421	72.495
t value	14.771	14.534
Municipal corporation	1.693	1.697
t value	2.798	2.791
Teacher:Student ratio	−0.003	
t value	−0.083	
Deprivation Index	−0.165	−0.165
t value	−9.153	−9.133
Lower class	−7.916	−7.911
t value	−1.676	−1.673
Middle class	0.612	−10.603
t value	−2.195	−2.190
Selection bias	−11.205	−11.198
t value	−6.077	6.061
No. of observations	510	510
R^2-BAR	0.304	0.302
F value	45.383	37.746

Table C. Results for the Nonreligious School Subsample, Dependent Variable, SIMCE, 1994

	MODEL 1	MODEL 2	MODEL 3
Constant	84.798	81.415	81.991
t value	20.174	47.271	48.804
Private school	2.585	2.649	2.494
t value	2.258	2.339	2.207
For profit	−1.317		
t value	−0.704		
Teacher:Student ratio	0.024		
t value	1.031		
Deprivation index	−0.252	−0.249	−0.262
t value	−8.374	−8.337	−9.189
Lower class	−4.867	−1.781	
t value	−1.335	−1.461	
Low-middle class	−3.155		
t value	−0.884		
Selection bias	4.507	4.750	5.827
t value	2.613	2.775	3.763
No. of observations	276	276	276
R^2-BAR	0.360	0.363	0.360
F value	23.144	40.106	52.544

Table D. Results for the Religious School Subsample, Dependent Variable, SIMCE, 1994

	MODEL 1	MODEL 2	MODEL 3	MODEL 4
Constant	88.032	87.960	87.489	88.999
t value	21.382	29.902	30.300	33.536
Private	1.992	2.014	1.904	
t value	1.325	1.364	1.297	
Teacher:Student ratio	−0.015	−0.019		
t value	−0.701	−0.875		
Deprivation index	−0.231	−0.237	−0.234	−0.238
t value	−5.271	−5.621	−5.583	−5.653
Lower class	−2.256			
t value	−0.606			
Low-middle class	−1.205			
t value	−0.377			
Selection bias	2.925	3.733	3.864	4.114
t value	1.238	1.938	2.015	2.147
No. of observations	80	80	80	80
R^2-BAR	0.470	0.481	0.482	0.478
t value	12.660	19.294	25.550	37.156

CHAPTER 3

The Impact of Three Institutional Innovations in Brazilian Education

Ricardo Paes de Barros and Rosane Mendonça[1]

Brazil's development process stands apart from Asian and other Latin American countries with similar income levels because of its remarkably low rates of school enrollment and the slow expansion of its education system. Indeed, most countries growing at rates equal to or greater than Brazil's have expanded their education systems at a much faster pace.

Development in Brazil, particularly its boom during the 1970s, can be described as unbalanced. Investments in physical capital and infrastructure always outweighed investments in human capital. The consequence of this strategy has been a wide gap between economic development and human development.

Despite the current relevance of the discussion over how Brazil could have experienced such remarkable growth without a simultaneous expansion of education, the issue now being posed is how to resume growth without first eliminating the huge and existing educational lag. All evidence seems to indicate that the educational system is one of the obstacles to the country's development and hence must be thoroughly redesigned.

Better educational performance can be attained by increasing either the amount of resources devoted to education or the efficiency with

[1] Ricardo Paes de Barros is a researcher at the Institute of Applied Economic Research (*Instituto de Pesquisa Econômica Aplicada - IPEA)* in Rio de Janeiro. Rosane Mendonça teaches at the Universidade Federal Fluminense in Rio de Janeiro.

which those resources are used. Public spending on education in Brazil is high (around 4 percent of GDP) compared with how much is spent in other Latin American countries with similar income levels. Thus there are indications that poor educational performance in Brazil must be linked to inefficient use of resources rather than to the amount of resources allocated.

Prominent among the possible reasons for the inefficiency of the Brazilian system is the way schools have traditionally been run. Direct elections for governor in 1982 marked the beginning of a process of spreading innovations in school management. This process varied in intensity, speed and degree of synchronization in the various state school systems and was based primarily on initiating three innovations: i) direct transfer of funds to schools, ii) election of principals, and iii) creation of local school councils.[2] The central purpose of this study is to evaluate the impact of these innovations on educational performance.

The uneven timing and extent to which these innovations were implemented is key to evaluating their impact on educational performance. First, the innovations went into effect at different times and in different states. Given how the process spread, the impact can be evaluated either by contrasting for a particular point in time the educational performance in innovative states with performance in those states with traditional systems (cross-section analysis); by contrasting for a particular state the educational performance before and after the introduction of these innovations in school management (time-series analysis); or by using both types of contrast simultaneously. Second, innovating states did not necessarily adopt the three innovations simultaneously, thereby making it possible to identify the impact of each of the three innovations on its own.

These contrasts are examined together through the use of cross-section pooling techniques, where each observation unit consists of a Brazilian state at a point in time. In addition, we examine differences in the quality of the family environment and of the teachers, which may also account for differences in educational performance between states and points in time. A

---

[2] The school council—a local group board made up of parents, teachers and community representatives—has a number of responsibilities that vary from state to state. In general it is responsible for administering resources for school maintenance and purchasing educational material. In some cases it also elects the school principal.

state-level longitudinal data base was constructed with information on the spread of innovations, measures of educational performance, and measures of the quality of family environment and the quality of available educational resources. The information base covers the 1981–1993 period and all geographical units in the country except the Federal District and the states in the north and the state of Alagoas. With information for 12 points in time[3] and 18 states, the data base has around 220 observations.

The measures of educational performance were i) the repetition rate, obtained from the school census, ii) the proportion of children outside school and two measures of grade-level lag obtained using the National Household Survey Sample (PNAD - *Pesquisa Nacional por Amostra de Domicílios)*, and iii) school performance indicators obtained from the National Basic Education Evaluation System *(SAEB - Sistema Nacional de Avaliação da Educação Básica).*

This chapter starts with a brief description of how each of the three innovations in management spread in Brazil over the past 15 years, focusing on their nature and the time when they were established in each of the states included in the analysis. The second section presents a theoretical discussion of the reasons and the way in which the innovations in school management may have influenced educational performance. The final section studies the relationship between innovations in management and educational performance, using state-level longitudinal information.

Institutional Environment

In Brazil, responsibility for providing public education is divided between the three levels of government: federal, state, and municipal. The main responsibility for primary school education (the first eight grades) falls formally on municipal governments. In most states, however, the state primary school networks end up being larger than municipal networks.[4]

---

[3] While the period covered is 1981–93, we only included 12 points in time because there is no information for 1991.

[4] State and municipal networks serve around 16 and 9 million students, respectively. The state network tends to be larger than the municipal one in the richer states in the country located in the South, Center-West and Southeast; the state of Rio de Janeiro is an exception, inasmuch as it has a municipal system with a relatively high share similar to the poor states of the Northeast.

Table 3.1. Number of Schools, Students and Teachers in the Brazilian Primary School System, 1993

States	Schools		Students*		Teachers*	
	State	Municipal	State	Municipal	State	Municipal
Maranhão (MA)	658	11,501	362	813	15	33
Piauí (PI)	975	6,780	256	281	12	13
Ceará (CE)	838	11,405	428	561	15	27
Rio Grande do Norte (RN)	1,079	3,045	253	218	10	10
Paraíba (PB)	1,144	6,072	265	282	12	14
Pernambuco (PE)	1,150	8,270	685	686	22	25
Alagoas (AL)	393	2,954	129	277	6	10
Sergipe (SE)	352	1,533	181	147	7	6
Bahia (BA)	3,490	20,653	1,161	1,111	44	46
Minas Gerais (MG)	6,083	11,242	2,465	723	107	38
Espírito Santo (ES)	3,172	876	434	122	17	5
Rio de Janeiro (RJ)	2,005	3,053	565	889	30	42
São Paulo (SP)	7,517	520	4,852	585	201	23
Santa Catarina (SC)	4,275	3,535	584	208	25	10
Paraná (PR)	2,219	8,772	945	673	41	34
Rio Grande do Sul (RS)	3,165	9,547	895	599	54	38
Mato Grosso do Sul (MS)	368	1,130	247	141	9	6
Mato Grosso (MT)	542	3,069	314	143	12	7
Goiás (GO)	1,365	4,222	625	273	22	11
Distrito Federal (DF)	460	—	307	—	12	—
Total	41,250	118,179	15,952	8,732	674	398

Source: Compiled from data in the *Sinopse Estatística da Educação Fundamental, Censo Escolar,* 1993, MEC.
Note: Excludes the North Region.
* In thousands of persons.

The primary school system is gigantic (Table 3.1): approximately 160,000 schools spread over a territory of over 8.5 million square kilometers enroll around 25 million children, employ over 1 million teachers, and have an annual budget of around $8 billion. The fact that the system is decentralized by state does not keep the size of some state systems from being of frightful proportions. In São Paulo, for example, the education system is composed of 8,000 schools spread over 249,999 square kilometers, serves 5.3 million students, employs 225,000 teachers, and has an annual budget of around $2 billion. The state of Minas Gerais has 17,000 schools has 3.1 million teachers, 145,000 teachers and an $800 million budget. It therefore seems obvious that a centralized and authoritarian management system subject to systematic political interference, as was typical of Brazil in the 1970s, would hardly be able to manage an educational system of such proportions with even minimal efficiency.

Since the beginning of the redemocratization process in the early 1980s, particularly after the opposition victory in the 1982 elections for governor, management of the Brazilian public education system has been thoroughly reorganized. This process received great impetus from the promulgation of a new Federal Constitution in 1988 and subsequent state constitutions and municipal laws. This institutional arrangement constitutionally bolstered democratic management of the education system, and had the effect that in the ten years following passage of the laws at least half of the funds used in education were devoted to primary school education and to eliminating illiteracy (Mello, 1992).

Initially, the demand for more democratic, participatory and decentralized management was almost an end in itself, and was basically a demand by teachers and other educational experts. By the end of the 1980s, demand for reforms in the management process came to be seen as a requirement for improving the efficiency and quality of the education system, besides embracing an ever wider range of the population.

The past 15 years in Brazil have seen a series of changes and experiences in school management at both the state and municipal level. However, these innovations have not been centrally coordinated and have been subject to stops and starts. State education systems have taken up school management with varying intensities and speeds. Reversals have also been common. Such is the case, for example, of the state of Minas Gerais, which was one of those leading the wave of reforms in 1983 with the implementation of school boards, but which underwent a sharp reversal when the process was interrupted from 1987 to 1991.

If this decentralized and unsynchronized process of changing school management in Brazil has produced a great wealth of experiences and innovations, it has also made it very difficult to monitor, and hence to evaluate its impact on educational performance. The wealth of these innovations, and the problems in evaluating them, are clearly shown in two IPEA studies by Xavier, et al. (1994 and 1995).

Three Fundamental Innovations

Despite the qualitative diversity of the innovative experiences in school management in Brazil, they may be grouped into three major categories. The first includes those intended to encourage the financial autonomy of schools by transferring funds. These innovations enable schools to decide on how best to allocate resources, making them accountable for doing so as efficiently as possible. Financial autonomy becomes the pillar of the process of decentralizing school management.

A second group is comprised of changes in school management linked to the selection of school principals. They are basically intended to have principals chosen by election, which becomes the pillar of the school democratization process.

The third group is comprised of changes aimed at organizing and institutionalizing participatory management, involving not only teachers and school officials but also parents, students and other members of the local community. These innovations lead basically to the establishment of a school council, which becomes the pillar of the process of developing a participatory model of school management.

Financial autonomy. Traditionally, the autonomy of the school unit was limited to setting its priorities. The school did not receive funds and hence had no knowledge of its true budgetary constraints because it was unaware of either the amount of funding available or of the cost of the supplies to be used. With financial autonomy, funds are transferred directly to the school, which consequently becomes fully aware of its budgetary constraints and is free to allocate those resources as it deems fit, albeit subject to certain restrictions.

The restrictions to which the school is subject are of two basic kinds. First, these funds cannot be used for payroll (salary, bonuses or other monetary incentives). Second, part of these transfers are tied to specific projects that can be proposed either at the initiative of the school or of the State Secretary of Education. In this case, resources can be spent only on activities and supplies needed to carry out the specific project to which they are connected.

Funds are generally set aside for building and equipment maintenance, teaching materials and supplies. In some states funds can be used for training courses and for hiring services.[5] Although the volume of resources transferred varies by state, the goal is to reach $300 a student per year.[6]

State systems differ in the criteria they use for distributing funds among the schools, in the means used to make the transfer, and the system used for follow-up and monitoring. The criteria that are applied may be the number of students, the number of courses, or the cost per student. In some states resources are distributed progressively in order to reduce inequalities.

The main problems encountered in transferring resources directly to schools are identified in the IPEA study as the bureaucracy involved in implementing the transfers, the inexperienced and unqualified people involved, and existing legislation that, ironically, does not allow a school to be a budgetary unit.

Among the three innovations, school financial autonomy is the oldest and most widespread. The first state to adopt it was Sergipe in 1977. This is somewhat surprising, given the fact that for almost 20 years that state did not introduce either of the other reforms (election of the principal and the school council). Santa Catarina followed Sergipe by implementing transfer of funds to schools in 1980.

Adoption of this innovation was given a major push by direct elections for governor in 1982. It was then adopted in four other states (Bahia, Pernambuco, Paraná and Goiás), followed by Mato Grosso in 1987. All the other states except Paraíba and São Paulo instituted a transfer of funds to the schools in the first two years of the 1990s. Table 3.2 shows how this innovation spread within state school systems in Brazil. By the end of 1993 it had been implemented in 16 states, and only two states (Paraíba and São Paulo) had still not adopted it.

Election of principals. Traditionally, school principals were chosen on the basis of political criteria, which were sometimes based entirely on political favoritism. With the redemocratization process that began in the 1980s, demand grew for a more democratic and transparent process for appointment of principals.

---

[5] On this issue, see Xavier, et al. (1995).

[6] In Minas Gerais, for example, transfers represented around $160 to $220 a student per year in 1993. See Xavier, et al. (1994, p. 95).

Table 3.2. Spread of the Transfer of Funds Process

State	1975	1976	1977	1978	1979	1980	1981	1982	1983	1984	1985	1986	1987	1988	1989	1990	1991	1992	1993	1994	State
Maranhão (MA)																	■	■	■	■	Maranhão (MA)
Piauí (PI)																		■	■	■	Piauí (PI)
Ceará (CE)																	■	■	■	■	Ceará (CE)
Rio Grande do Norte (RN)																■	■	■	■	■	Rio Grande do Norte (RN)
Paraíba (PB)																					Paraíba (PB)
Pernambuco (PE)									■	■	■	■	■	■	■	■	■	■	■	■	Pernambuco (PE)
Sergipe (SE)			■	■	■	■	■	■	■	■	■	■	■	■	■	■	■	■	■	■	Sergipe (SE)
Bahia (BA)								■	■	■	■	■	■	■	■	■	■	■	■	■	Bahia (BA)
Minas Gerais (MG)																	■	■	■	■	Minas Gerais (MG)
Espírito Santo (ES)																		■	■	■	Espírito Santo (ES)
Rio de Janeiro (RJ)																		■	■	■	Rio de Janeiro (RJ)
São Paulo (SP)																					São Paulo (SP)
Santa Catarina (SC)						■	■	■	■	■	■	■	■	■	■	■	■	■	■	■	Santa Catarina (SC)
Paraná (PR)									■	■	■	■	■	■	■	■	■	■	■	■	Paraná (PR)
Rio Grande do Sul (RS)										■	■	■	■	■	■	■		■	■	■	Rio Grande do Sul (RS)
Mato Grosso do Sul (MS)																■	■	■	■	■	Mato Grosso do Sul (MS)
Mato Grosso (MT)														■	■	■	■	■	■	■	Mato Grosso (MT)
Goiás (GO)										■	■	■	■	■	■	■	■	■	■	■	Goiás (GO)

Source: Compiled from data in Xavier, Sobrinho and Marra (1994).

Over the course of the past decade, new methods for choosing principals have been introduced, ranging from selection processes based on competitive examinations, as is the case in São Paulo, to methods based entirely on elections, in which school officials, parents and students over 16 have a right to vote.

Between the two extremes, there are procedures such as that of Minas Gerais, where appointment of a principal takes place in two stages. First, the candidates take part in written tests and present their degrees, so that their knowledge of specific skills needed to run a school can be evaluated. Second, the three most qualified, provided they have passed, "then draw up a working plan which is discussed with the community at a general assembly called by the school. Parents, students over 16, and school employees make up the electoral body which decides who the new director will be by secret ballot" (SEEMG, 1994, p. 25).

Systems for electing principals differ widely in terms of the relationship to the demands or qualifications to be satisfied by the candidates. Typical criteria for candidates include educational level, experience in school administration, and length of time spent teaching and as a government employee. Systems also differ with regard to the length of the term (generally between two and three years) and the method for evaluating the principal's performance. However, some states, such as Minas Gerais, have no centralized evaluation system; it is left to the community itself as represented by the school council.

Like the other educational innovations, election of principals gained momentum after the introduction of gubernatorial elections in 1982. Elections were adopted by the states of Paraná (1984), Ceará (1985), Santa Catarina (1986), Mato Grosso (1987), Rio de Janeiro (1988), and Rio Grande do Norte (1989). In the 1990s, election of principals has finally been adopted in four more states, Paraíba, Espírito Santo, Minas Gerais, and Mato Grosso do Sul. However, the election of principals was interrupted in Santa Catarina and Mato Grosso. Table 3.3 shows how this innovation spread among the states. By the end of 1983 it was operational in eight states, while still not adopted in 10 others (Maranhão, Piauí, Pernambuco, Sergipe, Bahia, São Paulo, Santa Catarina, Rio Grande do Sul, Mato Grosso, and Goiás).

School councils. The school council (called a *colegiado* in Brazil) is a consultative and deliberative body responsible for coordinating and evaluating pedagogical, administrative and financial activities of individual

Table 3.3. Spread of the Election of Principals

State	1975	1976	1977	1978	1979	1980	1981	1982	1983	1984	1985	1986	1987	1988	1989	1990	1991	1992	1993	1994	State
Maranhão (MA)																					Maranhão (MA)
Piauí (PI)																					Piauí (PI)
Ceará (CE)											■	■	■	■	■	■	■	■	■	■	Ceará (CE)
Rio Grande do Norte (RN)															■	■	■	■	■	■	Rio Grande do Norte (RN)
Paraíba (PB)																	■	■	■	■	Paraíba (PB)
Pernambuco (PE)																					Pernambuco (PE)
Sergipe (SE)																					Sergipe (SE)
Bahia (BA)																					Bahia (BA)
Minas Gerais (MG)																	■	■	■	■	Minas Gerais (MG)
Espírito Santo (ES)																■	■	■	■	■	Espírito Santo (ES)
Rio de Janeiro (RJ)														■	■	■	■	■	■	■	Rio de Janeiro (RJ)
São Paulo (SP)																					São Paulo (SP)
Santa Catarina (SC)												■			■	■					Santa Catarina (SC)
Paraná (PR)										■	■	■	■	■		■		■	■	■	Paraná (PR)
Rio Grande do Sul (RS)																					Rio Grande do Sul (RS)
Mato Grosso do Sul (MS)																	■	■	■	■	Mato Grosso do Sul (MS)
Mato Grosso (MT)													■	■	■						Mato Grosso (MT)
Goiás (GO)																					Goiás (GO)

Source: Compiled from data in Xavier, Sobrinho and Marra (1994).

schools. It is a basic unit used by states to organize and institutionalize the participation of teachers, employees, parents, teachers and members of the community in running schools. The school council is composed of the principal, who generally presides over it, representatives of teachers and other school employees, and representatives of parents and students. In over half the states, these representatives are elected for a one to two year term.

In Minas Gerais, school councils are responsible for approving the school's development plan and its curriculum. They also play a key role in monitoring the use of funds transferred by the Ministry of Education to the school's accounts (members of the school council generally comprise the control board for the school's financial accounts). Besides that, the school council supervises infrastructure investments, personnel changes and the process of evaluating school performance.

Adoption of school councils also received great impetus after 1982. Councils were instituted in the states of Minas Gerais (1983), Goiás (1984), São Paulo (1985), and Santa Catarina (1986) (see Table 3.4). By the mid-1980s, use of councils spread slowly and experienced some setbacks. In 1987, school councils were partially implemented in Mato Grosso but suspended in Minas Gerais and Santa Catarina; in 1989, councils were introduced in Espírito Santo. Thus, at the end of the 1980s the number of states with school councils was the same as it had been in the middle of the decade. However, this innovation spread rapidly in the early 1990s; school councils were implemented in seven states between 1991 and 1992, and reactivated in Minas Gerais. By the end of 1993, councils were operating in 12 and, only six (Ceará, Pernambuco, Sergipe, Rio Grande do Sul, Rio de Janeiro, and Santa Catarina) had not yet adopted them.

Simultaneity of Innovations

While previous sections discussed the nature and objectives of each of the three innovations, their complementarity is equally important to achieve a combined impact greater than the sum of each innovation. Introduction of direct transfer of funds has a greater impact on school performance if some form of school council has already been established, which enables the community to have institutional control over school spending. Likewise, competitive and democratic choice of the school principal is more important

Table 3.4. Spread of the Establishment of School Councils

State	1975	1976	1977	1978	1979	1980	1981	1982	1983	1984	1985	1986	1987	1988	1989	1990	1991	1992	1993	1994	State
Maranhão (MA)																	■	■	■	■	Maranhão (MA)
Piauí (PI)																	■	■	■	■	Piauí (PI)
Ceará (CE)																					Ceará (CE)
Rio Grande do Norte (RN)																		■	■	■	Rio Grande do Norte (RN)
Paraíba (PB)																	■	■	■	■	Paraíba (PB)
Pernambuco (PE)																					Pernambuco (PE)
Sergipe (SE)																					Sergipe (SE)
Bahia (BA)																	■	■	■	■	Bahia (BA)
Minas Gerais (MG)									■	■	■	■					■	■	■	■	Minas Gerais (MG)
Espírito Santo (ES)														■	■	■	■	■	■	■	Espírito Santo (ES)
Rio de Janeiro (RJ)																					Rio de Janeiro (RJ)
São Paulo (SP)										■	■	■	■	■	■	■	■	■	■	■	São Paulo (SP)
Santa Catarina (SC)												■					■				Santa Catarina (SC)
Paraná (PR)																■	■	■	■	■	Paraná (PR)
Rio Grande do Sul (RS)																					Rio Grande do Sul (RS)
Mato Grosso do Sul (MS)																	■	■	■	■	Mato Grosso do Sul (MS)
Mato Grosso (MT)													■	■	■	■	■	■	■	■	Mato Grosso (MT)
Goiás (GO)									■	■	■	■	■	■	■	■	■	■	■	■	Goiás (GO)

Source: Compiled from data in Xavier, Sobrinho and Marra (1994).

for school performance if there is more community participation in advising principals and evaluating what they do.

Finally, there is little point in experimenting with a democratic and transparent process for choosing the principal and having a fully operating school council if the school has no autonomy in making the financial decisions that could influence its performance. Thus, transfer of funds to schools can motivate both community participation and a good principal, helping them in turn have significant effects on educational performance.

So while coordination clearly is important, Tables 3.2 and 3.4 show that in Brazil, the three innovations were implemented in a coordinated manner in only four states: Rio Grande do Norte, Espírito Santo, Minas Gerais, and Mato Grosso do Sul. In Paraná and Santa Catarina, they were implemented in a rather unsynchronized manner and with reversals. In Paraná, transfer of funds was established in 1983, whereas school councils were established only eight years later. In Santa Catarina, school councils and election of principals were eliminated. In Mato Grosso, elections of school principals were eliminated, and in the remaining 11 states at least one of the innovations was never introduced.

Theoretical Aspects of the Relationship Between Management Innovations and Educational Performance

In the previous section we have described how innovations in school management spread. In this section we go on to discuss in theoretical terms the relationship between these innovations and educational performance.

Financial Autonomy

In discussing the impact of financial autonomy on educational performance, a basic distinction must be made between two degrees of autonomy. The first can be characterized as "restricted autonomy," in which the central agency informs each school unit of its budget and the prices of a basket of supplies. The local unit is then responsible for indicating how resources are to be allocated within the bounds of what is allowed. The central agency is responsible for making purchases and for distributing the goods and services to local units.

The second is "full autonomy," under which the central agency not only informs the local school unit what its budget is, but also transfers resources to be administered by the school itself. In this case, besides having autonomy to choose its priorities, the school has the freedom and responsibility to make purchases and monitor its expenditures.

The rationale for restricted autonomy rests on the idea that i) the local unit has access to important information about resource allocation that is not available to the central agency, and ii) due to community pressure and oversight, the objective function of schools more closely approximates the objective social function than the objective function of the central agency. The latter would in theory be more vulnerable to political interests and corruption. Besides having the same advantages as restricted autonomy, full autonomy has other advantages whenever there are significant local variations in the price and quality of goods and services, along with significant storage and transportation costs, which mean that centralized purchasing does not benefit significantly from the economies of scale and specialization that constitute its underlying rationale.

A potential disadvantage of both restricted and full autonomy arises when the objective function of the school unit differs significantly from its objective social function. In this case, there arises a problem of incentives that is typical of the "principal-agent problem." The agent has the information that is relevant for efficient allocation, but since his or her objective function is different from the social function, a complete transfer of decisionmaking power into the agent's hands may be socially undesirable. Community participation in managing school resources is one way to assure that their objectives are approximated by the school unit. In short, given asymmetrical information and community participation in administering school resources, restricted autonomy would tend to be socially desirable.

Moreover, full autonomy has the disadvantage of allowing the principal and other employees to spend some of their teaching time in the school making purchases, hiring services, and monitoring expenditures. With full autonomy, all the benefits of specialization of work and of scale are diluted. Thus, for example, instead of just a small group at a central agency surveying prices, there will be one at each school. Hence the argument for full autonomy should be based on the idea that there are factors that offset these apparent economies of scale and specialization. The one factor most commonly claimed is that both price surveying and centralized purchasing are inefficient when local prices vary significantly and when transportation and storage costs are significant. It is commonly argued that centralized purchasing creates more bureaucracy at the central agency; that even though in principle it can operate efficiently, in practice it is generally inefficient. Moreover, centralized purchasing is systematically subject to political pressure and is more susceptible to corruption than purchasing performed by local actors under community supervision.

Election of Principals

The most efficient mechanism for selecting the school principal depends on the objective function of the various actors involved and on the information they have. The simplest case would be one in which i) the school principal's performance is observable or can be inferred from his or her prior performance in other positions; ii) all relevant information about the performance of the current school principal and the candidate is available; iii) the objective function of the Ministry of Education is compatible with maximizing social welfare; and iv) the ministry is acting independently by appointing the principal. In such a case, if the principal were chosen directly by the ministry, the system would be completely efficient.

Should at least one of the foregoing requirements not be met, a system in which school principals are appointed directly by the ministry would be inefficient. With regard to Brazil, this is the most common argument to explain inefficiency, including the claim that the ministry either does not have the proper goals or does not enjoy full independence for making appropriate selections. In both cases, appointment of the school director is made with objectives that differ from the social objective, and they are not necessarily compatible with efficient functioning of the system.

Yet even a ministry that has the proper goals and the necessary independence may be unable to adequately choose school principals because the information on the capability of each candidate for the positions is not available in systematic form. This information may be lacking because the characteristics that identify a good school principal are hard to measure, or because such information was simply not gathered and organized in the past. In such an event, a centralized selection system is not feasible.

When the objectives of a centralized system are not clear, or when the necessary information is not available, the choice of school principals by school employees and the community is an alternative worth considering.

Election of principals may be a better solution than centralized choice when i) the objective function of the group with voting rights is closer to the social welfare function than the objective function of the Minister of Education, given the political pressures to which it is subject; and ii) the information available to the electorate enables it to evaluate the candidates better than the ministry.

With regard to the objective function, no one can better determine the welfare function that ought to be maximized than the community itself. In this sense, the participation of school employees can clearly be questioned, since it is easy to imagine that teachers and school employees have their own interests in conducting school affairs, which may be in conflict with the interests of the community.

In terms of information, it is not clear that the community has the information needed to evaluate the potential ability of the various candidates for school principal. As a rule, the community either does not have the necessary information or has difficulty processing existing information. In that case, the involvement of employees and teachers can be decisive, because they not only have a much greater amount of information on the performance of the candidates (both as a school principal or in other positions), but they are also better able to relate the previous experience of the candidates to their ability to run the school.

In short, as is typical of "principal-agent problems," those agents who have better information available (ministry and teachers) do not have the objective function closest to the ideal one (community). In such cases the optimal solution seems to be a mix: neither direct election nor a centralized decision but a combination of both. A noteworthy example would be the system in effect in Minas Gerais, where candidates are subject to examinations and other tests before the election.

School Councils

Before examining the role of the school council in running a public education system, it should be noted that their existence depends very much on the groups who have a right to be represented. As in the case of the election of the school principals, it is important to distinguish between the basis for participation of teachers and other school employees and that of parents and other members of the community.

To the extent that there is no competition between public education systems or between school units in a single system (at least at the basic education level), there is accordingly no external mechanism for imposing discipline on the objective function of those running the education system. Thus the school council, when it is made up of parents and other members of the community, is compatible with the aim of keeping the objective function of the school close to that of the community to which it belongs. This function would be operative when the school council is involved in devising the school's development plan and in monitoring and evaluating its implementation by the school principal. In short, to the extent that the school council has planning, evaluation and oversight functions, it can discipline the objective function of those running the system.

Community participation also has other functions. To begin with, even if those running the school were to have the proper objective function, they would be unable to design a plan of action for the school, because as a rule they would be lacking information on the demand profile, that is, what value the community places on the various kinds of services that could be offered by the school. In other words, a socially efficient allocation of educational resources requires the knowledge of both the costs of the various services to be offered and the value given to such services by their users. Thus, part of the rationale for community participation in the school council is to transmit inexpensively such information on the demand for educational services to those running the system. The school council performs this function when it operates as a consulting body.

Finally, community participation in the school council can serve to raise the quality and quantity of resources available to the school by encouraging parental involvement and hence prompting them to devote a greater proportion of their resources to their children's education.

One of the problems with the school council as a consultative body derives from the fact that in some cases appropriate decisions depend, in ways that are not always clear, on technical knowledge that requires years of experience and training in education. Communities can make wrong decisions if they fail to recognize the importance of such experience and training. In other words, the contribution of the community to school management has ill-defined limits which if not adequately recognized can lead to inefficient management.

With regard to the rationale for the participation of teachers and other school employees in the school council, the situation is more traditional, although less obvious. It is traditional in the sense that it is no different from the importance of workers being involved in any production process. Despite the voluminous literature on the role of self-management in labor productivity, the circumstances under which it is recommended are still debated. In principle, self-management would be desirable in situations where monitoring the labor process is costly and workers have private information on efficient handling of the production process. In such situations, self-management would be a useful way of encouraging worker cooperation. However, it remains to be seen to what extent such factors are present in the case of schools.

Anecdotal evidence indicates that monitoring teachers is not especially costly. Moreover, the fact that private school teachers and employees are not usually involved in running their schools suggests that there is little basis for teacher involvement in the school councils of public schools.

Empirical Evaluation of Determinants of Educational Performance

This section introduces the sources of information used for this chapter: the School Census, the National Household Survey Research (PNAD), and the National Basic Education Evaluation System (SAEB).

School Census. The School Census is the basic tool of the Education Statistics System. It involves seven surveys taken annually: preschool, basic (primary), middle (secondary), higher, special, and complementary education and educational financing. This chapter uses information from the survey on basic education for the 1981–1993 period, in which the information gathering tools remained essentially unaltered.[7]

These surveys are performed in a census-like manner, and they are carried out through the use of forms that must be filled out by all institutions, which are identified by a registry updated each year (MEC, 1996). The forms include information on the school, teaching staff and student body. The information on the students considers initial enrollment by grade and

---

[7] However, it should be mentioned that in 1994 there were a number of important changes in the School Census forms.

age in the current year, the initial enrollment of repeating students by grade, school changes (withdrawals due to transfer or dropout), and examinations results (passed or failed) in the prior school year.

On the basis of information on the student body, a variety of performance indicators can be constructed basically measuring the coverage and performance of the system.[8] This chapter uses only the repetition rate. In addition, on the basis of information on the teaching staff, we obtained an indicator of teacher quality provided by the proportion of teachers with higher education.

National Household Survey Research (PNAD) The PNAD is an annual survey that has been carried out regularly at the beginning of the third quarter of each year since 1976, except 1980 and 1991—to avoid overlap with the Demographic Census—and 1994, when this survey was temporarily suspended. Since 1992 the PNAD has been thoroughly reworked. Besides the quadrupling of the size of the questionnaire, a series of conceptual modifications have been added, effects of which have not yet been well evaluated.

This survey is based on a probability sampling of around 100,000 families (0.5 percent of the Brazilian population) and includes personal characteristics (sex, race and age), housing conditions (access to water, sewerage, etc.), schooling and employment.

With regard to the educational situation of the population, the PNAD has items on whether each family member over five can read and write, the grade and school level they attend, if attending school, and the last grade and school level attended, if the person has left school. On the basis of this information, it is possible to identify whether a boy or girl is attending school and the last grade completed. Estimates can then be made on the proportion of children not attending school (nonattendance rates), the average mean grade-level lag, and the proportion of children with some grade-level lag.

This chapter also used the PNAD to calculate a set of measurements of the quality of the family environment and the teachers. The quality of family environment was determined by per capita family income and average schooling of the adult population (used as an indicator of schooling of the

---

[8] See MEC (1995) for a description of various performance indicators that can be constructed with this database.

parents). For the quality of teachers, the mean salary of teachers in basic education and mean schooling of teachers in basic education were used.

National Basic Education Evaluation System (SAEB) The SAEB is a regular survey carried out by the National Institute of Studies and Educational Research (INEPE), the purpose of which is to serve as an innovative tool for formulating, reformulating and monitoring policies intended to improve basic education (MEC, 1995). Three evaluation cycles have now been carried out in 1990, 1993 and 1995. However, the results of this most recent evaluation were not used because they were not available when this chapter was being prepared.

In each evaluation cycle, around 3,000 schools throughout the country were chosen on a probability basis for the research. The research is based on three tools: a questionnaire for the principal, one for the teacher, and an examination of student performance.

In each cycle, 10 performance measures are obtained from the students in accordance with the grade and subject matter in question. Mathematics, Portuguese and science are the subject matters evaluated. Only ten measurements were used because the first and third grade exams did not test science.

In order to make the two basic cycles of SAEB performance tests comparable, a pilot application was carried out in a sample of 2,049 students from seven regional units of the country in such a way that the same student took the tests for levels 1 and 2. This procedure made it possible to adjust the results of the first level, making them comparable to those of the second. All the results used here having to do with the first cycle have already been adjusted.[9]

Indicators

This section defines the indicators of educational performance used, offers some general comments on the level, trends and spatial variation associated with these indicators, and considers the degree of association of these indicators with the introduction of management innovations.

---

[9] See MEC, 1995, p. 156, for a description of the method used for this adjustment.

Definitions are given below for the five performance indicators used in this chapter: repetition rate, proportion of children not in school, mean grade-level lag, proportion of children with some lag, and school performance. Estimates of the movement of the first four indicators for the 1981–1993 period by state are presented in Barros and Mendonça (1997), where it is possible to contrast i) for each available year the mean of the indicators in those states where the innovation was implemented with the mean in those where it was not implemented, and ii) for each state, the mean in those years when the innovation did not exist with the mean of the indicators in those years when the innovation was present. That study also presents estimates of school performance for both types of evaluation, by state and subject matter, as summarized in Table 3.5.

Repetition rate. The repetition rate, obtained from the School Census, indicates the percentage of students enrolled in the state system at the beginning of the year who failed at the end of the school year. It can therefore be obtained by dividing the number of students failed by the initial enrollment.[10]

Table 3.5 shows that the mean repetition rate in the period under examination in Brazil was 20.1 percent, the repetition rate at the beginning of the 1990s was around 4.2 percentage points lower than what it was at the beginning of the 1980s, and the difference between the states with the highest and lowest average repetition rates was 14.2 percent.

With regard to association with innovations in management, Table 3.5 also shows a clear tendency toward a lower repetition rate in states and in years in which at least one of the three innovations had been implemented. Taking all these years and states together, Table 3.5 shows that the repetition rate was on average 1.7 percentage points lower in those states and years where there was transfer of funds, 2.9 points lower in states and years where the school principal was elected, and 4.2 points lower in states and years where there was a school council.

Hence the differences in repetition rates favor the states and years in which there are innovations, and that differential is as large as the decline in repetition rates over the decade of the 1980s, but considerably lower than

---

[10] The complement to the repetition rate is not the same as the rate of passing, since this complement includes not only the pass rate but also the rates of school dropout, and transfers.

Table 3.5. Indicators of Educational Performance and Innovative Experiences in School Management

Indicator	Mean (1)	(1990–93)– (1981–83) (2)	Regional minimum- maximum (3)	Fund Transfer			Election of principal			Establishment of school council		
				Yes (4)	No (5)	Difference (4)–(5)	Yes (6)	No (7)	Difference (6)–(7)	Yes (8)	No (9)	Difference (8)–(9)
Repetition rate	20.10	–4.18	14.23	19.27	20.96	–1.69	17.96	20.88	–2.92	17.22	21.43	–4.20
Nonattendance rate	20.25	–10.22	19.37	18.11	21.75	–3.64	17.51	20.90	–3.39	15.12	21.76	–6.64
Mean grade-level lag	1.75	–0.37	1.61	1.68	1.80	–0.13	1.57	1.79	–0.23	1.47	1.83	–0.36
Proportion of children with some lag	69.03	–7.94	28.96	67.65	69.99	–2.34	65.42	69.87	–4.46	64.07	70.48	–6.41
Mean school performance	42.78	—	11.27	42.38	43.16	–0.79	43.62	42.23	1.39	43.96	42.34	1.62

Source: Compiled from Barros and Mendonça (1997).

Notes: (2) Difference between the mean in the 1990–93 period and the mean in 1981–83.

(3) Difference between the maximum and minimum of the regional means.

regional disparities. Moreover, it is clear that this differential is higher for school councils than for transfer of funds, while election of principals occupies a middle position.

Proportion of children not in school. The proportion of children not in school obtained from the PNAD was defined as the fraction of the population aged 7 to 14 that was not attending school at the beginning of the third quarter of the year.

Table 3.5 shows that the average proportion of children not in school in Brazil in the period examined was 20.3 percent, the proportion of children not in school at the beginning of the 1990s was 10.2 percentage points lower than what it was at the beginning of the 1980s, and the difference between states with the highest and lowest proportion of children not in school was 19.4 percentage points.

With regard to the connection with innovations in management, Table 3.5 reveals a clear tendency toward a lower proportion of children not attending school in states and years in which at least one of the three innovations had been instituted. Taking all the years and states together, Table 3.5 shows that the rate of nonattendance was on average 3.6 percentage points lower in states and years where resources were transferred, 3.4 percentage points lower in states and years where school principals were elected, and 6.6 percentage points lower in states and years where school councils were operating.

Hence, the differences in the proportion of children not in school favor those schools and years where innovations took place, and that differential is of a magnitude similar to half of the reduction in the proportion of children not in school that took place over the period under examination, but it is considerably lower than the regional disparities. Moreover, it can be seen that this differential, as is the case with the repetition rate, is higher for school councils than for transfer of funds. However, contrary to the case of repetition rates, election of the school principal does not assume a middle position.

Average grade-level lag. The average grade-level lag d is defined for each child as $d = i - s - 7$, where i denotes the child's age, and s the last grade attended. Thus a seven-year-old child who is attending the first grade would have $d = 0$. The mean grade-level lag refers to the mean for the population aged 7 to 14.

Table 3.5 shows that the mean grade-level lag in Brazil during the period under examination was 1.75 years, the mean grade-level lag at the beginning of the 1990s was around 0.37 points lower than it was at the beginning of the 1980s, and the difference between states with the highest and lowest lag was 1.61 years.

With regard to the association with innovations in management, Table 3.5 also shows a certain tendency for this indicator to be lower in states and years in which at least one of the three innovations had been instituted. Taking all years and states together, Table 3.5 shows that the mean grade-level lag was on average 0.1 years lower in those states and years where election of principals took place and 0.4 years lower in states and years where there were school councils.

Thus, as in the previous cases, it can be seen that the differences in the mean grade-level lag favor states and years in which there were innovations, and that differential is of a magnitude similar to the reduction of the mean grade-level lag over the period under examination, but considerably less than that of the regional disparities. Moreover, it is clear that, as with the repetition rate, this differential is higher for school councils than for transfer of funds, while election of school principals lies in between.

Proportion of children with some lag. The proportion of children with some lag was defined as the proportion of children aged 7 to 14 with a positive grade-level lag ($d>0$).

Table 3.5 shows the proportion of children with some lag in Brazil during the period under examination was on average 69 percent, the proportion of children with some lag at the beginning of the 1990s was 7.9 percentage points lower than it was at the beginning of the 1980s, and the difference between states with the highest and lowest proportion of children with some lag was 29 percentage points.

With regard to the association with innovations in management, Table 3.5 also shows a certain tendency for this indicator to be lower in states and years in which at least one of the three innovations had been instituted. Taking all the years and states together, Table 3.5 shows that the proportion of children with some lag was on average 2.3 percentage points lower in states and years in which there had been transfer of funds, 4.5 percentage points lower in states and years in which principals had been elected, and 6.4 percentage points lower in states and years where there were school councils.

Thus, as with the previous cases, it is clear that the differences in the proportion of children with some lag favor states and years in which innovations took place, and that differential is of a magnitude similar to the drop in the proportion of children with some lag over the period examined, but considerably less than the regional disparities. Moreover, it can be seen that, like the repetition rate and the mean grade-level lag, this differential is higher for the school council than for transfer of funds, while election of school principals lies in between.

School performance. School performance was defined as the simple arithmetic mean of the 20 scores[11] obtained in the two examination cycles for 1990 and 1993 (mathematics, grades 1, 3, 5 and 7; Portuguese, grades 1, 3, 5 and 7; and science, grades 5 and 7).

Table 3.5 shows that school performance in Brazil during the period of analysis was on average 42.8, and the difference between states with the highest and lowest school performance was 11.3 percentage points.

With regard to the association with innovations in management, Table 3.5 shows that in the states where transfer of funds took place, mean school performance was 0.8 points better; where election of principals had been instituted, it was around 1.4 percentage points higher; and in the states and years in which the school council was instituted, it was 1.6 points higher.

In short, Table 3.5 suggests that innovations in school management can have significant impacts on educational performance, and that the innovation that presents the sharpest, clearest and most promising indicators is election of principals. However, because the quality of the family environment and teacher qualification vary from state to state and over time and certainly influence educational performance, the differentials found above may be spurious. That is, they may simply reflect the fact that the states with the best family environment and best qualified teachers are more likely to adopt such innovations. In that case, the performance in more innovative states would be superior not because of the innovations, but because of the higher quality of the family environment and the teachers in the state. Hence, the next step in evaluating the impact of innovations in school management on educational performance is to calculate those differences by controlling for the quality of family environment and of teachers.

Before proceeding to estimate those controlled differentials, the next section discusses the controls for family environment and teacher quality

---

[11] The scores assume values of from 0 to 100.

and examines to what extent that quality tends to be better in states and years in which innovations had been instituted.

Quality of Family Environment and Teachers

This section presents the controls used for the quality of family environment and teachers in order to determine the extent to which these factors are related to the implementation of innovations.

Per capita family income in the state and mean schooling of the adult population are used to control for the quality of the family environment. To control for teacher quality, the mean salary and schooling of primary teachers along with the proportion of teachers with some higher education are calculated. Barros and Mendonça (1997) presents estimates of trends in these indicators in the 1980s and the early 1990s by state. Table 3.6 presents a summary of the main data.

Quality of family environment. Both measures of the quality of family environment were estimated on the basis of the 1981 and 1993 PNAD. State per capita family income is defined as the ratio of mean income from all sources of all families in the state divided by the population. This variable is used as an indicator of the purchasing power of families in each state.[12] The schooling of the adult population is defined as the mean number of full years of study of the population 25 or older in each state and is used as an indicator of the educational level of parents in each state.

The results presented in Table 3.6 reveal that both per capita family income and mean schooling of the adult population tend to be higher in the states and years in which innovations had been instituted.

The table also reveals that the income and schooling differences favor states and years with innovations, and this differential is higher for school councils than for election of school principals, and much more than for transfer of resources. This is in keeping with what was noted throughout the previous section, where the differential of educational performance between states and years with and without school councils was higher than that of the differential related to whether funds are transferred or school principals

---

[12] The usefulness of this variable as an indicator for the purchasing power of families in different states is limited by differences in the cost of living, age structure of the population, and income distribution.

Table 3.6. Measures of Quality of Family Environment and of Teachers with Innovative Experiences in School Management

Quality measures	Mean	Funds transfer			Election of principal			Establishment of school council		
		Yes	No	Difference	Yes	No	Difference	Yes	No	Difference
	(1)	(2)	(3)	(2) – (3)	(4)	(5)	(4) – (5)	(6)	(7)	(6) – (7)
Family environment										
Family income per capita of state										
(in multiples of 1990 minimum wage)	1.6	1.6	1.7	−0.12	1.7	1.6	0.11	1.9	1.5	0.33
Mean schooling of adult population										
(25 or more)	3.9	4.0	3.8	0.15	4.4	3.8	0.58	4.4	3.7	0.70
Teachers										
Mean salary of primary school teachers										
(in multiples of 1990 minimum wage)	4.7	4.5	4.9	−0.48	4.9	4.7	0.14	5.3	4.6	0.77
Mean schooling of primary school teachers	10.9	11.1	10.8	0.24	11.4	10.8	0.53	11.6	10.8	0.82
Proportion of teachers with some										
advanced education	35.5	34.6	36.3	−1.61	42.1	33.6	8.45	38.0	34.6	3.38

Source: Compiled from Barros and Mendonça (1997).

are elected. Thus it can be concluded that a closer relationship between the implementation of the school council and educational performance is the result of a similarly close connection between the institution of school councils and the quality of family environment.

Teacher quality. The mean salary and mean schooling of teachers in primary schooling were estimated on the basis of the 1981 and 1993 PNAD. The proportion of teachers with higher education was obtained through the School Census. The results presented in Table 3.6 reveal that the three indicators of teacher quality tend to be higher in the states and years in which at least one of the innovations had been instituted, except for transfer of funds. Moreover, the schooling and salary differences favor states and years in which there were innovations, and the differential is higher for the school council than for election of school principals.

This is in keeping with the observations throughout the previous section that the differential in educational performance between states and years with and without school councils was always higher than the differential associated with whether school principals are elected, and especially for transfer of funds. Likewise, the stronger correlation between initiation of school councils and educational performance is at least partly the result of a similarly stronger association between the institution of school councils and teacher quality.

In short, Table 3.6 presents strong evidence that the greater impact of the school council on educational performance found in the previous section is at least partly due to the fact that the initiation of school councils is more closely correlated with the salary level and schooling of teachers, the schooling level of the population, and per capita income of states. The aim of the next section is to determine exactly what portion of the differential of educational performance shown in the previous sections between states with and without one of the three innovations will remain after controlling for the quality of family environment and of teachers.

Impact of Innovations in School Management
on Educational Performance

In the previous section we found that educational performance is considerably higher in states and years in which innovations in management had been instituted. In general, the differential in educational performance between states and years with and without innovations in management was of the same general magnitude as the improvement of educational performance that took place in the course of the 1980s.

Even though they indicate that there is a significant impact of innovations in management on educational performance, these differentials tend to overestimate it for two reasons. First, they at least partly benefit from the fact that the innovative states are precisely those in which the quality of family environment and teachers is better, as was shown in the previous section. Second, because there is a tendency for the innovations to be instituted at the same time, the estimated differentials tend to overestimate the true value of the impact of a particular innovation, insofar as the impact of the other innovations instituted is not isolated.

In order to eliminate these two sources of overestimation, this section investigates the relationship between educational performance and each of the innovations in school management, controlling for family environment and teacher quality, and the institution of the other innovations. The analysis will proceed in two stages. The first estimates a set of six basic models for the relationship between educational performance and school management, while controlling for the quality of the family environment and teachers. The second investigates to what extent the results are robust when a linear trend is included in the model, and to what extent the results change when the analysis is limited to subperiods. The longitudinal nature of the data is then used to examine to what extent the results are robust vis-à-vis controls for unobservable characteristics of the states, which may not vary over time but which nonetheless influence educational performance.

Basic Models

The basic model to be calculated is as follows:

$$e_{it} = \alpha + \beta_1 r_{it} + \beta_2 d_{it} + \beta_3 c_{it} + \eta f_{it} + \varphi q_{it} + \varepsilon_{it}$$

where e denotes educational performance; r, d and c are indicators of the existence of transfers of funds to schools, election of principals, and the school council, respectively; f denotes the quality of the family environment, q the quality of teachers, and ε is the sum of the remaining unobserved variables that influence educational performance. The parameters to be estimated are

Table 3.7. Basic Models Used

| | Teacher quality | | |
	Mean schooling of primary school teachers	Proportion of teachers with advanced education	Mean salary of primary school teachers
Quality of family environment			
Mean school of adult population	Model 1	Model 2	Model 3
Family income per capita	Model 4	Model 5	Model 6

α, β_1, β_2, β_3, η, ε, φ, where β_1, β_2, β_3 capture the impacts of innovations in management. The subscripts i and t indicate the state and year, respectively.

This model really represents six models, because, as discussed previously, there are two options for the family environment indicator and three for the teacher quality indicator. Table 3.7 presents the six models used and the variables used in each for controlling for quality of family environment and teachers used in each. Thus, for example, model 1 uses mean schooling of the adult population as an indicator of family environment and mean schooling of teachers in basic education as an indicator of teacher quality.

These models were calculated using the four indicators obtained from the PNAD and the School Census as the educational performance measure. On the basis of these four educational performance indicators (repetition rate, rate of nonattendance, mean grade-level lag, and proportion of children with some grade-level lag) and the six models, 24 regressions were calculated. Table 3.8 presents the coefficients β_1, β_2, β_3, (and the corresponding P-values) associated with the three indicators of innovations in school management under study. The table shows the estimated parameters for each of the six models, and the mean for these estimates. To simplify, only the mean parameters are shown.

Repetition rate. Table 3.8 reveals that the three innovations bring the repetition rate down. The impact of each lies between 0.8 and 2.9 percentage points; the school council produces a greater impact than transfer of funds, while electing principals is in between.

The combined impact of the three innovations is 5 percentage points. From a substantive standpoint, this impact on the repetition rate can be

Table 3.8. Regression Coefficients: Innovations in School Management, Basic Models

Model	Transfer of funds	Election of principal	Establishment of school council	Combined impact
		Repetition rate		
	Temporal variation: 4.2		**Regional variation: 14.2**	
1	−0.6	−1.5	−2.9	−4.9
	52	*19*	*1*	
2	−1.1	−0.7	−2.7	−4.5
	31	*54*	*2*	
3	−0.4	−1.4	−2.9	−4.7
	68	*21*	*1*	
4	−0.6	−1.6	−3.0	−5.2
	52	*14*	*1*	
5	−1.2	−1.0	−2.7	−4.9
	23	*42*	*2*	
6	−0.6	−1.7	−3.1	−5.5
	52	*11*	*0*	
Minimum	−1.2	−1.7	−3.1	−5.5
Maximum	−0.4	−0.7	−2.7	−4.5
Mean	−0.8	−1.3	−2.9	−5.0
		Proportion of children not in school		
	Temporal variation: 10.2		**Regional variation: 19.4**	
1	−2.5	1.2	−2.3	−4.8
	0	*3*	*0*	
2	−2.8	1.3	−2.4	−5.2
	0	*5*	*0*	
3	−2.4	1.4	−2.3	−4.7
	0	*2*	*0*	
4	−2.6	0.0	−2.7	−5.4
	0	*95*	*0*	
5	−4.3	0.3	−4.1	−8.3
	0	*74*	*0*	
6	−3.4	−0.6	−3.3	−7.3
	0	*47*	*0*	
Minimum	−4.3	−0.6	−4.1	−8.3
Maximum	−2.4	1.4	−2.3	−4.7
Mean	−3.0	0.6	−2.8	−6.0

Table 3.8. *(cont.)*

Model	Transfer of funds	Election of principal	Establishment of school council	Combined impact
			Mean grade-level lag	
	Temporal variation: 0.37		Regional variation: 1.61	
1	−0.05	0.04	−0.03	−0.08
	14	*33*	*51*	
2	−0.09	0.11	−0.04	−0.14
	3	*4*	*40*	
3	−0.09	0.04	−0.03	−0.12
	1	*33*	*48*	
4	−0.08	−0.04	−0.04	−0.16
	3	*43*	*33*	
5	−0.19	0.02	−0.12	−0.31
	0	*72*	*3*	
6	−0.16	−0.09	−0.09	−0.34
	0	*14*	*11*	
Minimum	−0.19	−0.09	−0.12	−0.34
Maximum	−0.05	0.11	−0.03	−0.08
Mean	−0.11	0.02	−0.06	−0.19
			Proportion of children with some lag	
	Temporal variation: 7.9		Regional variation: 29.0	
1	−0.9	0.4	−0.3	−1.3
	21	*67*	*73*	
2	−1.9	2.0	−0.7	−2.6
	3	*8*	*54*	
3	−1.6	0.5	−0.4	−2.0
	5	*0*	*69*	
4	−1.4	−1.0	−0.6	−3.1
	8	*30*	*52*	
5	−3.6	0.5	−2.2	−5.8
	0	*67*	*7*	
6	−2.8	−2.0	−1.5	−6.4
	1	*11*	*20*	
Minimum	−3.6	−2.0	−2.2	−6.4
Maximum	−0.9	2.0	−0.3	−1.3
Mean	−2.1	0.1	−1.0	−3.5

Note: Values in italics represent the *P*-values (x 100).

regarded as significant, inasmuch as the decline in this indicator during the 1980s was around four percentage points. Nevertheless, this impact is still small when compared with the differential between states, which is about 14 points.

In statistical terms, only the estimates for the impact of school councils are significant.[13]

Proportion of children outside school. Table 3.8 shows that contrary to the situation with the repetition rate, when educational performance is measured by the proportion of children outside of school, transfer of funds and school councils have impacts of a similar magnitude. In quantitative terms, it can be seen that transfer of funds and school councils individually lower the rate of nonattendance by 3 and 2.8 points, respectively, while election of principals has a perverse effect.

The combined impact of these two innovations is around six percentage points. In substantive terms, this impact on the rate of attendance can be regarded as significant, inasmuch as it rose 10 percentage points in the 1980s. However, this impact is still small when compared with the differential between states, which is close to 19 percentage points.

In statistical terms, the impact of both school councils—which for the repetition rate was significant—and of transfer of funds is statistically significant.[14] The impact of the election of school principals, besides being perverse, is statistically significant in half of the models.

Mean of grade-level lag. Table 3.8 reveals that both transfer of resources and school councils reduce the mean grade-level lag. In quantitative terms, it is apparent that the impact of transferring funds is close to 0.11 years; school councils have an impact of 0.06 years. Election of school principals again shows a perverse effect.

The combined impact of the first two innovations is around 0.19 years. From a substantive standpoint, this impact on the mean of grade-level lag may be considered relatively unimportant, considering that it fell by about

---

[13] All estimates for the impact of the school council on the repetition rate are statistically significant with all *P*-values under 5 percent. For transfers of funds and election of school principals, the estimates are not statistically significant insofar as all *P*-values are over 20 percent and 10 percent, respectively. All the *P*-values considered here refer to testing, under the null hypothesis that the innovation has no impact.

[14] The *P*-values for the test are all under 1 percent.

0.4 years during the 1980s. Moreover, this impact is even smaller when compared to the differential between states, which is around 1.6 years.

In statistical terms, only the impact of transferring funds is statistically significant.[15] As in the case of the rate of nonattendance, the impact of electing school principals appears to have a perverse effect. However, for the mean grade-level lag this impact is statistically insignificant in all the models.

Proportion of children with some grade lag. Table 3.8 shows that both transfer of funds and school councils lower the proportion of children with some lag. In quantitative terms, it can be seen that the impact of transferring funds is 2.1 points, while the school council has a 1-point impact. Election of school principals has a perverse effect.

The combined impact of the two innovations is 3.5 percentage points. In substantive terms, this impact on the proportion of children with some grade lag is of scant importance, because that lag declined by around 8 points in the 1980s and the differential between states is around 29 percentage points.

In statistical terms, only the impact of transfer of funds is statistically significant.[16] As in the case of the mean grade-level lag, election of principals has a perverse effect, but is always statistically insignificant.

National Basic Education Evaluation System (SAEB)

The SAEB provides 20 measurements of school performance for both school evaluation cycles taken together. Because the SAEB provides information for a high number of closely related indicators and only for two relatively close moments in time, the model used to estimate the impact of management innovations on school performance becomes in effect an adaptation of the basic model. Basically, the adaptation entailed using information from the 10 school performance measurements of the two evaluation cycles for the 18 states in order to estimate a single combined impact of the management innovations. However, it allowed the intersection of the regression to vary by subject matter, grade and evaluation cycle. In short, we are assuming that the level of school performance may vary by subject matter, grade and evaluation cycle, but that the impact of the innovations on school perfor-

---

[15] *P*-values are all (except in model 1) under 5 percent.
[16] *P*-values are all 5 percent or less (except for models 1 and 4).

mance is the same for all subjects and grades in both cycles. Specifically, the model took the following form:

$$e_{itds} = \alpha_{1t} + \alpha_{2ds} + \beta_1 r_{it} + \beta_2 d_{it} + \beta_3 c_{it} + \eta f_{it} + \varphi q_{it} + \varepsilon_{itds}$$

where the subscripts for α_2, d and s indicate the subject matter and the grade of the examination, and the other indices and variables have the same significance as in the basic model introduced earlier.

The difference between this and the basic model is that in this instance, due to greater scarcity of information, we are assuming that the impact of management innovations, and of the quality of family life and of teachers is the same for the 20 available measurements. However, the mean level of performance varies widely by subject matter, grade/year and cycle, as was the case with the basic model. Hence, this model actually represents a set of four models, because there are two possibilities for choosing the quality of family environment indicators and two options for the teacher quality indicator. In this instance, there are not three options for the teacher quality index, since information on the proportion of teachers who have some higher education was not available for 1993.

The results obtained on the basis of this model for the impact of management innovations on school performance (see Table 3.9) show that of the three innovations, only the implementation of election of school principals tends to raise school performance. The impact is only one percentage point, however. In substantive terms, a one-point impact is clearly of little importance, inasmuch as the difference between states with highest and lowest mean school performance is 12 points. In statistical terms, the impact is significant only in half of the models.

In short, the results obtained with the basic model reveal that after controlling for quality of family environment and teachers, introducing transfer of funds to schools is the innovation of the three studied that has greatest impact on indicators of educational performance (except for the repetition rate and school test scores). Instituting school councils lies in between, with impacts similar to those noted for introducing a transfer of funds, but to a lesser extent. With regard to election of school principals, this innovation has a significant impact only on the repetition rate and school test scores. For the other indicators, the impact of this innovation is small and, as a rule, perverse and statistically insignificant.

Table 3.9. Regression Coefficients: Basic Models, Cycles 1 and 2

	Models with innovation			
Model	Transfer of funds	Election of principal	Establishment of school council	Combined impact
1	0.4	0.4	0.1	0.9
	54	*47*	*93*	
3	0.6	1.0	-0.9	1.6
	41	*11*	*22*	
4	0.2	1.2	-0.8	1.4
	81	*3*	*19*	
6	0.3	1.5	-1.2	1.8
	67	*1*	*6*	
Minimum	0.2	0.4	-1.2	0.9
Maximum	0.6	1.5	0.1	1.8
Mean	0.4	1.0	-0.7	1.4

Note: Values in italics represent the *P*-values (x 100).

Trend over Time and Subperiods

This section examines whether the results obtained with the basic model are robust with the inclusion of a linear trend in the model, and to what extent it generates similar results when certain subperiods are excluded.

Alterations in the Basic Model and Their Rationale

Because there is a natural tendency for educational indicators to improve over time, and because management innovations spread gradually from one state to another, the impact of innovations on educational indicators obtained in the previous subsector may be overestimated. That is so because, along with their true impact, these estimates also embody the influence of certain historic trends. In order to avoid this overestimation, we introduced a linear trend into the basic model. The results are presented in Table 3.10.

Direct election of governors starting in 1982 led to a series of thorough changes in the way state education systems were managed, as well as to changes in school-level management that were thereby set in motion. Thus,

Table 3.10. Regression Coefficients: Innovations in School Management, Basic Models with Linear Trend

Model	Transfer of funds	Election of principal	Establishment of school council	Combined impact
			Rate of failure	
	Temporal variation: 4.2		Regional variation: 14.2	
1	−0.3	−1.3	−2.6	−4.3
	72	*25*	*2*	
2	−1.3	−0.8	−2.9	−5.0
	27	*50*	*2*	
3	−0.3	−1.3	−2.7	−4.3
	78	*25*	*1*	
4	−0.3	−1.4	−2.6	−4.3
	74	*22*	*2*	
5	−1.2	−1.0	−2.7	−4.9
	28	*43*	*3*	
6	−0.3	−1.4	−2.7	−4.4
	77	*20*	*2*	
Minimum	−1.3	−1.4	−2.9	−5.0
Maximum	−0.3	−0.8	−2.6	−4.3
Mean	−0.6	−1.2	−2.7	−4.5
			Proportion of children not in school	
	Temporal variation: 10.2		Regional variation: 19.4	
1	−1.6	2.0	−1.3	−2.9
	0	*0*	*1*	
2	−1.7	2.3	−1.2	−2.9
	0	*0*	*5*	
3	−1.7	2.1	1.2	−2.9
	0	*0*	*2*	
4	−1.4	1.5	−0.9	−2.2
	1	*2*	*17*	
5	−1.8	2.2	−0.8	−2.6
	0	*0*	*26*	
6	−1.6	1.5	−0.7	−2.3
	1	*3*	*33*	
Minimum	−1.8	1.5	−1.3	−2.9
Maximum	−1.4	2.3	−0.7	−2.2
Mean	−1.6	1.9	−1.0	−2.6

Table 3.10. *(cont.)*

Model	Transfer of funds	Election of principal	Establishment of school council	Combined impact
		Mean grade-level lag		
	Temporal variation: 0.37	Regional variation: 1.61		
1	−0.10	0.00	−0.08	−0.17
	1	*99*	*6*	
2	−0.13	0.08	−0.08	−0.20
	0	*14*	*14*	
3	−0.12	0.02	−0.07	−0.19
	0	*70*	*11*	
4	−0.08	−0.04	−0.04	−0.16
	4	*44*	*35*	
5	−0.13	0.07	−0.05	−0.18
	1	*29*	*43*	
6	−0.11	−0.03	−0.02	−0.17
	3	*59*	*70*	
Minimum	−0.13	−0.04	−0.08	−0.20
Maximum	−0.08	0.08	−0.02	−0.16
Mean	−0.11	0.02	−0.06	−0.18
		Proportion of children with some lag		
	Temporal variation: 7.9	Regional variation: 29.0		
1	−1.3	0.0	−0.7	−2.1
	9	*96*	*44*	
2	−1.9	2.0	−0.6	−2.5
	5	*9*	*59*	
3	−1.7	0.3	−0.6	−2.3
	4	*73*	*55*	
4	−1.1	−0.6	−0.1	−1.8
	19	*56*	*93*	
5	−1.9	1.8	−0.1	−2.0
	7	*17*	*95*	
6	−1.6	−0.5	0.2	−2.1
	12	*66*	*84*	
Minimum	−1.9	−0.6	−0.7	−2.5
Maximum	−1.1	2.0	0.2	−1.8
Mean	−1.6	0.5	−0.3	−2.1

Note: Values in italics represent the *P*-values (x 100).

the improvement in educational performance at the beginning of the 1980s was not solely the result of the three innovations under study but of other changes in education after the 1982 election. In order to evaluate the importance of this potential bias, we reestimated the basic model utilizing only information for the 1983–93 period, that is, we eliminated the analysis of the 1981–82 subperiod. The results obtained can be seen in Table 3.11.

As mentioned previously, the PNAD was thoroughly changed after 1992. Hence, the combined use of information for the 1980s and 1990s may be creating a bias in the impacts of the innovations on educational indicators. In order to check the importance of this potential bias, we reestimated the basic model using only information for the 1981–91 period; that is, we eliminated the analysis of the 1992–93 subperiod. The results obtained are presented in Table 3.12.

Results

Including a linear trend and eliminating the subperiods tend to reduce the estimates of the impact of the three innovations. This reduction is especially significant for the proportion of children outside school because the combined impact of the transfer of funds and the creation of school councils, which under the basic model had an impact of six percentage points, is reduced to 2.6, 4.7 and 3.3 points with the inclusion of the linear trend, and the elimination of the 1981–82 and 1992–93 subperiods, respectively.

The influence of the other changes in the basic model on the impact of introducing the transfer of funds and the institution of school councils on the proportion of children with some lag declines moderately, particularly when the 1992–93 subperiod is excluded; the combined impact declines from 3.5 to 2.3 percentage points.

Finally, these changes have only a slight influence on the mean grade-level lag and on the repetition rate, except when the 1992–93 subperiod is included, and then the impact of the institution of school councils declines substantially.

Control for Unobserved Heterogeneity

Comparing the results derived from the basic model, in which there are controls for quality of family environment and teachers, as seen in Table 3.8, with the results in which there are no such controls, presented in Table 3.5, we see that the estimates are in fact sensitive to introducing such controls.

Nevertheless, with regard to differences between states, the basic model controls only for observed characteristics. It is possible that unobserved differences between states are as important as those that are observed. This section uses the longitudinal nature of the available information to introduce controls for this kind of unobserved heterogeneity between states. It should be emphasized that this method makes it possible to control only for those unobserved characteristics that do not vary over time. More specifically, this section calculates the basic model allowing the intersection of the regression to vary by state; that is, it calculates the following extension of the basic model:

$$e_{it} = \alpha_i + \beta_1 r_{it} + \beta_2 d_{it} + \beta_3 c_{it} + \eta f_{it} + \varphi q_{it} + \varepsilon_{it}$$

where the subscript i in α_i indicates in this model that each state has its own intercept. The unobserved heterogeneity captured by α_i can be arbitrarily correlated with the other independent variables introduced in the regression, that is, the three innovations in school management and the controls for the quality of family environment and teachers. Table 3.13 presents estimates of coefficients β when the control for unobserved heterogeneity is introduced. These estimates are analyzed below.

Repetition rate. Table 3.13 reveals that introducing controls for unobserved characteristics concentrates the entire impact of innovations on transfer of funds, thereby causing the repetition rate to drop by around 2.8 points. In substantive terms, this impact on the repetition rate can be considered relatively insignificant insofar as it declined 4.2 percentage points in the 1980s. Moreover, this impact is quite small when compared with the differential between states, which is 14.2 points.

In statistical terms, only the impact of transfer of funds is significant.[17] The impact of the election of school principals and school councils is not statistically significant.[18]

---

[17] *P*-values are all under 3 percent for Models 2, 4, 5 and 6, and under 7 percent and 13 percent, respectively, for Models 1 and 3.

[18] *P*-values are all over 30 percent.

Table 3.11. Regression Coefficients: Innovation in School Management, Excluding 1981–82

Model	Transfer of funds	Election of principal	Establishment of school council	Combined impact
		Rate of repetition		
	Temporal variation: 4.2	Regional variation: 14.2		
1	−0.6	−1.5	−2.9	−4.9
	52	*19*	*1*	
2	−1.1	−0.7	−2.7	−4.5
	31	*54*	*2*	
3	−0.4	−1.4	−2.9	−4.7
	68	*21*	*1*	
4	−0.6	−1.6	−3.0	−5.2
	52	*14*	*1*	
5	−1.2	−1.0	−2.7	−4.9
	23	*42*	*2*	
6	−0.6	−1.7	−3.1	−5.5
	52	*11*	*0*	
Minimum	−1.2	−1.7	−3.1	−5.5
Maximum	−0.4	−0.7	−2.7	−4.5
Mean	−0.8	−1.3	−2.9	−5.0
		Proportion of children not in school		
	Temporal variation: 10.2	Regional variation: 19.4		
1	−1.9	1.5	−2.2	−4.1
	0	*0*	*0*	
2	−2.1	1.6	−2.2	−4.4
	0	*0*	*0*	
3	−1.8	1.5	−2.2	−4.0
	0	*0*	*0*	
4	−1.9	0.4	−2.4	−4.3
	0	*48*	*0*	
5	−2.9	1.4	−3.1	−6.0
	0	*7*	*0*	
6	−2.4	0.0	−2.8	−5.2
	0	*95*	*0*	
Minimum	−2.9	0.0	−3.1	−6.0
Maximum	−1.8	1.6	−2.2	−4.0
Mean	−2.2	1.1	−2.5	−4.7

Table 3.11. *(cont.)*

Model	Transfer of funds	Election of principal	Establishment of school council	Combined impact
		Mean grade-level lag		
	Temporal variation: 0.37	Regional variation: 1.61		
1	−0.05	0.04	−0.03	−0.08
	14	*41*	*50*	
2	−0.09	0.11	−0.04	−0.13
	8	*5*	*40*	
3	−0.09	0.04	−0.03	−0.12
	2	*35*	*52*	
4	−0.08	−0.03	−0.03	−0.14
	4	*55*	*51*	
5	−0.15	0.06	−0.09	−0.24
	1	*32*	*13*	
6	−0.14	−0.07	−0.07	−0.29
	1	*26*	*23*	
Minimum	−0.15	−0.07	−0.09	−0.29
Maximum	−0.05	0.11	−0.03	−0.08
Mean	−0.10	0.03	−0.05	−0.17
	Proportion of children with some lag			
	Temporal variation: 7.9	Regional variation: 29.0		
1	−0.9	0.5	−0.1	−1.0
	29	*65*	*92*	
2	−1.6	2.4	−0.5	−2.1
	12	*5*	*66*	
3	−1.6	0.6	−0.1	−1.7
	8	*57*	*92*	
4	−1.3	−0.7	−0.1	−2.2
	13	*48*	*91*	
5	−2.8	1.6	−1.3	−4.0
	2	*23*	*31*	
6	−2.5	−1.6	−1.0	−5.0
	3	*24*	*45*	
Minimum	−2.8	−1.6	−1.3	−5.0
Maximum	−0.9	2.4	−0.1	−1.0
Mean	−1.8	0.5	−0.5	−2.7

Note: Values in italics represent the *P*-values (x 100).

Table 3.12. Regression Coefficients: Innovation in School Management, Excluding 1992–93

Model	Transfer of funds	Election of principal	Establishment of school council	Combined impact
	Rate of repetition			
	Temporal variation: 4.2	Regional variation: 14.2		
1	−0.6	−1.6	−2.9	−5.0
	61	*30*	*6*	
2	−1.5	−0.8	−2.0	−4.3
	29	*65*	*31*	
3	−0.3	−1.8	−3.2	−5.3
	77	*22*	*4*	
4	−0.4	−2.0	−3.2	−5.6
	73	*17*	*4*	
5	−1.5	−0.7	−1.3	−3.5
	29	*72*	*54*	
6	−0.2	−2.0	−3.0	−5.2
	83	*18*	*6*	
Minimum	−1.5	−2.0	−3.2	−5.6
Maximum	−0.2	−0.7	−1.3	−3.5
Mean	−0.7	−1.5	−2.6	−4.8
	Proportion of children not in school			
	Temporal variation: 10.2	Regional variation: 19.4		
1	−2.0	1.2	−1.5	−3.4
	0	*9*	*4*	
2	−2.4	1.6	−1.2	−3.5
	0	*7*	*21*	
3	−2.1	1.4	−1.4	−3.5
	0	*4*	*5*	
4	−1.5	−0.2	−1.6	−3.3
	1	*80*	*8*	
5	−2.5	1.4	−1.0	−3.5
	0	*24*	*46*	
6	−1.9	0.3	−0.8	−2.7
	1	*79*	*43*	
Minimum	−2.5	−0.2	−1.6	−3.5
Maximum	−1.5	1.6	−0.8	−2.7
Mean	−2.1	0.9	−1.2	−3.3

Table 3.12. *(cont.)*

Model	Transfer of funds	Election of principal	Establishment of school council	Combined impact
	Mean grade-level lag			
	Temporal variation: 0.37	Regional variation: 1.61		
1	−0.06	−0.01	−0.05	−0.13
	7	*83*	*30*	
2	−0.12	0.12	0.00	−0.12
	1	*6*	*98*	
3	−0.11	0.05	−0.02	−0.13
	1	*36*	*74*	
4	−0.05	−0.07	−0.03	−0.16
	20	*15*	*54*	
5	−0.13	0.11	0.05	−0.13
	2	*18*	*58*	
6	−0.10	−0.03	0.02	−0.13
	7	*64*	*81*	
Minimum	−0.13	−0.07	−0.05	−0.16
Maximum	−0.05	0.12	0.05	−0.12
Mean	−0.10	0.03	−0.01	−0.13
	Proportion of children with some grade-level lag			
	Temporal variation: 7.9	Regional variation: 29.0		
1	−0.9	−0.8	−0.6	−2.3
	22	*46*	*58*	
2	−2.1	2.1	0.4	−2.1
	3	*12*	*78*	
3	−1.7	0.2	0.0	−1.7
	4	*87*	*99*	
4	−0.7	−1.9	−0.2	−2.8
	39	*8*	*85*	
5	−2.3	1.8	1.1	−2.3
	4	*24*	*51*	
6	−1.5	−1.2	0.7	−2.7
	14	*37*	*66*	
Minimum	−2.3	−1.9	−0.6	−2.8
Maximum	−0.7	2.1	1.1	−1.7
Mean	−1.5	0.0	0.2	−2.3

Note: Values in italics represent the *P*-values (x 100).

Table 3.13. Regression Coefficients: Innovation in School Management, Models with Fixed Effect

Model	Transfer of funds	Election of principal	Establishment of school council	Combined impact
		Rate of repetition		
	Temporal variation: 4.2	**Regional variation: 14.2**		
1	−2.1	0.1	0.8	−2.1
	7	93	44	
2	−2.4	−0.6	0.9	−3.0
	2	55	36	
3	−1.7	0.0	0.7	−1.7
	13	97	50	
4	−2.9	−0.2	−0.1	−3.2
	1	87	90	
5	−2.9	−0.4	0.0	−3.3
	0	71	98	
6	−3.0	−0.4	−0.2	−3.6
	1	75	82	
Minimum	−3.0	−0.6	−0.2	−3.6
Maximum	−1.7	0.1	0.9	−1.7
Mean	−2.5	−0.2	0.3	−2.8
		Proportion of children not in school		
	Temporal variation: 10.2	**Regional variation: 19.4**		
1	−2.0	1.7	−1.2	−3.2
	0	2	6	
2	−2.5	1.4	−1.0	−3.5
	0	10	20	
3	−2.2	1.4	−1.1	−3.3
	0	3	8	
4	−4.2	1.0	−3.0	−7.2
	0	24	0	
5	−6.0	0.6	−4.2	−10.2
	0	64	0	
6	−5.7	−0.1	−3.3	−9.2
	0	92	0	
Minimum	−6.0	−0.1	−4.2	−10.2
Maximum	−2.0	1.7	−1.0	−3.2
Mean	−3.8	1.0	−2.3	−6.1

Table 3.13. *(cont.)*

Model	Transfer of funds	Election of principal	Establishment of school council	Combined impact
			Mean grade-level lag	
	Temporal variation: 0.37		**Regional variation: 1.61**	
1	−0.07	0.02	−0.05	−0.12
	0	*27*	*1*	
2	−0.07	0.02	−0.05	−0.12
	1	*38*	*5*	
3	−0.07	0.02	−0.05	−0.12
	0	*37*	*1*	
4	−0.16	0.00	−0.12	−0.27
	0	*96*	*0*	
5	−0.20	0.00	−0.16	−0.36
	0	*91*	*0*	
6	−0.20	−0.03	−0.13	−0.36
	0	*28*	*0*	
Minimum	−0.20	−0.03	−0.16	−0.36
Maximum	−0.07	0.02	−0.05	−0.12
Mean	−0.13	0.00	−0.09	−0.23
			Proportion of children with some lag	
	Temporal variation: 7.9		**Regional variation: 29.0**	
1	−0.5	0.7	−1.9	−2.4
	40	*27*	*0*	
2	−0.6	0.7	−1.7	−2.3
	46	*38*	*3*	
3	−0.6	0.6	−1.9	−2.5
	37	*31*	*0*	
4	−2.5	0.2	−3.4	−5.9
	0	*80*	*0*	
5	−3.4	0.1	−4.1	−7.5
	0	*93*	*0*	
6	−3.5	−0.5	−3.5	−7.6
	0	*52*	*0*	
Minimum	−3.5	−0.5	−4.1	−7.6
Maximum	−0.5	0.7	−1.7	−2.3
Mean	−1.9	0.3	−2.7	−4.7

Note: Values in italics represent the *P*-values (x 100).

Proportion of children not in school. Table 3.13 reveals that when controls for unobserved characteristics are introduced, both transfer of funds and school councils lower the proportion of children not in school, as in the basic model. However, the impact of school councils becomes considerably smaller than that of transfer of funds, while in the basic model it was similar to that of transfer of funds. Election of school principals continues to display a perverse effect.

The combined impact of transferring funds and school councils is around 6.1 percentage points, which is practically identical with the estimate under the basic model. In substantive terms, this impact on the proportion of children not in school can be regarded as relatively significant, inasmuch as it fell by 10.2 points during the 1980s. This impact is still small, however, in comparison with the 19.4 point differential between states.

From a statistical standpoint, just as in the basic model, the impacts of transfers of funds and of councils are statistically significant, while the impact of election of school principals is small and statistically significant in only a portion of the models.

Mean grade-level lag. Table 3.13 shows that both transfers of funds and school councils reduce the grade-level lag, as in the basic model results, while the impact of election of principals continues to be perverse.

The combined impact of transfer of funds and school councils is 0.23 years. In substantive terms, this impact can be regarded as relatively significant inasmuch as the mean grade-level lag fell by 0.37 over the 1980s. This impact is still small, however, when compared with the differential between states, which is around 1.61 years.

From a statistical standpoint, the estimates for both transfer of funds and school councils are statistically significant. As in the basic model, the impact of election of school principals is perverse, but it is not statistically significant.

Proportion of children with some grade-level lag. Table 3.13 shows that both transfer of funds and school councils lower the proportion of children with some grade-level lag, as in the basic model results, while election of school principals has a perverse effect. In this sense, it resembles the basic model with the introduction of controls for unobserved heterogeneity. Nevertheless, the impact of school councils, contrary to the results in the basic model, becomes larger than the impact of transferring funds.

The combined impact of school councils and transfers of funds is around 4.7 points. In substantive terms, this impact may be regarded as relatively significant, inasmuch as the proportion of children with some lag fell by 7.9 percentage points during the 1980s. That impact is still very small, however, when compared with the differential between states, which is approximately 29 points. In statistical terms, only the impact of school councils is statistically significant. The impact of electing school principals remains statistically significant, as was the case in the basic model.

In summary, introducing controls for unobserved heterogeneity changed the estimated effects on repetition rates by concentrating the impact of management innovations on the transfer of resources to schools, and rendering the impacts of school principal election and school councils insignificant.

With regard to the proportion of children who are not attending school and the mean grade-level lag, introducing a control for unobserved heterogeneity did not change the main results. That is, transfer of resources and school councils have positive effects, with the former having a greater impact. In addition, the impact of electing school principals is negative but not significant.

Finally, with regard to the proportion of children with some degree of grade-level lag, the basic result—that transfer of funds and school councils have positive effects—still stands. There is a change in the relative impact of the school council, which was less than that of transfer of funds under the basic model, and here becomes greater. The perverse impact of the election of school principals remains.

Summary and Conclusions

This chapter has investigated the impact on educational performance of the three main innovations in school management over the past 15 years. To evaluate that impact, the chapter took advantage of the unsynchronized manner in which these innovations spread. Two aspects of this lack of synchronization were analyzed. First, the fact that the innovations were implemented at different times in different states made it possible to evaluate the impact of these innovations by contrasting for a particular point in time the educational performance in innovating states with performance in states with traditional systems (cross-section analysis); by contrasting educational performance for a particular state before and after the introduction of these innovations in school management (time series analysis); or by using both types of contrast simultaneously. Second, the fact that innovating states did not necessarily adopt the three innovations simultaneously made it possible to identify the impact of each of the three innovations in isolation. These contrasts were analyzed together by using cross-section pooling techniques, where each unit of observation consists of a state in Brazil and a point in time.

The measures of educational performance used were i) the repetition rate obtained from the School Census, ii) the proportion of children not attending school, iii) the mean of grade-level lag, iv) the proportion of students with some grade-level lag obtained from the National Household Survey Sample (PNAD), and v) a series of indicators of school performance, obtained from the National Basic Education Assessment System (SAEB).

The analysis was carried out in three stages. First, we estimated differentials of performance between states and points in time where the innovations had been instituted compared to the performance of the states and points in time where they had not. The results appear in Table 3.5 and are summarized in Table 3.14. They show that educational performance tends to be better in the states and at points in time where any of the three management innovations examined (transfer of funds to schools, creation of school councils, and election of school principals) had been adopted. The only exception is that school performance is lower in states and points in time where transfer of resources to schools had been instituted. With regard to the magnitude of the differentials, it can be seen that those connected to the institution of school councils are higher than the others, and those connected to transfer of funds turn out to be lower. Differentials related to instituting election of school principals accordingly occupy a middle ground.

Although these differentials show that innovations in management have an impact on educational performance, they tend to overestimate this impact for two reasons. First, these differentials partly reflect the fact that the innovative states are the ones with a higher quality of family life and teachers. Second, because there is a tendency for the three innovations to be instituted to some extent simultaneously, the estimated differentials tend to overestimate the true value of the impact of a particular innovation, insofar as the impact of the other innovations is not isolated.

Hence, at a second stage, we introduced controls for the quality of family environment and teachers in order to isolate the impact of each of the three innovations. Inasmuch as family environment and teacher quality tend to score higher in the states and at the times of greater innovation, introducing and isolating their impact on each of the innovations had the effect that the estimated impacts of innovations on school performance are generally lower than the differentials previously calculated. In addition, introducing controls and seeking to isolate the impact of innovations affected in a differentiated way the relationship between the previously calculated differential and the estimated impact of each of the innovations on school performance.

We found that of the three innovations studied, the one that had the greatest impact on educational performance is transfer of funds (except with regard to the repetition rate and school performance). Implementing election of school principals has a positive impact only on the repetition rate and school performance. The institution of school councils, which was the innovation associated with greater gross differentials, occupies a middle position, its impact being generally positive but less than those observed for instituting transfer of funds. However, the impact of implementing school councils is higher than that of other innovations for the repetition rate but negative for school performance.

Even though introducing controls leads to a reduction in the impact of the three innovations on educational performance from the estimated gross differentials, taken together their impact on the repetition rate continues to be very significant in quantitative terms. The impact on the proportion of children not in school and on indicators of grade-level lag becomes less significant, and comes to explain only about half of the variation noted over the decade. With regard to school performance, the impact of introducing transfer of resources and election of principals is positive but relatively insignificant in magnitude.

In the third stage of the analysis, we carried out a series of extensions of the model and tests for robustness. Because this stage has to take advantage of the longitudinal nature of the data, it cannot be performed for the indicators of school performance. Two extensions were made. In the first we sought to check whether the results obtained were sensible to the introduction of a linear trend or to estimation restricted to subperiods. The results, presented in Tables 3.11 to 3.13, indicate little sensitivity to these changes, but the impact of the innovations tends to decline with these modifications, particularly the impact on the proportion of children not in school.

Table 3.14. Impact of School Management Innovations on Educational Indicators

	Transfer of funds	Election of principal	Establishment of school council	Combined impact
Repetition rate				
Effects:				
Without any control	−1.7	−2.9	−4.2	−8.8
With basic controls	−0.8	−1.3	−2.9	−5.0
+ Linear trend	−0.6	−1.2	−2.7	−4.5
Excluding 1981–1982	−0.8	−1.3	−2.9	−5.0
Excluding 1992–1993	−0.7	−1.5	−2.6	−4.8
Fixed effect	−2.5	−0.2	0.3	−2.8
Differentials:				
(1990–93) − (1981–83)*	−4.2	−4.2	−4.2	−4.2
Regional best-worst**	−14.2	−14.2	−14.2	−14.2
Proportion of children not in school				
Effects:				
Without any control	−3.6	−3.4	−6.6	−13.7
With basic controls	−3.0	0.6	−2.8	−5.9
+ Linear trend	−1.6	1.9	−1.0	−2.6
Excluding 1981–1982	−2.2	1.1	−2.5	−4.7
Excluding 1992–1993	−2.1	0.9	−1.2	−3.3
Fixed effect	−3.8	1.0	−2.3	−6.1
Differentials:				
(1990–93) − (1981–83)*	−10.2	−10.2	−10.2	−10.2
Regional best-worst**	−19.4	−19.4	−19.4	−19.4
Mean grade-level lag				
Effects:				
Without any control	−0.13	−0.23	−0.36	−0.72
With basic control	−0.11	0.02	−0.06	−0.17
+ Linear trend	−0.11	0.02	−0.06	−0.17
Excluding 1981–1982	−0.10	0.03	−0.05	−0.15
Excluding 1992–1993	−0.10	0.03	−0.01	−0.11
Fixed effect	−0.13	0.00	−0.09	−0.22
Differentials:				
(1990–93) − (1981–83)*	−0.37	−0.37	−0.37	−0.37
Regional best-worst**	−1.61	−1.61	−1.61	−1.61

Table 3.14. *(cont.)*

	Transfer of funds	Election of principal	Establishment of school council	Combined impact
	Proportion of children with some school lag			
Effects:				
Without any control	–2.3	–4.5	–6.4	–13.2
With basic control	–2.1	0.1	–1.0	–3.0
+ Linear trend	–1.6	0.5	–0.3	–1.9
Excluding 1981–1982	–1.8	0.5	–0.5	–2.3
Excluding 1992–1993	–1.5	0.0	0.2	–1.5
Fixed effect	–1.9	0.3	–2.7	–4.6
Differentials:				
(1990–93) – (1981–83)*	–7.9	–7.9	–7.9	–7.9
Regional best-worst**	–29.0	–29.0	–29.0	–29.0
	1st and 2nd cycles			
Effects:				
Without any control	–0.8	1.4	1.6	–0.8
With basic controls	0.0	1.1	–0.7	–0.7
+ Linear trend	—	—	—	—
Excluding 1981–1982	—	—	—	—
Excluding 1992–1993	—	—	—	—
Fixed effect	—	—	—	—
Differentials:				
(1990–93) – (1981–83)*	—	—	—	—
Regional best-worst**	11.3	11.3	11.3	—

Notes: * Difference between means in 1990–93 and 1981–83.

    ** Difference between the best and worst mean regional value.

In the second extension of the model, with the introduction of a control for unobserved heterogeneity, the combined impact of the innovations was little changed, the most important observed in the distribution among the innovations. Introducing this control meant that the impact of the innovations on the repetition rate and the proportion of children not attending school is concentrated on the introduction of transfer of funds to schools, and to a lesser extent, that the impact on the two grade-level lag indicators is concentrated on the institution of school councils. The combined impacts of introducing transfer of funds and the institution of school councils remained substantially as important as before the introduction of these controls, and hence they remain equal to half of the change that occurred in the 1980s.

Conclusions

This chapter has shown that, taken together, the three innovations explain only half of the modest improvement in educational performance that took place in Brazil during the 1980s. Thus, if the evidence presented here indicates that these innovations had some impact, there is also evidence that in substantive terms such impact is modest.

Before assuming a relatively pessimistic position on the chances that these innovations can lead to substantial changes in the Brazilian educational system, it is important to highlight some limitations of this study that may have led to an underestimation of the impact of these innovations.

First, the innovations studied here have to do solely with the state education system, while the measures of educational performance reflect measures for the entire education system (state, municipal and private). Inasmuch as enrollment in the state system represents only around half of total enrollment, it can be inferred that the true impact of the innovations may be as great as double what is estimated in this study.

Second, even though some innovations were already established in states more than a decade ago, the nature of their content has changed over time. The innovations that took place in the early 1990s, even though they were labeled the same as those taking place in the mid-1980s, are different and deeper in nature. Thus the impact that calculated here is to some extent a mixture of the modest impact resulting from innovations in the mid-1980s with the significant impact of typical innovations of the early 1990s, and hence may be underestimating the impact of the deeper changes taking place since the beginning of this decade. Third, the estimated impact largely measures only the short-term impact of these innovations, while long-term impacts tend to be significantly greater.

Given their enormous importance and the great expectations that these innovations have raised, it is important that subsequent studies be carried out with new data bases, different methods and greater depth in order to re-evaluate the impact of these innovations. In short, the evidence gathered throughout this chapter shows a generally positive but modest impact of these innovations on educational performance. The evidence is especially pessimistic with regard to the importance of electing school principals, but is less pessimistic with regard to the importance of instituting transfer of funds and establishing school councils.

References

Barros, R., and R. Mendonça. 1997. O Impacto de Gestão sobre o Desempenho Educacional. Working Paper Series R-301, OCE-BID.

Barros, R., and L. Ramos. 1992. *A Note on the Temporal Evolution of the Relationship Between Wages and Education Among Brazilian Prime-Age Males: 1976–1989.* IPEA Discussion Paper 279, Rio de Janeiro.

Boletim de Indicadores Educacionais. *Imagens da educação* 5, MEC, INEP, Brasília.

Marques, A. 1991. *Despesas governamentais com educação: 1986/1990.* IPEA Discussion Paper 243, Rio de Janeiro.

MEC. 1975–96. Censo escolar. Sinopse Estatística da Educação Fundamental, Brasília.

Mello, Guiomar de. 1992. Autonomia da Escola: Possibilidades, Limites e Condições. *Qualidade, eficiência e eqüidade na educação básica.* IPEA Discussion Paper 136, Brasília.

Mendonça, R. 1993. *A qualidade da educação básica no Brasil e igualdade de oportunidades.* Rio de Janeiro: PUC (DM).

Pesquisa Nacional por Amostra de Domicílios. 1981–1995. Rio de Janeiro: IBGE.

SEEMG. 1994. *A Política Educacional de Minas Gerais: Prioridades, Compromissos, Ações.* Belo Horizonte: SEEMG.

Sistema Nacional de Avaliação da Educação Básica. 1990–93. MED, SEDIAE, SAEB, Brasília.

Souza, Alberto de Mello e. 1979. *Financiamento da educação e acesso à escola no Brasil.* Coleção Relatórios de Pesquisa 42, IPEA, Rio de Janeiro.

United Nations. 1990. *Human Development Report. 1990.* Oxford: Oxford University Press.

Xavier, A., Guiomar de Mello, J. Sobrinho, et al. 1994. Gestão educacional: desafios e tendências. IPEA Discussion Paper 143, Brasília.

________. 1995. Gestão educacional: experiências inovadoras. IPEA Discussion Paper 147, Brasília.

Xavier, A., J. Sobrinho, and F. Marra. 1994. *Gestão escolar: desafios e tendências.* Brasília: IPEA.

CHAPTER 4

Federal, State and Nonprofit Schools in Venezuela

Juan Carlos Navarro and Rafael de la Cruz[1]

This chapter presents the results of a study of the economic organization of education services in Venezuela. The broadest frame of reference is that of the economic theory of organization, and the primary motivation lies in recognizing the severe problems confronting education in Venezuela. The chapter first introduces the contextual elements required for adequately understanding the approach of the study and recent trends in the supply of education in Venezuela. The second part presents the analysis of the economic organization of education services in three education systems (the national and state systems and one private system) in Mérida, a state in western Venezuela. It also contains the elements required to understand the theoretical frame of reference and the description of the research strategy, as well as the results of the analysis of the data and the conclusions.

Educational Organization in Venezuela and Mérida

National Education System

As is common throughout Latin America, the Venezuelan education system today is heir to an early tradition of strong state involvement in the development of education. When the country returned to democracy in the 1960s,

---

[1] Juan Carlos Navarro, former Director of the IESA Public Policy Center, is a senior education specialist with the Inter-American Development Bank. Rafael de la Cruz is Director of Masters Studies at the School of Political Science at IESA.

the role of the state in social policy had to be redefined, especially in education. As part of what political parties were offering society, government agreed to assure legally and financially that education would be compulsory and free, taking advantage of the economic opportunities presented by the boom in oil revenues.

Throughout most of this century public education was organized along very centralized lines. However, for historical reasons and because of the federal system that has at various times flourished in Venezuela, education has been spread through the various levels of government. On average, about 25 percent of enrollment in basic and diversified education (the first 11 years of the system) has been handled by the states, approximately 3.5 percent by municipal schools, and over 60 percent (varying from state to state) by the national government. Slightly over 18 percent of teachers work for state governments, 3 percent for municipalities, 62 percent for the national government, and slightly less than 17 percent in the private sector. With regard to the number of schools, the states administer around 35 percent, the municipalities less than 3 percent, the national government 35 percent. Approximately 16 percent are private and another 12 percent are combined government institutions with funds and staff from at least two levels of government.

Even though Venezuela gives the appearance of having a system in which different educational systems operate side by side, until very recently the three levels of government administered their respective school systems under the educational, organizational, and financial guidelines of the national government through the Ministry of Education. Until a few years ago, state governors were appointed by the president, while city councils had a system for electing their council members that did not allow local governments autonomy in decisionmaking. We will return to this point below when we examine the decentralization of the public sector now taking place as part of political reforms that have led to elections of governors, mayors and members of state and local legislatures since 1989.

In short, strong control by the central government over formulation of policy and performance of education services made government administration uniform in almost all respects. Only within private education was there room for differences from the national education system. The *Fe y Alegría* schools, which are private (though subsidized by the national government) schools that target poor children, are the most independent and autonomous schools going back many years. The system of state schools bears the legacy of several decades of centralism, although the democratization process has opened such possibilities as the *Escuelas Integrales* (Comprehensive Schools) in the state of Mérida.

Even before decentralization began in the late 1980s, the central government recognized that the national education system was too large (250,000 employees) for efficient centralized management. Thus, the ministry undertook various efforts at "deconcentration," understanding that to mean setting up ministry offices in a number of regions in the country to carry out administrative operations closer to where services were being provided.

Even though they are not really decentralized units for education, these offices constitute the only formal organizational and administrative mechanism closer to the communities through which the central body can perform its functions. Originally in 1969 there were eight education regions. In 1987, the Organic Law of Education established a region for each federal territorial entity, hence creating 23 education regions (20 states, two federal territories, and the federal district).

Despite these efforts to regionalize education and the positive effects that in principle regionalization could have had as part of a process of decentralization, the weak structure of the education regions, which have no substantive functions, makes it obvious how centralized the national public education system remains.

Current legislation recognizes particular regional features and authorizes the Ministry of Education to adjust the levels and modalities of the education system to each region so as to adapt the general educational goals issued by the central level (Art. 15, Organic Law of Education). However, the structure continues to adhere to the principles of unity and coordination, thereby reinforcing its centralist tendencies (Casanova et al., 1993).

With the declared purpose of guaranteeing the unity and integration of education policies, the system is organized by levels and modalities. The *levels* encompass preschool education (one to two years); basic education (nine years); middle education (two years); and diversified and professional education and university education. Each of these systems makes up an interrelated educational network. The *modalities* refer to other areas of education, such as special education, education for the arts, military education, adult education, and off-campus education.

Among its other functions, the Ministry of Education is responsible for establishing the system by which teachers compete to fill teaching positions, and for organizing the seniority system and pay scales for national teaching employees. It is also empowered to design and change areas or subject matter in the curricula for each education level.

Decentralization and its Potential Impact on Incentives in the Public Sector

The decentralization process that has been underway in Venezuela in recent years has already affected the institutional structure of the state as well as the system of incentives and the industrial organization of government services.

Because the government has so many tasks to perform and is overly centralized, it cannot efficiently and effectively carry out all of its responsibilities. Many local matters are neglected because they have to be decided at the top levels of ministries or even at the presidential level. Under such an arrangement, communities do not have access to the decisionmaking process (because it takes place far away from them), and many problems that could be resolved if state and municipal governments had the authority to handle them remain unresolved. The principle underlying these ideas is very simple: having more functions handled by administrative offices closer to the population will facilitate handling those functions better. In turn, having the central government handle fewer administrative functions would enable it to be concerned with decisions of a strategic nature. That is the aim of decentralization.

The rediscovery of federalism and of new forms of decentralization in much of the West is linked to recovering the very idea of democracy as a system that assures efficiency, liberty, citizen participation and justice in the formulation of public policies. The meaning of decentralization on the threshold of the 21st century is that of returning control over states to communities by making government administratively closer and more responsive to voters.

The government structures and administrative mechanisms that have been set up in Venezuela since the late 1980s reflect the various efforts to create adequate incentives to progress toward an efficient federal system that will correct the distortions of excessive centralism. The more noteworthy of these structures and mechanisms are:

- New ways of electing governors and mayors that will prompt these officials to behave with greater accountability toward voters who are close by;
- Redesign of how authority and services are spread among levels of government;
- Fiscal federalism that develops financing mechanisms appropriate for decentralized governments.

Clearly, Venezuela does not have all the conditions for assuring successful decentralization. The electoral system is still not stable, and the way legislative bodies are elected, both at the central and decentralized levels, is still unsettled. There is no clear agreement between the different sectors concerned with this issue on what the final arrangement ought to be.

In Venezuela, the transfer of services and authority of the national government to states and municipalities, especially those related to social welfare, has just begun. A persistent mistrust of decentralization in parts of the central government can slow the pace of the transfer of administration, even though in previous years important activities were entrusted to the states, such as management of ports, airports, mines, salt mines, freeways, and even (in 12 states) health care.

Finally, should the centralized model of public financing persist, and if state and municipal taxes are not developed to help finance the responsibilities that state and municipal governments are taking on, the country will find itself in a few years frustrated with the presumed virtues of decentralization. But if these fiscal reforms are carried out and government services are provided at the local level honestly, fairly and efficiently, citizens will have even more reasons to pay taxes, and the lesson that the public sector is costly but beneficial when it is under the community's watch will have been learned.

These limits must not, however, stand in the way of recognizing that the admittedly imperfect process of decentralization in Venezuela has already produced some successes. This chapter indeed is about one of the accomplishments of decentralization: the fact that some governors, who have been directly elected since 1989, took the initiative to reform educational systems in their states in response to the critical situation of education under the Ministry of Education. Such was the particular case of the state of Mérida.

Decentralization of Education in Mérida

The state of Mérida sits in the Andes mountains at the far western side of Venezuela. Geographically, it covers only 1.2 percent of the country, and its population, estimated at 639,921 in 1994, represents just 3 percent of the national total.

Economically and socially, Mérida is one of the most agricultural states in the country. The population is 27 percent rural, 11 percent higher than the national average. Similarly, almost 30 percent of the economically active population works in the agricultural sector, in sharp contrast to the national average of 11.4 percent.

Besides being agricultural and rural, the state has two additional features. First, Mérida seems to have experienced little economic growth in recent decades. Even though there are no figures on changes in its GDP, the last two censuses have shown that the state has had a net migratory outflow and that the population is very poor. Some 60 percent of households live in poverty; the illiteracy rate (14 percent in 1990) is considerably above the national average of 9 percent; and the infant mortality rate (1.3 percent) is among the highest in the country (sixth among 23 territorial divisions).

Basic Education in Mérida

In the 1994–95 school year, 139,170 students were enrolled in basic education in Mérida, that is, 90 percent of the population between the ages of 5 and 14. The level of coverage was only slightly lower than the national average in 1990 (Table 4.1). The coverage could in fact be regarded as high in comparison to the rest of the country, taking into account the difficulty of providing basic education to remote farming communities.

Table 4.2 shows that basic education in Mérida is provided by national schools directly under the Ministry of Education, state government schools, municipal schools, private schools with or without public subsidies, and "combined" schools, which consist almost entirely of joint initiatives between the governor's office and the Ministry of Education. While the proportion of enrollment covered by national schools represents 40 percent of the total, these schools cover only 20 percent of rural enrollment. By contrast, while state schools represent only 13 percent of total enrollment, they represent 25 percent of rural enrollment. Likewise, the combined schools

Table 4.1. School-age Population and School Enrollment: Venezuela and the State of Mérida

	Population aged 5 to 14	Enrollment: basic education	Enrollment/ population %
Mérida (1994)	155,002	139,170	89.78
Venezuela (1990)	4,400,792	4,052,947	92.09

Table 4.2. Schools and Enrollment, State of Mérida, 1995

System	Schools Mérida	Enrollment	Rural schools	%	Rural enrollment	%
National	204	56,456	128	63.0	10,980	19.4
State	333	18,943	319	96.0	13,773	73.0
Municipal	25	714	25	100.0	714	100.0
Combined	288	45,591	245	85.0	24,740	54.3
Private	27	5,866	1	3.7	248	4.0
Nat. subsidized	18	6,955	1	5.5	209	3.0
Ofic. subsidized	10	4,665	2	20.0	602	13.0
Total	905	139,190	721	80.0	51,266	36.8

Source: Ministry of Education, 1995.

that represent 33 percent of total coverage represent 48 percent of rural enrollment. Because almost all the combined schools are connected to the Mérida state government, we can conclude that the state education system plays a key role in providing education in the rural areas.

Finally, the rural combined schools (Ministry of Education and state government) have an average enrollment of 100 students, while the rural state schools have an average enrollment of 40 students. This difference in size suggests that the state government of Mérida assumes responsibility for reaching the more remote and less populated areas of the state.

In addition to an apparent policy of expanding coverage in rural areas, the Mérida state government has been taking steps to improve the quality of education, particularly for rural children. The Program to Improve Preschool and Basic Education (PMEBP), created in the 1990's, was headed by a teacher, Antonio Luis Cárdenas, who years later was appointed Minister of Education. This initiative was the basis for creating the *Escuelas Integrales* school program, and in 1995 the "Don Juan de Dios Picón" regional center for training and retraining teachers was established. The purpose of the *Escuelas Integrales* schools program is to offer a quality education and at the same time make up for those deficiencies that hinder the learning of peasant children in marginal areas. Thus far, 23 mainly rural schools have been incorporated into the program. The governor's office has begun to gradually expand this program to other state-run schools, but it has set itself the target of bringing this kind of education to all schools in Mérida, provided that the national government grants the state the responsibility for running its schools. All teachers in the state must be retrained at least two weeks a year at the regional center for teacher support.

Currently, the prospects for *Escuelas Integrales* to be consolidated and extended throughout Mérida are uncertain. The program has moved ahead thanks to strong political support from the governor, who has made improvement of state education the banner of his administration. His successor will probably have to maintain the level of quality and expectations that this experience has created, but that remains to be seen. On the other hand, the program is expensive in terms of the initial investment required—though not necessarily in operating costs, as will be seen below—and will not be able to expand if the only funds for that purpose are those transferred from the national government to the state. That will be even less likely if it is expanded to all the state schools and to the national school system, which is soon to be transferred. (Mérida has been requesting that national education be decentralized to the state since December 1993).

Administration of National Education in Mérida

All public and private education in Mérida is governed by Education Region No. 8 of the Ministry of Education, located in the city of Mérida, the state capital. Its authority over the entire education system includes supervising schools, gathering educational statistics, and certifying school buildings and degrees. Education Region No. 8 is also responsible for administering national welfare programs in all government schools, such as the school "glass of milk" program, the lunch program, student scholarships, and the school supplies program. Finally, with respect to the national school system, the region has limited functions in the areas of administering teaching staff and equipping schools.

Education regions are flawed in several ways because of their lack of autonomy and administrative capability. The regions cannot set educational policies, partly because they cannot set their own budget. They have no flexibility for allocating resources, nor is there clear information on how much each school and program is allocated. Hence, the region has neither the capacity nor the authority to set goals and priorities in allocating resources. Likewise, funds for maintenance are managed by a separate entity (the Foundation for Educational Buildings or *Fundación de Edificaciones Educativas*, FEDE) which is under the Ministry of Education in Caracas. The region also lacks administrative authority and hence various processes are hindered. For example, in paying teachers, it acts only as a post office between the ministry headquarters in Caracas and the school. This means that in order to dock pay from a teacher for missing work, the school principal has to travel to the regional office, and then the head of the region has to ask Caracas to rewrite one of the 300,000 checks that it issues every two weeks. That is why hours missed are never deducted from pay. Similar problems happen with regard to retirements, dismissals and transfers of teachers.

Likewise, the region seems to lack the administrative ability to perform proactive tasks intended to improve the quality of education and the condition of school facilities, or to pressure the national government for more funds. There is no plan for maintaining school buildings by setting short and medium-term priorities; no effort is made to make requests for resources from municipalities, state government, or regional development corporations for upkeep of school buildings; there are no systematic procedures for equipping schools; supervisors are not given ongoing training for providing help in the classroom; and tests are not applied systematically to determine student and teacher needs.

State Educational Administration

State schools and teachers are under the Department of Education of the government of the state of Mérida. This office was created in 1990 when what was formerly the Department of Education, Culture and Sports was restructured. It has four coordinating offices, one each for basic education, preschool education, adult education and services. In contrast to the National Education Region, the state Department of Education is a small body, with only 18 employees, including four coordinators and the director. Payroll for the 1,780 state teachers and the equipping of schools are handled in a centralized manner by this department. Maintenance works and improvements, however, are performed not by the Department of Education but by the State Office of Public Construction (*Oficina de Construcciones Públicas del Estado*, OCP). Even so, requests to the OCP are made through the Department of Education.

In addition to the OCP, the Mérida state government's Regional Unit for Coordination and Execution (*Unidad Coordinadora y Ejecutora Regional - UCER*) was created in 1994 to plan and implement improvements in the equipping and infrastructure of state schools, using funds from multilateral agencies. The UCER also coordinates Education Region No. 8 and the Department of Education of the State of Mérida.

Finally, as noted above, the state government of Mérida has a Commission for the Improvement of the Quality of Preschool and Basic Education which reports directly to the state governor. This unit was created in 1990 and has been responsible for getting the *Escuelas Integrales* underway. Its budget is separate from that of the Department of Education and includes outlays added to the regular budget of those schools that have been converted into *Escuelas Integrales,* such as an additional bonus for the classroom teachers who work in the afternoon, payments for music and computer teachers, special supplies (books and computers), and funds for child nutrition in the *Escuelas Integrales.* This commission also has four supervisors of comprehensive education, plus the commissioner himself, who are responsible for providing technical and pedagogical consulting for teachers in the 23 schools participating in this program.

Administration of the Fe y Alegría System in Mérida

Fe y Alegría is a religiously-based institution devoted primarily to providing education to low- income sectors. It began operating in 1965 and has spread throughout the country. Since it is national in scope, *Fe y Alegría,* like the Ministry of Education, operates on three levels: the main office (in Caracas), the regional offices, and education centers (schools). The main office is responsible for strategic aspects of planning, financing and supervising the activities of the network of schools. The regional offices transmit plans and goals to schools for a particular period and advise them in drawing up their education plans, financing strategies and personnel selection. Finally, the schools operate autonomously within the framework of guidelines from the central office.

Fe y Alegría has a Regional Office in Mérida that was set up in 1989 because its educational work was expanding rapidly in the Andes region. Currently in Mérida, it has two basic schools and one technical high school, a tourism training center, and a craft training center.

Economic Organization of Education Services in Venezuela

Three education systems with contrasting organizational features exist side-by-side in the state of Mérida, but they are similar in terms of the kind of school population they serve. This section explores differences in performance between the systems and seeks to determine to what extent such differences can be attributed to their differing economic organization more than to other variables normally associated with causing variations in school performance.

School Performance in the Literature

It has been amply documented that two major variables influence learning in school. One is family circumstances surrounding the student, including the family's socioeconomic status, the parents' education level, and the availability of books in the home. The other is characteristics in the schools themselves: spending per pupil, quality of teachers, and the availability of textbooks and other learning materials. Both variables exert a powerful influence in all settings, although the literature favors the idea that the more developed a society, the more decisive become factors in the surroundings and the family. In less developed societies, on the other hand, the influence of factors directly related to the school may be greater. Another recurring finding in studies is that the unexplained variation in performance becomes greater the more underdeveloped the particular country (Farrel and Oliveira, 1993), suggesting the presence of significant determining factors in school performance that have not been well studied, probably due to the difficulty of finding an appropriate measure of such factors.

A certain basis can also be found in a number of currents of the literature for speculating that school performance is influenced by aspects such as discipline within the school, a clear definition of the principal's authority, parent involvement in school decisionmaking, and an orderly environment within the school (Levin and Lockheed, 1993).

On the other hand, it is easy to find studies criticizing the ability of education systems in Latin America to effectively promote learning, both because of inefficient management of school resources and a failure to encourage the emergence and maintenance of those human qualities associated with effective learning. Such is the particular case of Venezuela, where severe problems have been uncovered in the effectiveness of government spending and in the internal efficiency of educational institutions: the schools offer abundant evidence of mismatched inputs (more teachers than can actually teach, combined with an average of one textbook for every 17 students in elementary school), deteriorating facilities, low level of labor discipline, and little community participation in school decisionmaking. Principals are often unable to work effectively because they are deprived of professional authority (often appointed on political grounds rather than merit) and administrative authority (principals do not manage budgets, nor do they choose, sanction or dismiss teachers or others who work with them, high degree of unionization, etc.) (World Bank, 1993). The education system as a whole, as explained in the first part of this chapter, has been the target of criticism and reform proposals because of what observers identify as its overly centralized administration (Casanova, et al., 1993).

This internal inefficiency clearly has a negative influence on student performance in Venezuela. For years, government spending per student has been relatively high in Venezuela when compared to other Latin American countries with a comparable level of development. But its school system has yielded results considerably lower than those achieved by societies that devote relatively fewer resources to education. Thus, the issue is not solely one of resources or of the situation of the relative poverty or wealth, but of the way the education system is organized so as to make the best possible use of its resources, or, if you will, to counteract the deficiencies that the children bring to school as a result of a family setting that is not conducive to study.

Such conditions seem to call for something other than the traditional approaches to school performance based on studying the presence or amount of particular family inputs, or of certain contextual conditions that affect learning. One option is to use the contemporary approach of organization theory, in which the performance and effectiveness of an organization depend on the incentives that its members encounter. Attention is focused on the costs and distribution of information, transaction costs in general, and the contractual problems that any organization has to resolve in order to operate. These costs are affected by the technology available for generating supervisory performance indicators, the physical aspects of the assets, the nature of acts of exchange (how often they are repeated, for example), and the institutional framework of the society in which the organization is operating (for example, the relative ease with which property rights are defined and enforced).

Milgrom and Roberts (1992) suggest that analysis from this standpoint include legal aspects influencing the behavior of the organization's members, patterns of resources and information flows; relationships of authority and control; distribution of real decisionmaking power; allocation of responsibilities; rights of decision, organizational routines and decisionmaking processes; methods for attracting, retaining and remunerating staff; ways of adapting to changing circumstances and absorbing innovations; and means for attaining convergence between the expressed aims of the organization and those of the individuals involved in it. This last point encapsulates, by itself, the heart of the contract dilemma faced by organizations, which has been analytically approached through the principal-agent model: international experience indicates that systems that reward teachers on the basis of their performance are quite rare and questionable in terms of their results (Farrel and Oliveira, 1993). There is no expectation that significant differences will be found with regard to this aspect of the labor contracts typical of the education system. However, some differences can be expected in relation to the specificity of labor contracts. One of the caveats of all economic analysis of organization is that it is impossible to write contracts so perfect as to anticipate all the contingencies that can possibly arise for those involved in a contractual relationship. Given this impossibility of foreseeing all contingencies, the general practice is to adopt an intermediate degree of specifying obligations that guarantee the parties that what is set forth in the contract will be fulfilled, while at the same time reconciling that guarantee with the flexibility needed to deal with the unforeseen.

In this regard, there is a tendency toward overspecifying labor contracts, generally as the result of pressures from unions to spell out in as much detail as possible how much work can be demanded by the principal, in this instance the government. If we follow Eggertsson's (1994) claim that contractual overspecification leads to a high level of dissipation of wealth and therefore to inefficiency, then this area should be one of the points considered in a study of the performance of education systems from the standpoint of the economics of organization.

Moreover, if contractual overspecification is generally the result of labor union pressure, high degrees of unionization seem to be associated with various rigidities in administration of the system, particularly constraints on the discretionary power of administrators to make decisions on teaching staff (selection, promotion, transfers, rewards and sanctions, removals). Indeed, the situation can reach the point of placing these decisions in the hands of the unions themselves. Such circumstances may limit the ability of the system to operate with efficient resource allocation and an appropriate mix of inputs, as well as labor discipline and a chance for school principals to fully play their role.

Finally, similar effects that limit performance may result from a divergence between the place where information resides and the place where the decisions that ought to be affected by such information are made. Presumably, a highly centralized system like Venezuela's must make thousands of tiny decisions on the allocation of all kinds of resources (staff, budget, etc.) from a distant center and on the basis of general rules that can create or enhance inefficiency in the numerous education units to which they are applied. If such is the case, there ought to be a positive correlation between the degree of decentralization of allocation decisions and the efficiency (and hence performance) of education systems.

In short, the set of hypotheses that have been derived from organizational economic analysis with regard to the potential crucial determinants of internal inefficiency, and thereby the poor performance of the school system in Venezuela, would be the following:

- Systems ought to differ in their supervision technology and in the authority and scope of the principal's decisionmaking role, with those systems with better supervision technology and a more clearly defined role for the school principal correspondingly attaining more efficient allocation of resources in schools, and presumably more effective learning and better school performance.

- Systems ought to differ in the degree of contract specification of teachers' obligations. The greater the overspecification, the greater will be the inefficiency and the worse the performance.
- Those education systems that are more decentralized in decision-making on budgets and staff ought to be more efficient and produce better school performance. A complementary hypothesis is that there should be a positive correlation between more intense community participation in school matters and school efficiency, since participation is a means for revealing preference on the kind of educational service that the customers want to receive, and hence it enhances decisionmaking ability.
- More highly unionized education systems are more inefficient and produce worse results in learning and performance.

Design of the Research

There is a methodological problem of how to isolate the effect of the economic organization variables on school performance, since the specialized literature says that such performance also depends on the contextual and input factors mentioned at the beginning of this section. Strictly speaking, the ultimate aim of a study of the performance of school systems ought to be to explain the variation in performance between schools and students after controlling for the effect of variables connected to students' family background, such as their socioeconomic status, and also of the variables traditionally included in studies of school inputs, such as cost per student, class size, and teacher qualification and experience.

Carrying out such studies requires a considerable volume of information for a large number of schools for which relevant aspects of economic organization can be contrasted. In particular, we need detailed information on:

- The family context of the students in schools. Traditionally this is done by obtaining information on such variables as urban or rural student origins, family income, father's or mother's work, and mother's schooling level, or a combination of them.
- The cost of schools, and the amount and quality of inputs placed in them. This is generally measured through variables such as spending

per student, qualification and experience of teachers, and students per class.

- Characteristics of the economic organization of the schools being examined, including places in the organization where key decisions are made regarding personnel and budget, characteristics of the contracts governing actors in the system, financing mechanisms, the nature of supervision, and community participation in decisionmaking.

- The state of decisions regarding resource allocation within schools. How appropriate is the mixture of inputs (measured, for example, by the proportion of the budget allocated to categories other than payroll)? How much labor discipline is there, and to what extent does it get the work done in the schools? This last point is important, because the economic theory of organization indicates that better incentives and a better supervision system ought to be reflected in more efficiently organized education, that is, a better job done by teachers, greater availability of resources for learning, and school buildings in better condition and better adapted to what users want. At this point, however, we have to depend upon studies that show the factors that are decisive for school performance and tell us that the presence of the characteristics listed above improves learning in schools. Schematically, the causal chain can be presented as shown in Figure 4.1. Note that inputs both in quantity (spending per student) and quality (experience and studies of teachers) appear in this scheme as external to economic organization. The implication is that the economic organization of school systems affects their efficiency in the use of such inputs, assuming that their level and quality are given. This may well not be exactly the case: the fact that a system is highly centralized, for example, may not only create problems about the allocation of resources within schools, but also create distortions in the very level of spending itself. Nevertheless, for the sake of simplicity and unless otherwise stated, for purposes of analysis they will be assumed to be external.

- School performance, through standardized tests that measure the learning taking place in schools at regular intervals, along with measurements of school performance such as retention, repetition and dropout rates.

Figure 4.1. Analytical Framework of the Research

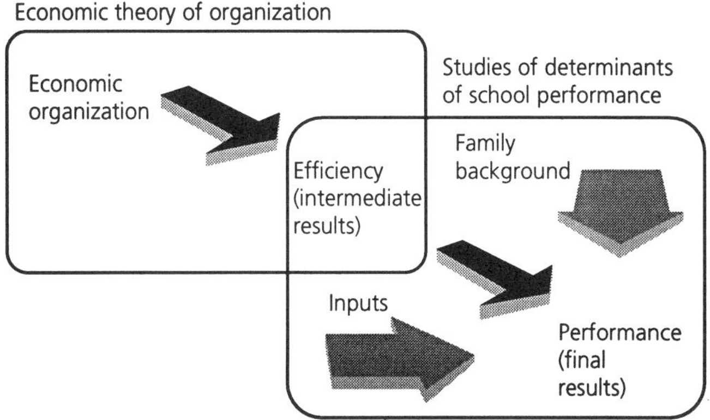

Unfortunately, educational examinations are not carried out regularly in Venezuela, making it difficult to follow the quality of learning in the different levels of the education system. Moreover, while tools for gathering data on many characteristics of the operation of schools exist formally, these tools are not used with regularity by those in charge, nor are they processed by the central offices so as to make it easy to manage the information that may be gathered. Likewise, there is no systematic information on the social and economic variables describing the students.

That being the case, it was necessary for this research to gather information from primary sources both with regard to the economic organization of schools and for student performance, school inputs, and intermediate results (as we have termed them: input mix, labor discipline, and so forth). At the same time, we attempted to control as much as possible for those socioeconomic variables that affect schooling, but for which it was impossible to obtain detailed information within the limits of this study.

For that reason, it was decided to study schools located in a single state, Mérida, where schools presumably quite different in terms of their economic organization can be found standing side by side because they are part of three different education systems: the national education system under the Ministry of Education; the *Fe y Alegría* system, a private system of schools for children in low-income areas; and the system of *Escuelas Integrales* organized and directed by the state of Mérida.

The interest in comparing these systems is based on the fact that they share a series of characteristics normally associated with variations in school achievement and performance, while they differ critically in the way their educational services are organized, at least insofar as they have been studied previously. Among the shared features that make them more comparable are:

- The social and economic background of the students enrolled in the three systems. Both the *Fe y Alegría* system and the comprehensive schools of Mérida have been set up specifically with students from low-income families in mind, while Ministry of Education schools in Venezuela typically serve children of low socioeconomic levels as a result of the flight of middle class children toward private education. None of the systems under examination can be regarded as elitist.
- All three cases are systems, not experiments limited to a single school or a specific neighborhood. While the Mérida program covers only the state and is therefore specific to one region, it has been applied on a considerable scale statewide. The most important limitation is that this system was created only recently (the oldest schools date from only 1992), and hence it could be argued that not enough time has passed for the system to take on a distinctive character or clearly influence its children or teachers.
- Teachers in the three systems are similar because they are primarily graduates from the same schools of education and pedagogical institutes. No particular system would contract only employees from a particular school or teacher training institute. In fact, it often happens that the same teacher works part-time in two of these systems concurrently. In addition, the pay scales in the three systems are practically identical,[2] with the exception of retirement benefits, which are similar for the national system and the *Escuelas Integrales*, but practically nonexistent for *Fe y Alegría* teachers beyond the minimums set by the Labor Law.

---

[2] Average hourly pay for a teacher with 12 years experience in the national system and at *Fe y Alegría* is $10. Teachers in the state system who work in *Escuelas Integrales* work more hours per day but receive a compensatory bonus that is less than proportional to their base pay, leaving their hourly wage at $9. All these pay levels are applied uniformly within each system, and hence there are no variations between individual schools.

- The three systems can be studied in the same location, since *Escuelas Integrales* and Ministry of Education schools exist side by side with some *Fe y Alegría* schools.

The following are, in turn, some of the contrasts connected to the economic organization of the school systems in Mérida:

- As a general organizational pattern, one system is private and the other two public, and one of the public systems is highly centralized under the Ministry of Education, while the other is decentralized in the sense that it is under a regional rather than the national government.
- Strong traits of autonomous management at the individual school level in the case of *Fe y Alegría,* as compared with almost none for the Ministry of Education schools. The comprehensive schools fall in between.
- The labor systems in the three systems are different in terms of the degree of unionization and the role of collective bargaining in decisionmaking.
- The method for choosing personnel is different in the three systems. Teachers are fed into national schools through a selection process organized by the Education Region on the basis of competitive credentials. The decisionmaking body is a commission, chaired by the head of the region, and on which teachers' unions have a majority. Once in the system, the teacher is assigned by the region to the school where there is a need. For *Escuelas Integrales,* the method used to be the same, and hence most of the teachers now teaching in them were originally hired in the same manner; however, the *Escuelas Integrales* program in 1991 introduced a teacher examination for entry into all state schools. Teachers for *Fe y Alegría* schools are chosen individually by the school principal and hired for a one-year probation period before being offered long-term contracts.
- Supervision, budget and planning are different in the three systems.
- Community participation and the degree to which there is some kind of accountability are different. The *Fe y Alegría* schools and *Escuelas Integrales* are quite participatory, while the Ministry of Education schools are not.

- Financing sources of the three systems are obviously different, particularly between the private system and the two public systems. Users are charged modest fees in the private system.
- Prior research suggests that there are significant contrasts between the three systems in terms of cost-effectiveness (González and Navarro, 1994), and performance (Herrera, 1994). Nevertheless, there is no research examining the three systems in detail, nor of the connection between such differences and the system's economic organization.

Given the limitations of time and resources, a sample of 18 primary schools was chosen, eight under the Ministry of Education, eight *Escuelas Integrales* under the state government, and two from the private *Fe y Alegría* system,[3] which are the only primary schools in this network operating in the state of Mérida.

Within a set of eight municipalities that had been previously chosen because they were more accessible to the research team, the sample was deliberately selected to maximize the comparability of the students' social and economic background through criteria based on the neighborhoods where the schools are located. As will be seen in detail below, the *Fe y Alegría* schools are found only in the town centers, while the *Escuelas Integrales* are generally rural or are located in poor neighborhoods of small towns. Taking that as a given, a set of national schools was chosen so as to resemble in their outward features the schools in other systems as much as possible. The features taken into account were as follows. First, in terms of the socioeconomic environment, a combination of national schools was deliberately chosen from rural environments, poor city neighborhoods, and the downtown area of medium-sized towns, all in order to facilitate comparison with *Escuelas Integrales* and *Fe y Alegría* schools located predominantly in such areas. Secondly, in terms of size, a group of small national schools was selected (six grades, one section per grade) to improve comparability with the *Escuelas Integrales,* and some larger size national schools were chosen to facilitate comparison with *Fe y Alegría* schools. Available statistical and geographical information about

---

[3] In practice, the entire analysis that follows contains information on 17 schools, since one of the holistic schools had the roof repaired the very week when the school performance test was to be administered.

the state of Mérida was used to make the selection, along with the judgment of the director of information of the Education Region of the state.

The information on which the analysis presented below is based was obtained through a combination of several sources and instruments:

- Material from secondary sources such as statistics, record books, labor contracts, manuals, regulations and collections of rules of operation.
- In-depth interviews with school principals and those in charge of head offices or supervisory offices on the regional level, such as the Education Region. Eighteen school principals were interviewed, as were the head of the Education Region of the Ministry of Education in the state, the commissioner for the state government in charge of comprehensive schools, and the regional head of *Fe y Alegría*.
- A written survey of teachers about their perception of their duties and expectations in performing their jobs. The analysis includes information taken from 101 interviews with teachers.
- Visits to schools to observe their features directly and gather on-site primary information about enrollment, number and description of teachers, socioeconomic conditions of students, and so forth.
- Observations on a standardized achievement test given to 376 fifth-grade students from each of the schools visited.

The data gathering effort made it possible to compile information that did not always lend itself to analysis through econometric techniques. In the course of the analysis, some statistical techniques of lesser power were used when necessary. Because of this limitation, it has not been possible to perform the most desirable analysis of the information, particularly of selection bias, as is appropriate in econometric studies of related issues (Cox and Jiménez, 1990). The conclusions are tentative and in the nature of a first approximation, rather than having more solid corroborating power.

The analysis unfolds as follows: first, we provide a rough initial description of student achievement and learning indicators in the three systems, presuming for the time being that the children in the various types of schools are indeed comparable. Second, the education systems are compared regarding the availability of inputs, with a view to examining to what extent the influence of relative abundance or quality of inputs can be regarded as controlled. Next, the most important agency relationships in the three systems are described so as to check whether there are significant differences between them, as well as between the indicators of internal efficiency that may be attributed to the form such relationships take. Finally, having established that there are significant differences in the realm of economic organization, the crucial issue is broached: the degree to which these differences explain a significant portion of the variations of performance observed between the systems when the influence of variables from students' socioeconomic context is controlled. The general conclusions of the chapter are then presented, and the findings connected with the foregoing hypotheses.

Performance of School Systems in Mérida

From the outset, both the research design in general and that of the particular sample of schools chosen were influenced by the intention to isolate the influence of the differing economic organization of the systems from the effect of other variables which, according to existing literature, influence learning. In this sense, for practical purposes, it will be taken for granted from the outset that the three educational systems in fact constitute three ways of organizing agency relations in carrying out education. We can then devote attention to the issue of the degree to which there is a true difference between agency relations in the three systems, and to what extent the measured differences in performance can be attributed to variables other than economic organization.

Performance

Table 4.3 summarizes standardized test results for mathematics, reading and spelling by fifth-grade students in each of the schools included in the study, aggregated by education system.

Fe y Alegría schools consistently come out on top in performance tests. The two public school systems lag behind, with similar results in mathematics and writing, where the balance shifts slightly toward the Ministry of Education schools, while the results in reading more clearly favor the state government's *Escuelas Integrales*. In both mathematics and reading comprehension there is greater variation among the *Escuelas Integrales*, indicating that the performance of students in state schools varies more widely. In-

Table 4.3. Point Scores of Students in School Performance Test, by Type of School

	Escuelas Integrales	National	*Fe y Alegría*
Mathematics			
Mean	34.11	35.67	53.03
Standard deviation	16.61	14.16	3.49
Reading			
Mean	60.45	53.46	66.79
Standard deviation	21.93	17.87	19.98
Writing			
Mean	23.94	26.77	39.68
Standard deviation	16.8	11.81	29.72

deed, one of the *Escuelas Integrales,* John XXIII, is consistently among the top three performing schools in the three subjects studied, while another, the Mitisús school, is consistently among the two worst. The two *Fe y Alegría* schools in the state are never below seventh place in any regard.[4]

Pursuing a different approach, Table 4.4 presents further information on the performance of the three school systems, based not on student scores on standardized tests, but on the repetition rate in first grade and the proportion of students that schools in each system can keep from first to sixth grade in primary education.

Fe y Alegría schools again perform better than the other two systems, and on both measures the *Escuelas Integrales* are above the national schools. Thus, while it cannot be said that students in the *Escuelas Integrales* are learning more in every sense of the word, these schools do seem to have a greater ability to hold onto those children who are enrolled there.

These differences are possibly related to certain peculiar features of the situation in the schools. It is widely believed by the general public that *Fe*

---

[4] In the test used, the scale for mathematics was 0 to 15, for reading 0 to 11 and for writing 0 to 18. Points have been standardized to a base of 100 to facilitate analysis and presentation of results.

Table 4.4. Indicators of School Performance by Type of School
(In percent)

Performance	*Escuelas Integrales*	National	*Fe y Alegría*
Retention rate			
1st to 6th grade	59.26	42.44	100.00
Repetition rate,			
1st grade	19.26	59.66	0.00

y Alegría schools offer a quality education, and hence there are waiting lines of parents trying to register their children in the only two of these schools in the state. As far as could be determined, *Fe y Alegría* schools make a deliberate attempt to keep children coming from low-income families, but they do not select the students on the basis of talent or ability. However, this observation cannot be corroborated more systematically without a much longer and more careful study of how they operate.

With regard to the greater ability of *Escuelas Integrales* to hold onto students, the reason could be that since these are rural schools, the parents who enroll their children there have no other options. Although that cannot be ruled out, the retention of children in these schools in contrast to national schools is also evident in schools located in urban areas, where parents do have alternatives.

Thus, at first glance, certain differences in student performance can be noted between the three systems. But if they really constitute different kinds of organizations with respect to the contractual relationships implicit in each of them, these relationships ought to be compared with the results by contrasting them in the manner suggested in the hypotheses stated above. Naturally, attention must be devoted to controlling for other variables that may possibly help cause the differences between systems.

Inputs

Table 4.5 presents information on the characteristics of teachers working in the three systems, particularly their years of experience and academic credentials.

Table 4.5. Years of Experience and Professional Qualifications of Teachers in Schools by Type of School

	Teachers with university studies	Teachers with normal school studies	Total	% university	Average years of experience
Integrales	18	27	45	40.00	10.84
National	34	40	74	45.95	13.10
Fe y Alegría	26	18	44	59.09	13.65
Total	78	85	163	47.85	—

As is evident, the teachers with the least experience, on average, are those in the state schools, while those in *Fe y Alegría* and the national system are similar. *Fe y Alegría* teachers have studied longer than the teachers of national and state-run comprehensive schools, which have similar averages. If any conclusion can be drawn, it should be that the advantage displayed in test scores of students in the *Fe y Alegría* system could be explained at least partly by the higher quality of teachers in those schools, and that any relative disadvantage shown by students in the *Escuelas Integrales* could be attributed to the relative inexperience and lesser education of their teachers.

Spending per pupil is found to be significant in almost all studies of the determinants of school performance. Table 4.6 estimates school operating costs per pupil, which includes teachers' salaries, teaching materials, administration and minor maintenance of school facilities. Costs of meals and other social and economic benefits provided for the children in the various types of schools have been excluded, as have investment expenditures needed for building or remodeling school buildings. However, in addition to the direct operating costs of the school, we have added the school's share of administrative costs of the system to which it belongs.

Several points stand out. First, the costs of the national system and the *Fe y Alegría* system are quite similar, despite considerably different results produced in the students. Secondly, spending per student in the *Escuelas Integrales* appears to be higher. However, while the cost per student in these schools is 15 percent higher than that of the Ministry of Education, *Escuelas Integrales* while they are kept open for a full day—that is, they have the children four hours longer than in national schools. This means that the cost per student-hour taught is actually lower in *Escuelas Integrales*. The cost is $24, $32 and $31 per student/hour in *Escuelas Integrales*, national and *Fe y Alegría* schools, respectively. Only if the food costs that are part of the *Escuelas Integrales* program are included are costs per student/hour the same as in national schools. These estimates point to a tentative conclusion that in the area of resources, as measured by spending per pupil, the systems are not very different: all three seem to be devoting a similar economic effort to educating their students, although, as will be seen, the allocation of those resources and their effectiveness varies from one system to the other.

The other aspect to take into account in the area of inputs is to what extent contributions from parents are complementing the resources contributed by the various school systems. Both the national system and the state system are officially free. By contrast, *Fe y Alegría*, as a matter of policy charges its students enrollment and monthly payments, although the amount of such payments is quite modest, amounting to 5 percent of the operating costs of the system. In practice, however, in the course of visits to the schools and interviews, it could be established that in both public systems, it was common practice to collect sums from parents, sometimes in the form of a lump sum at the time of enrollment, in others in the form of a monthly contribution. In fact, these are the only funds that a school principal actually administers, and they are generally devoted to minor repairs, emergencies, and for providing lighting, plumbing or carpentry work needed for the school's daily operation. It was difficult to precisely determine the amount of such payments, because the informants were not very willing to reveal such information. Although it cannot be determined whether it is a representative case, one national school in a poor municipality collected 3 percent of the school's operating cost from families. Similar situations were identified in *Escuelas Integrales*.

Internal Efficiency of Education Systems

The *use* made of these resources is another matter. What is at stake at this point is efficiency in the allocation of resources rather than their absolute availability, which has been seen to vary rather little between the systems.

Information on efficient use of resources by education service providers is hard to obtain, but direct observation of schools, interviews with those in charge, and the financial information provided enough material to make possible the following observations:

- With one exception the eight national schools included in the study had inadequate facilities, either because of prolonged deterioration or because the original site itself was inadequate. Even the sole exception, a school built six years ago, was showing signs of advancing deterioration.
- Equipping of schools by the Ministry of Education with textbooks and reference books and other learning tools was consistently the worst among the three systems. Schools of the ministry often have a library, but encyclopedias are several decades old and there are few textbooks. Several librarians who had been serving for at least five years could not recall the acquisition of any books since their arrival except for the occasional gift from commercial publishing houses. By contrast, with a couple of exceptions, *Escuelas Integrales* rarely have a school library, but the libraries that exist are consistently well supplied with textbooks and complementary materials, such as maps and educational games, little or none of which are found in national schools. *Fe y Alegría* schools are well supplied with books and teaching materials.
- Labor discipline shows major differences within the three systems. While teacher pay is similar in all three cases, reflecting the similarity of costs per student already described, the teachers within the different schools behave differently, as indicated by the interviews and observations carried out on-site by the research team. Indeed, only principals in national schools mentioned teachers' failure to perform work as a serious problem. Neither in *Fe y Alegría* schools nor in *Escuelas Integrales* was this mentioned as a problem, with one exception. Some of the teachers in the *Escuelas Integrales* were not under the state government, but have been assigned to the schools by the ministry to plug gaps in the state government. Principals of *Escuelas Integrales* repeatedly stated that discipline problems with staff in their schools primarily involved national teachers, who are less inclined to acknowledge the authority of the principal.

Table 4.6. Comparison of Expenditures and Attitudes of Teachers, by Type of School

	Integrales	National	Fe y Alegría
Teachers' attitudes			
"Teachers in the school are absent more than they should be"*	3.05	2.83	3.73
"I'm satisfied with my work"*	3.75	3.57	4.02
Expenditures			
Percentage of operating expenses devoted to purposes other than payroll (%)	4.70	0.94	12.37
Operating expenses per pupil (US$/month)	190.35**	160.16	155.29

* Average point score on a scale of 1 to 5, where 5 means complete agreement.

** In making this comparison, costs of feeding students, which forms part of the regular activities of these schools, have been left out of school spending.

In what at first sight would seem to contradict this information supplied by principals, teachers in the three systems displayed widely varying attitudes with regard to showing up for work. Thus, as shown in Table 4.6, it was precisely in the national schools, where teacher absence is a clearly identified problem, that teacher responses to a question intended to measure teacher attitude about failure to show up for work reflected the least concern about the problem. At the other extreme, the *Fe y Alegría* teachers seem to be relatively more concerned about missing their classes, although that does not seem to be a problem worthy of attention in the judgment of the principals of those schools. These differences are statistically significant in a simple test of differences of means for comparing *Fe y Alegría* schools with both types of public schools. The difference between *Escuelas Integrales* and national schools is too small to be significant in that same test.

The conclusion seems to be that labor discipline is less strict in Ministry of Education schools: teachers at those schools see missing work as a relatively less serious problem than their *Fe y Alegría* colleagues, although in fact it is precisely in the national system that missing work is a much more serious problem. The situation of *Escuelas Integrales* is less clear cut in this regard, and that may be related to the fact that changes have recently been made in the way these schools operate.

The motivation level of teachers in the different schools also varies. Observation in the field consistently found considerable enthusiasm for and commitment to their work by teachers at both *Fe y Alegría* schools and *Escuelas Integrales*. There were a few exceptions, such as, for example, some teachers in *Escuelas Integrales* who are unhappy over what they regard as insufficient pay for the extraordinary amount of work that they do. Manifestations of motivation in national schools are less consistent, varying from instances where teachers seemed discouraged, to others where they were highly motivated. These field reports seem to be confirmed by interviews of teachers in which the systems line up by the degree of motivation expressed by their teachers, as shown in Table 4.6.

While the differences are small, they are large enough to be statistically significant in a test of difference of means at a 0.05 level of significance. Again, this result is not so clear for comparing national schools and *Escuelas Integrales*, but the fact that the latter in practice have a significant albeit minority presence of national system teachers may explain the narrowness of the difference.

Finally, there is the matter of the mix of inputs. As is well known, one of the more common observations about schools and educational systems in a number of Latin American countries—and Venezuela is certainly among them—is that the budget tends to be concentrated disproportionately on payroll costs at the expense of outlays for books, school supplies, maps, and so forth. Although a precise definition of just what constitutes the optimum mix of inputs has always been difficult, the imbalance observed in some education systems is too great to satisfy almost any reasonable position on the matter. An indicator of a greater degree of distortion in the mix of inputs is the fact that a particular system and its schools devote a greater proportion of spending to payroll; or, if one prefers it the other way around, that given the most common imbalance, a greater proportion of expenses on items other than payroll may indicate a mix of inputs that is closer to an optimal mixture. This proportion for the systems being studied is also presented in Table 4.6.

These figures bear out the previous observation that the order of internal efficiency in the use of resources is, from best to worst, *Fe y Alegría*, *Escuelas Integrales*, and national schools. The latter spend 1 percent on inputs other than pay for teachers and other kinds of payroll, excluding expenditures on school facilities that are not counted in the calculation of any of the systems. At the other extreme are *Fe y Alegría* schools, where the proportion of expenditures devoted to items other than payroll reaches 12 percent, with *Escuelas Integrales* in between. Observations made during school visits confirmed that these estimates correspond to reality: national schools are commonly found to lack the most elementary materials for learning, and have few discretionary funds to fill gaps in this area or to undertake any kind of special project.

There seems to be sufficient evidence, then, that allocation of resources within schools is more efficient in the *Fe y Alegría* and state government schools than in the national schools. This conclusion is important in the analysis for two reasons.

First, characteristics such as availability of books, appropriate mix of inputs, teacher motivation and discipline are generally acknowledged to have a significant impact on learning in schools. It would be reasonable to believe, then, that the learning process in *Fe y Alegría* schools is more effective than in the public systems, since the former's resources, which are not very different from those of the public system, are used with greater internal efficiency. A similar comparison can be made between the *Escuelas Integrales* system and the national schools. What is striking is that the evidence presented at the beginning of this section seems to partially contradict this last statement (with the exception, that is, of the minor corrections having to do with learning to read). As you may recall, student test scores measuring academic performance are on average lower for *Escuelas Integrales* than for the Ministry of Education schools (with the exception noted). We will return to this contradictory result later.

The second reason why the evidence just presented is relevant is that according to our framework of analysis, such differences can be taken into account from the standpoint of the economic theory of organization and conceptualized as the result of the impact of the existing contract relationships within the economic organization of each educational system. If it is agreed that the economic organization of an education system and its service provider units affect resource allocation within the system, then the indicators of internal efficiency such as those shown ought to indicate the existence of different incentive systems implicit in the organization of the three types of schools. Some of these incentives will be more conducive than others to the efficient use of resources and therefore more compatible than others with producing effective learning. The question is whether such differences in contract relationships and incentive systems between the education systems examined can be determined with precision. And do those differences tend to corroborate the hypotheses presented?

Contract Relations and Incentives in School Systems

The survey filled out by teachers contained a pair of items devised to establish which were the relevant agency relationships to teachers in their work: who did they regard as their superior, to whom were they responsible, and who did they regard as a resource when they needed help. Figure 4.2 compares the three systems through an index calculated on the basis of teacher replies.

National teachers rely on two categories of people for dealing with labor issues: superiors within the school (the school principal) and the union. *Fe y Alegría* teachers do not even mention the union—hardly surprising since they are not unionized—but teachers in the *Escuelas Integrales* do not mention unions either, even though they are members. The community figures as a moderately important body for the teachers in the *Escuelas Integrales* and a little less for *Fe y Alegría*. These teachers also look to an entity outside the school for support: in the *Escuelas Integrales*, they seek out program supervisors, and in the *Fe y Alegría* schools they seek out the Regional Office to resolve labor problems. One reading of these results is that the school principal's authority in such cases is limited or controlled by a higher level, but that this higher level is close enough that teachers consider it to be accessible. However, it would be worth asking why the same is not the case with the Educational Region of the ministry, which is not mentioned by the teachers even though it is a fully operative agency and has broad powers over teachers in the state.

The most plausible conclusion seems to be that, in practice, national schools tend to be disconnected in terms of being able to offer teachers resources beyond the school itself) from any higher administrative level—and from the community as well, which likewise goes unmentioned in connection with national schools, even though by law every national school must establish an organization of parents and representatives. These findings are supported by similar patterns of response to related questions having to do

Figure 4.2. Higher Levels Approached by Teachers for Handling Labor Problems

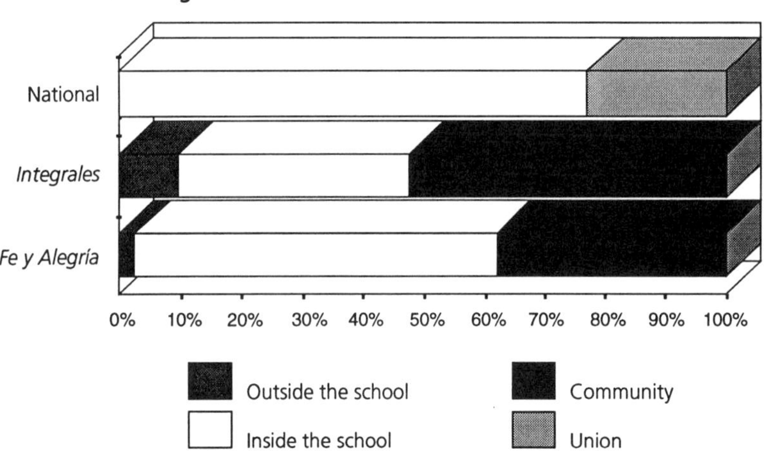

with the attitude of teachers regarding involvement in union activities, for example.

These data are of course a first approximation to phenomena that are complex and difficult to interpret, but they indicate quite clearly that i) labor unions seem to play a more important role in national schools than in the other two systems, ii) the community plays a more active and closer role in *Escuelas Integrales* and *Fe y Alegría* schools; and iii) the levels immediately above the *Escuelas Integrales* and *Fe y Alegría* schools play a significant role in the work of teachers, one that the corresponding level in a more centralized system like that of the ministry seems to eschew.

These preliminary conclusions tend to corroborate several of the hypotheses of this chapter, particularly those suggesting that education systems are more internally efficient if they are organized along less centralized lines, have greater community involvement, and are influenced less by unions. This is precisely the situation of *Fe y Alegría* schools and *Escuelas Integrales*, in contrast to those of the Ministry of Education. The conclusions are likewise bolstered by what has been observed in investigating the organization and operation of personnel administration and budgeting in the three systems.

In budgeting, there is a continuum extending from a "bottom up" system for *Fe y Alegría*, where the school prepares an annual draft budget which is then discussed and approved with modifications by the "head office" of the system, to the national schools, where no one in the system knows the budget of a particular school because funds from the capital are allocated in the form of overall "items" (payroll, equipment, etc.) These budgeted inputs are never calculated at the school level, and are barely reviewed at the Education Region. *Escuelas Integrales* occupy a middle ground where, although people work with overall items from the state capital, the system at least has the capacity to budget by school, and principals have a degree of liberty to reallocate a limited proportion of resources. For the *Escuelas Integrales*, there is even an incentive system to mobilize community resources; the state government puts up half the funds for minor repairs to the school building on the condition that the community raises the other half. The arrangement seems to be working well as an additional source of funds for maintaining the *Escuelas Integrales*.

Decisionmaking patterns for staffing are similar to those of budgeting. Staff changes such as transfers, promotions, retirements and hiring in the national system are ultimately decided in Caracas, and hence the regional chief often has to travel to the capital to "move files along." Even teachers sometimes have to make the trip in person. The typical school principal in the national school system cannot choose the staff with whom he or she works, or punish or reward. The case is reversed in the *Fe y Alegría* system, where the school principal and the school administration generally evaluate and make decisions on staff. In the *Escuelas Integrales*, flexibility in administering staff lies in between. As one school principal said, "if employees are under the state government you can do something (by way of sanctions) but if they're under the national government, there's nothing you can do." Along the same lines, one of the national schools had just changed school principals because the previous principal tried to sanction a teacher who did not perform up to standard, and ultimately the region chose to replace the principal, not the teacher. By contrast, teachers and even a school principal have been known to be removed from *Escuelas Integrales* for performing unsatisfactorily.

Thus, principals at Ministry of Education schools typically are powerless to manage either the budget or the employees at the school for which they are responsible. It could be said that there is no such thing as a school budget. The Education Region has data on budgets by categorized inputs, but it does not have information on spending per school for use in planning its activities or making decisions. Moreover, for the most part, the allocation of budget items is determined directly by the ministry in Caracas, although this past year the regions have been invited to submit estimates of needs for certain items to be taken as a baseline for the budget issued by the central ministry. The only exception to this centralized budgeting is the contributions from parents. Generally, national school principals use these small sums to finance minor needs such as replacing light bulbs and locks.

Principals in *Fe y Alegría* schools, by contrast, are actively involved along with their teaching staff in formulating the annual school budget, which must be consistent with the school's education plan. The regional *Fe y Alegría* office provides schools a certain amount of technical assistance in preparing the budget.[5] At an *Escuela Integral,* the school principal is much less independent, since the state department of education plays the role of the ministry in setting spending items. Nevertheless, the *Escuelas Integrales* are partially under the special authority of the office of the commissioner in Mérida, which issues funds for special programs (instructors for music and computing, educational materials, bonuses for teachers who spend extra time in schools). That authority in turn maintains a close and horizontal connection to school principals and teachers. As a consequence, in practice the school principal is more fully involved in the school's economic decisions.

Thus far little has been said about the hypotheses having to do with supervision and overspecification of contracts. One of the aims of this study was to investigate the labor contracts governing employee relationships in education systems in order to find symptoms of overspecification or other distortions that would make it possible to establish differences between systems. Here it is easy to distinguish between *Fe y Alegría* and the public sys-

---

[5] The greatest differences between the organization of information and flow of resources at *Fe y Alegría* and the Ministry of Education are, first, that budgets are prepared from the bottom up. That is, each school must develop a budget with revenues and expenditures on the basis of its planned activities, given the guidelines from the central office and its own priorities. These budgets are revised and consolidated at the central level. Within this system, *Fe y Alegría*—in contrast to the Ministry of Education—knows the cost of each school and the programs taking place there. It therefore has the information needed to set priorities when resources are limited. Second, each month the central headquarters gives each school the total sum of funds to be administered. Thus, contrary to what happens at state and Ministry of Education schools, payroll and administration of teachers, and costs for repairing and equipping the school are handled by the school principal and not directly by headquarters. The school principal and administration therefore have the power to reorganize spending if they deem it necessary.

tems, since the former is covered by individual contracts between the school and each teacher. These contracts are two pages long and speak in general terms about the obligations of the parties, with reference to the country's legal framework. This is a clear-cut case of a labor contract that is not overspecified.

By contrast, the collective bargaining agreements signed by the Ministry of Education with teachers' unions, and between the government of the state of Mérida and the regional teachers' unions for the state system, are quite extensive and specifically spell out the obligations and rights of the parties, although it is admittedly difficult to consider it so specific as to interfere with efficient allocation of labor effort in schools. Bearing in mind this result, a series of items was included in the questionnaire which was applied to teachers in each school. Organized in the form of a Likert scale, the questions were designed to study teacher attitudes about the obligations of the employer (the school system in question) toward them, in comparison with the obligations that each of the teachers perceive he or she has toward the system. On the basis of this scale it was possible to develop an operating definition of contract overspecification in the form of the symmetry or asymmetry with which teachers face their employers in terms of the rights and obligations of the parties.[6] The main assumption is that, while the collective bargaining agreements of the public system are much more detailed in their provisions than the individual *Fe y Alegría* labor contracts, much of what is plainly contract overspecification is seen only in the everyday labor practices in schools and has to do with the specific interpretation made of written norms and teachers' attitudes toward those norms, rather than with their actual written form. Based on responses given by the teachers, an index of symmetry between their obligations and duties was drawn up.

On this index, zero means that the perception of the teacher's rights (employer's obligations) and duties (employer's prerogatives) is perfectly symmetrical. The result was 0.05 for *Escuelas Integrales*, 0.72 for national schools, and 0.24 for those of *Fe y Alegría*. These figures indicate that the prevailing attitude among teachers in all systems is that the employer's obli-

---

[6] This operational approach to studying contract relations draws its inspiration from the literature on "psychological contracts" (Barksdale and McFarlane, 1995).

Figure 4.3. Supervisory Level Acknowledged by Teacher, by Type of School

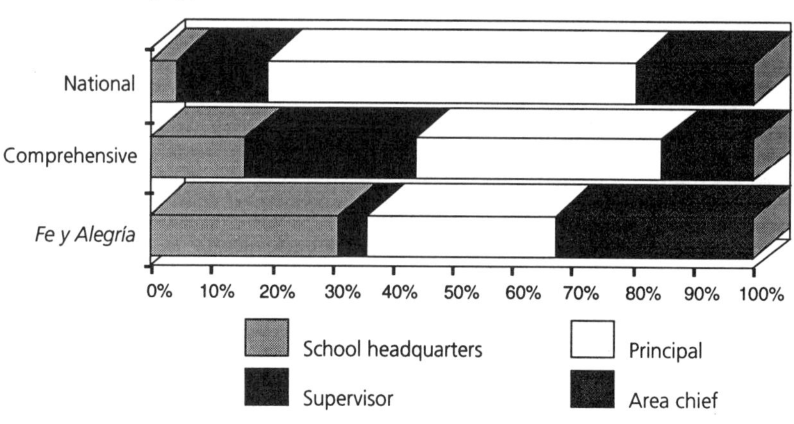

gations are stronger and more extensive than those of the teachers: the system owes them more than they owe their work. Even so, there are clear differences between systems: teachers in *Escuelas Integrales* come much closer to a perfectly balanced attitude, *Fe y Alegría* teachers somewhat less so, and, quite in keeping with our hypotheses, the national system displays the greatest asymmetry, with teachers believing they are owed the most in exchange for the fewest obligations (by the operating definition of contract overspecification).

Regarding the remaining issue of supervision, Figure 4.3 shows how teachers in schools perceived themselves with regard to supervisory relationships. This was measured by a complex question that asked teachers to rank supervisory levels with regard to whether they thought it important to have a good relationship with that authority.

Studying how the systems operate by interviewing those in charge in Mérida made it possible to draw up a picture of relationships that fits quite well with the perceptions of the teachers, and moreover provides some keys for interpreting them. Thus what stands out in the *Fe y Alegría* network is not only the importance of the school principal, but also that of the area chiefs who are members of the team in charge of the school, and for whom supervising the work and helping teachers is an important task. Also involved in this network supervising the work of teachers are staff from the *Fe y Alegría* "head office" in the state, which follows the work carried out in the schools in the Andean area as a whole quite closely. There is also the figure of a "supervisor" properly speaking, but that role is considerably less important than the three just mentioned, since these are Ministry of Education supervisors who have authority over private schools. *Fe y Alegría* teachers generally regard them as external agents who are supportive but who also demand certain formalities required by Ministry of Education regulations.

The supervisor is a more imposing figure in the *Escuelas Integrales*, but this depends on which supervisor you are talking about. Interviews with principals and teachers confirmed there are two very different kinds of supervision. First is that of the ministry, repeatedly described as formal, not very useful, punitive ("like police," said one principal), and centered on formal aspects such as number of objectives covered, number of sheets filled out, etc. Second is supervision under the *Escuelas Integrales* program itself, which was almost unanimously described as useful, friendly and frequent.

The national schools show a reduced role for the Education Region (their "head office") and of area chiefs, which exist but do not have the same weight that they have in the *Fe y Alegría* system. The perception of school principals as strong is striking, especially when all other information sources indicate that their role is weak and that they exercise little authority and control over what happens in schools. The best interpretation is probably that the scope attributed to their leadership position in responses is due primarily to a lack of other levels, both inside the school and elsewhere, rather than to any actual power in the role of the principal as such.

It is well to note that the aspect most criticized in all the education regions in Venezuela is the task of supervision. The state of Mérida has 140 supervisors to cover approximately 1,000 preschools and basic and secondary schools. In theory, with one supervisor for every seven schools, supervisors ought to pay frequent visits to schools and offer technical and pedagogical help to classroom teachers. But that does not happen. Supervisors are organized into four school districts, which divide up the territory of the state. Each district has its headquarters in a town and is headed by a district chief, who organizes the tasks of supervisors and transmits information to and from the regional office. Such an arrangement looks rational, but it is undermined by the fact that visits are not actually made, largely because education supervisors have neither vehicles nor travel expenses. Most supervisors live in the state capital, so if they are responsible for schools located in a number of towns, they tend to make only sporadic visits. School principals in larger towns with access to a telephone maintain contact with the supervisors in that way. Rural schools, lacking such means, are more affected. Another reason why supervisors do not visit schools is that the workload is unevenly divided among them. Information for 1995 shows that only 43 supervisors were assigned to visit schools, which means that on average each of these supervisors is assigned 23 schools. The other supervisors (approximately 100) stayed in regional and district offices. Therefore, supervisors are limited to occasionally visiting or phoning school principals, and to collecting and requesting statistics and other documents. They have neither the time, resources nor training to focus their efforts on helping classroom teachers.

The three systems, then, practice different forms of supervision. One form is private and based predominantly on the work of area chiefs. Another, the state system, takes advantage of its proximity to decisionmaking in Mérida to stay frequently and thoroughly in contact with teachers. The third more traditional and dispersed approach of the Ministry of Education is based on the work of supervisors who formally gather information on fulfilling curricular targets, without establishing a dialogue or collaborative process with teachers. Their activity is also spread out irregularly over time and area of the state.

It should be pointed out that teaching is not easy to observe. The supervision technology of the ministry identified some indicators of teaching activity and has ended up (at least as indicated by the information gathered) so focused on these indicators that it has lost contact with the substance of education and learning. The supervisory methodology of the *Escuelas Integrales* is from the outset more complete, because it has to respond to the needs for supervising an innovative pedagogical method that the schools are putting into practice: teaching by projects. Whatever the pros and cons of each procedure, teachers obviously perceive the supervision of *Escuelas Integrales* as a help and that of the Ministry as a nuisance that demands compliance.

Finally, there is the important point of the incentives systems to which supervisors themselves are subjected. In the case of the *Escuelas Integrales*, the commissioner works closely with supervisors (indeed, he himself also works as a supervisor) thereby facilitating decisionmaking and supervising the work of supervision. The lack of a supervision mechanism in the *Fe y Alegría* system seems to be compensated for by the vigorous monitoring and assistance provided by school principals and area chiefs, while the regional office of the network is restricted to the task of evaluating and supervising the principal. Likewise, there is a close relationship between teachers and those in charge of the *Escuelas Integrales* program. The office has on occasion taken action to replace a school principal who has not performed satisfactorily. It is not easy to determine whether any similar system operates in Ministry of Education schools. Interviews with Education Region staff and study of collective bargaining agreements clearly convey the impression that becoming a supervisor is seen as a natural promotion to which many teachers aspire because of its associated pay bonuses and lighter workload, but not necessarily as a job vital to the functioning of the system. Indeed, it is difficult to determine exactly how many supervisors there *are* in the national system, let alone provide an account of what they actually do.

There are, then, very well-defined patterns of agency relationships in each of the three systems. As outlined in our hypotheses, these patterns correspond to the systems' differing abilities to take advantage of the resources that society provides them to operate. The patterns extend from a system highly suited to making schools operate efficiently *(Fe y Alegría)* to the rigidities of the national system, the other extreme, where there are supervision gaps and information overload at a center far removed from the location where education is provided. In the middle stands a system which at its recent starting point (recall that the *Escuelas Integrales* program is only a few years old) was probably rather like that of the national schools, but into which changes have gradually been introduced to make resource allocation better.

The task of this study would now be completed except for the fact that little or nothing has been considered on the possible influence that children's social and economic factors might have on the performance indicators used above.

Socioeconomic Context of Students and Schools and Their Economic Organization

Until now, this analysis has presumed that all schools in the sample are strictly comparable. Schools were deliberately selected to allow for some degree of control over variables connected to the socioeconomic status of students, which are generally recognized as having a powerful influence on the learning.

This section aims to examine the matter somewhat more carefully, but there is little detailed information from students themselves about their social and economic condition. Except for the two *Fe y Alegría* schools and a couple of the *Escuelas Integrales*, individual schools had no detailed information on the family income of the children who were tested, nor were related variables such as the parents' work or schooling available.

Nevertheless, it is possible to make some reasonable comparisons of schools with regard to the social and economic situation of the students. It is known, for example, that the level of households in poverty, and particularly of school-aged children who come from poor households, varies considerably between the different districts where the schools are located. By drawing a dividing line between municipalities where over 50 percent of the school age children are poor and those where fewer than 50 percent are poor, schools in the study can be split into two groups. Two schools are located in relatively "rich" municipalities, and 11 in "poor" municipalities. Table 4.7 shows the general averages obtained by students classified not only by the school system to which they belong but also by how many are in a richer or poorer municipality.

This table serves primarily to adjust the assessments made earlier. When the students' standardized test scores are broken down by the poverty level of the municipality where the schools are located, the students in *Escuelas Integrales* in the more prosperous municipalities do somewhat better in learning than those from national schools, contrary to what seemed to be the case when the schools were considered in the aggregate. The previous impression of better learning was probably due to the relatively poor performance of students in state schools in poor municipalities, which could be clearly seen in students in *Escuelas Integrales* in municipalities with a lower poverty index. All these differences, except for the comparison between *Escuelas Integrales* for the point scores in written expression, were found to be statistically significant at the 0.05 level in testing differences between means.

Those differences were not found between national schools and the two kinds of municipalities, where student performance is sufficiently alike as to be practically indistinguishable. While the national system sometimes shows performance levels lower than the other two systems, its performance is similar across the different socioeconomic environments. The exception is found in learning mathematics, where national schools located in richer municipalities are clearly superior.

Table 4.7. Average Point Score on Standardized Test, by Type of School and Poverty Level of the Location

School	Municipality	Mathematics	Reading	Writing
Integrales	Rich	44.0	71.3	23.1
	Poor	30.2	56.1	24.3
National	Rich	25.4	50.6	22.2
	Poor	39.1	54.4	28.3
Fe y Alegría	Rich	53.0	67.0	39.6
	Poor	—	—	—
Mean	Rich	40.8	59.6	28.3
	Poor	35.0	55.2	26.5

No similar judgment can be issued with the information presented about *Fe y Alegría,* inasmuch as its two schools in Mérida are in richer municipalities, and thus no internal comparison can be made. Within the richer municipalities, however, they attain the highest performance level.

In general, as was expected, the performance of students in the schools located in richer municipalities is generally better on average than that of students in schools in poor municipalities, thus indicating a strong influence of socioeconomic status of the student's family academic performance. That influence, however, need not necessarily mean that the economic organization of schools and school systems is irrelevant to results in the area of learning. Although for the schools in poorer municipalities the pattern of relationships is less clear, between schools located in richer districts the data are quite compatible with the presumption that economic organization is important, since ministry schools are systematically the least effective.

As a further corroboration, a regression analysis was carried out in which the point score obtained by each of the 376 students tested for performance in the three areas considered—mathematics (MATHSTD), reading (READSTD) and writing (WRITESTD)—was defined as a function of the type of economic organization of the student's school, the poverty level of the kind of municipality where the student lived, and a measurement of the kind of inputs going into the education process in his or her school. The same model was also calculated for the combined point score of the three areas (SOPES).

Since there are three kinds of economic organization in schools, the following dichotomous variables were used:

SYSd1: where 1 indicates *Fe y Alegría* and 0 otherwise, and
SYSd2: where 1 indicates *Escuela Integral* and 0 otherwise.
The type of municipality was included as another dichotomous variable.
SED7: where 1 indicates that the student lives in a poorer municipality and 0 in a richer municipality as defined above.

The educational level of the teachers in each school was included as an input variable, measured as the proportion who have higher or advanced education (TEDUC). As seen in Table 4.5, this variable displayed certain significant differences between schools, while spending per student is almost indistinguishable between schools in the three systems. Systematic information was also available on the "work experience of teachers," but the fact that it was highly correlated negatively with the educational level of the teachers suggested that it should be eliminated from the model. This decision was naturally open to the criticism that a bias was thus being introduced in the specification, but the matter appears less serious if one takes into account the conclusion of the review carried out by Farrel and Oliveira (1993). Their research into the decisive factors in academic performance in developing countries found there is no strong and consistent association between the work experience of teachers and school performance. Nor did they find a relation for such variables as class size or teachers' salaries.

A further variable was included in the equation to bring greater refinement to capturing the differences in the socioeconomic status of students' families. Schools are located in three clearly different environments: completely rural, in the middle of poor outlying neighborhoods of towns, and in the middle of medium-sized towns ("town schools" with a clientele quite different from the others in social and economic terms). Thus, a student may live in a richer municipality, but if he or she attends a school in the middle of a poor neighborhood, his or her social and economic status will be lower in the equation than that of someone attending a school located in the urban center of a poor municipality. Two additional variables were defined as follows:

ENVd4: where 1 indicates rural school, 0 otherwise.

ENVd5: where 1 indicates school in the center of a town, 0 otherwise.

The results of the analysis, based on calculations utilizing 376 observations, are shown in Table 4.8. In the results presented for Model 1, based on the SOPES equation, all the parameters estimated for the variables make it possible to reject the null hypothesis with a 5 percent significance level. This is a powerful indication that belonging to different systems (which, as has been shown previously, differ in their economic organization) partly explains the differences in performance of the students tested, even after making allowance for the influence of the social and economic status of the student's origin.

Beyond this general observation, it is obviously advantageous to study in *Fe y Alegría* schools, and it is better to study in an *Escuela Integral* than in a national school, although only moderately so. This is the case for the equation calculated for the combined point score of the three dimensions. We begin to find exceptions to this statement when the equation is calculated to explain the behavior of point scores for writing, in which belonging to both systems is disadvantageous in comparison to the Ministry of Education schools. However, this coefficient is insignificant at the 5 percent level. Nor were the coefficients for SYSD2 significant for the MATHSTD and READSTD equations, suggesting that when controls are set up for the effect of socio-economic origin and inputs into the school system, *Fe y Alegría* schools continue to offer students an advantage, but the difference between the state and national schools vanishes.

As was to be expected, all the equations calculated coincide in corroborating the idea that the higher the social and economic level, the better is school performance. The negative sign for SED7 can be understood when one bears in mind that the correct interpretation of its coefficients consists in the marginal performance differential for children who live in poor municipalities with those who live in richer municipalities. The coefficients of the ENVD4 and ENVD5 variables are significant at the 5 percent level and positive in all cases, thus showing that even while controlling for the level of critical poverty of the student's municipality of origin, there is a marginal advantage in the state of Mérida in the school performance for children who study in schools located in a socially diverse town center, as compared to those who study in rural areas. Likewise, those studying in rural schools

Table 4.8. Results of Regression Analysis of School Performance

	Model 1				Model 2
	SOPES	**MATHSTD**	**READSTD**	**WRITESTD**	**AGENCY**
C	35.34	28.69	53.74	23.58	34.01
	(9.34)	(5.63)	(7.83)	(5.01)	(9.02)
SYSD1	7.68	19.39	10.85	−7.20	10.85
t	(2.13)	(4.01)	(1.66)	(−1.61)	(2.80)
Agency					−49.52
t					(−2.43)
SYSD2	−4.75	−2.37	−5.63	−6.23	
t	(−2.13)	(−0.79)	(−1.39)	(−2.25)	
ENVD4	15.48	9.66	23.24	13.54	17.27
t	(5.03)	(2.33)	(4.16)	(3.54)	(5.14)
ENVD5	5.64	6.35	13.11	−2.51	4.43
t	(2.28)	(1.90)	(2.92)	(−0.81)	(1.98)
SED7	−10.77	−5.30	−14.15	−12.88	−8.63
t	(−4.43)	(−1.61)	(−3.21)	(−4.26)	(3.25)
TEDUC	14.05	12.47	4.41	25.26	21.26
t	(3.11)	(2.05)	(0.53)	(4.50)	(3.25)
F	17.22	9.42	9.67	14.17	17.51
Adj. R^2	0.21	0.12	0.12	0.17	0.21

have an advantage over those in poor outlying neighborhoods. Here the exception is that of the equation calculated for the score on writing, where students in outlying neighborhood schools do somewhat better than those in rural schools. It is difficult to interpret these estimates more precisely in the absence of more disaggregated data: one possible reading would be that these variables are picking up the beneficial effects of social diversity in schools; another could be that they are showing the effect of the differentiated social conditions experienced in the three different environments.

Model 2 was added to explore the usefulness of a specification that would include variables operationally defined as part of the economic organization of the school. The variable of the degree of contract overspecification (AGENCY) was chosen, since this study contains an estimate of this variable for each school developed on the basis of answers by teachers to a written survey. Direct observation also suggested that there are significant differences between schools in this area. The survey was used because a reading of the labor contracts for each system pointed to clear differences between *Fe y Alegría* and the public systems, but practically none between the latter two, and hence an effort was made to develop a measurement of the implicit contracts above and beyond the general written rules regulating the labor relationship. For all these reasons, Model 2 retains SYSD1, which makes a distinction between *Fe y Alegría* schools and others, capturing their differences in the area of economic organization. But it replaces SYSD2 with AGENCY, a continuous variable that seeks to capture the difference in the implicit contracts between *Escuelas Integrales* and the Ministry of Education schools. The value of this variable is zero if teaching staff perceive a perfect balance between their duties and rights. Positive values indicate an attitude towards their work in which rights are much more prominent than obligations or, if you will, how much can be legitimately demanded by the employer or superior.[7]

The estimates of this equation display significant coefficients at the 5 percent level for all variables, and the AGENCY sign is negative, as expected (that is, the greater the degree of contract overspecification, the worse is performance). The signs of the other variables remain in their expected direction, suggesting that the specification is good, since there is no evidence of any other kind of econometric problems in the model. This result suggests the desirability of including measurements of variables of economic organization in models of school performance as precise operational definitions of these variables are developed.

Conclusions

This chapter has established that the economic organization of the three education systems studied in Mérida affects the internal efficiency of schools in a manner that is consistent with the hypotheses. The evidence seems to

---

[7] For purposes of analysis, each teacher was located on the scale according to the index made up by his or her answers to items from a scale designed to capture the teacher's attitude toward rights and obligations. Examples include: "It is my duty to help with school maintenance;" "The most important thing is to cover the program, although doing so may require some extra effort—working extra days or hours;" "If the principal asks me for an extraordinary effort, I ought to help;" and "It is fair to halt school activities to protest nonfulfillment of the collective bargaining agreement."

indicate that the less centralization there is, and the less the weight of labor unions and contract overspecification, the better is the mix of inputs and labor discipline, and the more motivated is the corps of teachers. Likewise, greater proximity and community participation seem to be associated with better "intermediate results," as we have called them.

Less firm is any conclusion related to the learning of children in schools, because methodological limitations have made it impossible to satisfactorily and completely isolate the effect on learning of variables connected to the social and economic context of students. While limitations remain, insofar as it has been possible to isolate the effects on learning by controlling for variables of input, a glance at the analysis presented at the outset suggests that the inputs of the system are not so different as to cause an appreciable difference in the results. Bearing in mind those qualifications, the econometric analysis developed at the end of the chapter is encouraging in the sense of corroborating the hypotheses, especially the general idea that the economic organization of schools, their agency relationships, and their incentives systems have a bearing as determinants of school performance, even when controls are introduced for input variables and the socioeconomic origin of the students.

In terms of the school systems, and with all the cautions mentioned above, the *Fe y Alegría* private school system consistently presents the best intermediate and final performance indicators, coming in highest both with respect to the school performance test results and indicators of internal efficiency. The *Escuelas Integrales* system presents a mixed picture, with an excellent performance on some indicators when compared with the other public system, while lagging behind in others. It is well to keep in mind, however, that *Escuelas Integrales* represent recent educational reforms that are not yet well established, even in several of the schools visited, which for two or three years have undergone reform. Nevertheless, there are many encouraging signs, especially with regard to indicators of internal efficiency. The Ministry of Education schools are alternately behind and ahead of the *Escuelas Integrales* among the public systems, depending on the indicator used. In intermediate indicators, however, they appear to be especially problematic because they consistently display the worst mix of inputs, the worst labor discipline, and the lowest staff morale.

This chapter was able to approximate an empirical measurement of agency relationships that can undoubtedly be improved, but whose results were in line with what was to be expected from the body of hypotheses used, flowing from the economic theory of organization. On balance, this study provides clear indications that variables of industrial organization are relevant for studying the efficiency and effectiveness of schools and education systems, and that continuing along this line of research is potentially fruitful.

References

Barksdale, K., and L. McFarlane. 1995. A Typological Approach to Examining Psychological Contracts. Memphis. Mimeo.

Casanova, R., R.A. González, L. Hung, and J.C. Navarro. 1993. La descentralización de la educación: mejor y más democrática. In *Descentralización, gobernabilidad, democracia*, ed. R. de la Cruz. Caracas: COPRE-PNUD, Editorial Nueva Sociedad.

Cox, D., and E. Jiménez. 1990. The Relative Effectiveness of Private and Public Schools: Evidence from Two Developing Countries. *Journal of Development Economics* 43 (1–2).

De la Cruz, R. 1993. *Descentralización, gobernabilidad, democracia*. Caracas: COPRE-PNUD, Editorial Nueva Sociedad.

Eggertson, T. 1994. The Economics of Institutions in Transitional Economies. In *Institutional Change and the Public Sector in Transitional Economies*, ed. S. Schiavo-Cambo. World Bank Discussion Papers No. 241. World Bank, Washington, D.C.

Farrel, J., and J. Oliveira. 1993. *Teachers in Development: Improving Effectiveness and Managing Costs*. EDI. Washington, D.C.: World Bank.

Hanushek, E., et al. 1994. *Making Schools Work: Improving Performance and Controlling Costs*. Washington, D.C.: The Brookings Institution.

Hausmann, R. 1993. Sustaining Reform: What Role for Social Policy? Study prepared for the IDB-OCDE International Forum on Latin American Perspectives, Paris, France.

Herrera, M. 1994. Estudio de caso de la red Fe y Alegría. Centro de Investigaciones Culturales y Educativas, Caracas. Mimeo.

Jiménez, E., M. Lockheed, and V. Paqueo. 1991. The Relative Efficiency of Private and Public Schools in Developing Countries. *The World Bank Research Observer* 6, July.

Levin, H., and E. Lockheed, eds. 1993. *Effective Schools in Developing Countries.* London: The Falmer Press.

Milgrom, P., and J. Roberts. 1992. *Economics, Organization and Management.* New Jersey: Prentice Hall.

Tirole, J. 1994. The Economic Organization of Government. United States Agency for International Development, Washington, D.C. Mimeo.

World Bank. 1993. *Venezuela Poverty Study: From Generalized Subsidies to Targeted Programs.* Washington, D.C.: World Bank.

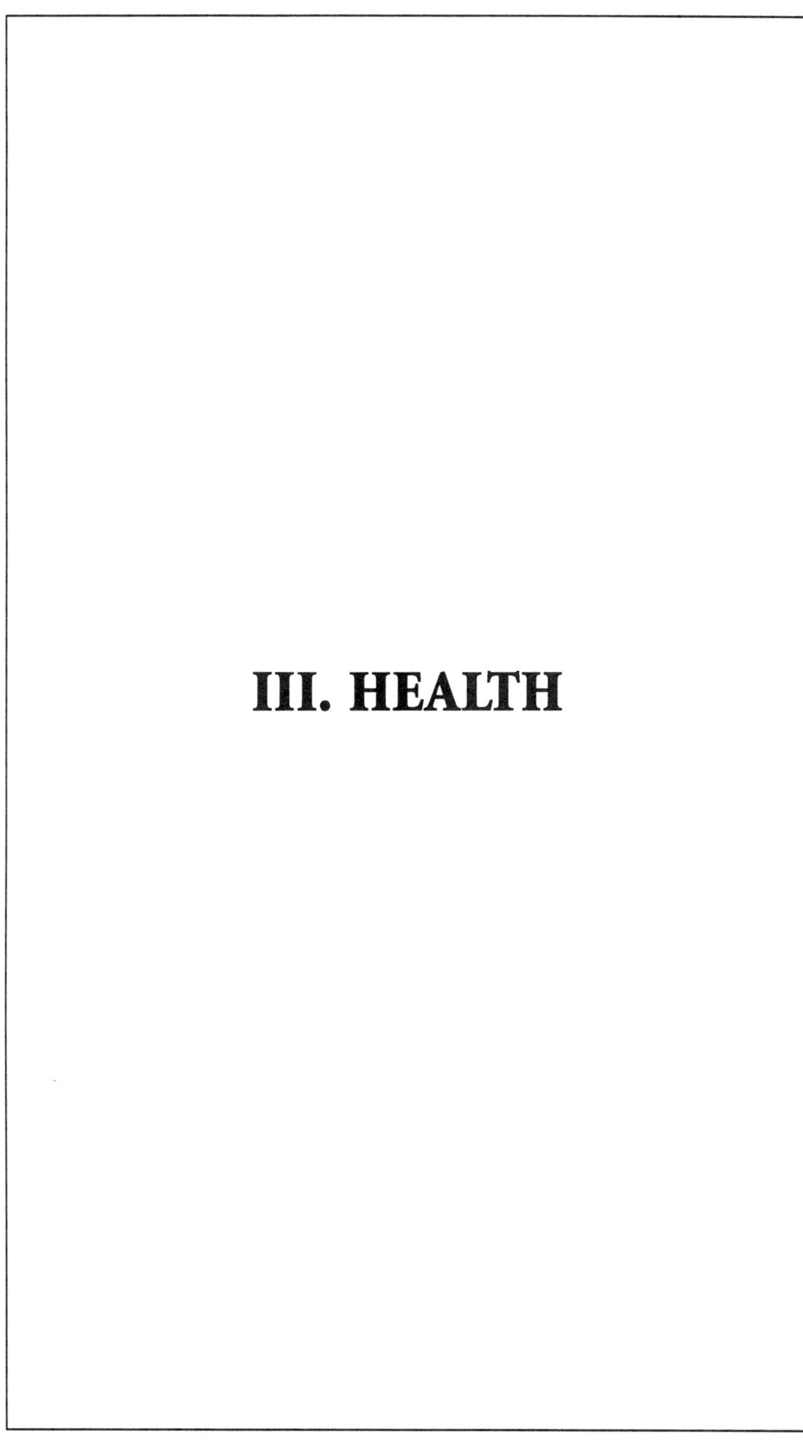

III. HEALTH

CHAPTER 5

Social Security and Private Prepayment Plans in the Dominican Republic

Isidoro Santana[1]

This chapter contains the results of a research project carried out by ECOCARIBE on the industrial organization of delivery of health services in the Dominican Republic. The cases covered are medical services provided through the network of facilities of the Dominican Social Security Institute (IDSS), as compared with the private medical managed care plans known as *Igualas*.[2] Both are systems that provide prepaid health services. However, while the former is organized under a state production mode, with centralized management, obligatory payments and assigned providers, the latter are private entities with decentralized management, governed by private contracts that are unregulated by the state, and financed voluntarily by the client.

This research aims to determine how the elements defining the structure of the industry affect the allocation of resources, amount and structure of costs, productivity and operating efficiency, and how this is reflected in service delivery. These elements include ownership, number and kind of providers, legal bases, financing mechanisms, degree of budgetary freedom, types of operation, relationships between the participating agents (the one

---

[1] Isidoro Santana, an economist and social and fiscal policy researcher, is a consultant with ECOCARIBE, S.A. in Santo Domingo, and a member of the Fundación Siglo 21.

[2] The term *iguala* is commonly used in the Dominican Republic to refer to a "retainer fee". In the health sector, "*Igualas*" are private firms that offer prepaid medical plans in "equal" monthly installments.

financing, the one producing, and the one for whom the service is intended), and the customer's ability to monitor.

Specifically, this chapter evaluates users' perceptions of the quality of service. An attempt is also made through limited statistics to determine the size of the market covered by both systems and to evaluate the motivation of consumers.

Notes on Methodology

This study begins with an institutional evaluation and a description of the degree of autonomy of the agents involved, along with capacities and models of management. Attention is given to examining the legal, institutional or economic conditions determining the user's choice of one service provider or another, and the degree of control or monitoring ability that the user has to influence the provider's performance or to change providers.

Unit costs were estimated for IDSS medical care on the basis of financial and statistical information on services provided, and indicators of economic efficiency and productivity in providing services were calculated. Although there was no way to measure effectiveness in terms of the final outcomes of services, the perception that users have of the quality of service could be assessed through interviews and by reviewing the literature.

The amount of statistical information on the country's managed care companies is meager, since no official agency oversees or gathers information on them. Basic information for this study came from reviewing the recent research literature and from interviews with the president of the companies' umbrella association, as well as with the presidents of three private companies. Information was also obtained from two other managed care companies.

Institutional Organization of Health Service Delivery

The health service delivery system in the Dominican Republic includes a broad range of public and private institutions. The body guiding sector policy is the Secretary of Public Health and Social Assistance (SESPAS), which also operates as a direct service provider.

On the whole, SESPAS's regulatory performance is weak because it is too centralized, has modest budget resources, and hence a weak operating capacity. SESPAS has therefore not been effective in issuing policies and in regulating and monitoring the health care system. Consequently, the other agents involved in health care delivery act quite independently.

SESPAS also plays a limited role as a service provider. Combined with the practical failure of social security mechanisms as the option for workers to gain access to health programs, that means that a very large portion of poor families is left literally outside the public medical care system. Many do not use medical services regularly, except in emergency situations, when access to SESPAS hospitals is always available. Although the service is free, poor operating conditions lead to significant costs for patients, especially for prescription medicines and diagnostic services. According to data from the 1991 Demographic and Health Survey (ENDESA-91), many of the chronically ill receive no treatment, including over half of those with cancer, asthma or arthritis, and lower percentages of those ill with diabetes or tuberculosis.[3]

A significant portion of households regularly use private services. Data from ENDESA-91 show that 67 percent of the people who went to see a doctor went to private establishments.[4] That explains the development of a wide range of private establishments for delivery of medical services, which reflect various types of industrial organization. In terms of the financing and organization of the production of medical care, there are a variety of options in the country covering major segments of the population, namely:

- Free delivery, government production, centralized management, financing by budget allocations from the tax system. This is the service delivered by SESPAS through the network of primary, secondary and tertiary establishments. Service employees are paid fixed salaries. This system is open and does not require previous membership.

  Although SESPAS is obliged to provide health services to the entire population not covered by social security, some studies indicate that in practice fewer than 40 percent of households regularly use its services.[5] Naturally, since this covers a good deal of preven-

---

[3] *Instituto de Estudios de Población y Desarrollo* (1993).
[4] *Oficina de Coordinación Técnica de la Comisión Nacional de Salud* (1995).
[5] Ibid.

tive care, and because delivery of curative services does not bind the user to the provider, people switch between using government services with those of other subsystems, to the extent that it is impossible to obtain precise figures on the proportion of the population covered.

- Prepaid care, government production, centralized management, financing by obligatory deductions. This is the service provided by the IDSS and the Institute of Social Security of the Armed Forces and the National Police (ISSFAPOL). Both are closed subsystems aimed at defined segments of the population.

  The IDSS covers only some groups within the working class, and hence its coverage is limited, extending nominally to 6.6 percent of the population in 1994, basically in curative care. The ISSFAPOL has fewer restrictions because it does not set limits by rank or salary level, and also covers the complete nuclear family. Its coverage is estimated to be 4 percent of the total population.

- Prepaid care, privately provided, decentralized management along the lines deemed best by the provider, voluntary private financing, usually by groups, sometimes individual or family. This characterizes the *Igualas*, which coexist with the public health insurance system, and which generally offer health plans to full-time employees of companies and institutions. They operate with no government control or regulation. Their clientele has been growing rapidly and it is now estimated to extend to 7.6 percent of the population, higher than that of the IDSS.

- Prepaid care, private production, decentralized management organized to suit the consumer's convenience, voluntary private financing by groups. These are self-managed medical insurance firms which are another institutional device similar to the *Igualas* except that these are typically consumer associations.

- Prepaid care, privately provided, decentralized management influenced by the customer's convenience, voluntary private financing, by groups, individual or family (insurance companies).

- Direct payment for services, private production, decentralized management, influenced by the consumer's convenience, individual private financing. This may be the most extensive segment of health care, embracing a wide range of establishments involved in the market and offering medical care services through clinics of the most diverse sizes and categories, doctors' offices, diagnostic testing centers, and so forth, equipped with differing levels of technology. There is little supervision or state control. This category responds to a diversified demand and includes companies offering the highest quality services along with others offering poor services.

- Free or subsidized care or care subject to reimbursement, private delivery, decentralized management, combined financing (private, state and international aid). This group includes a wide range of nongovernmental organizations that offer medical care, particularly in specialized hospitals.

The Dominican Social Security Institute (IDSS)

The IDSS, the basic government agency that provides prepaid medical services, is a state-managed institute under public law, although it is governed by a Board of Directors representing the government, employers and workers. In practice, the general director is appointed by the executive and must follow its lead. Historically, labor and employer representatives on the board have played a negligible role in defining and managing policy.

The IDSS was created in 1948 to protect workers and low-wage private employees, in an international context that led to an expectation that over time the system would bring about universal coverage. Like other Latin American social security systems, the IDSS has not changed after almost a half century of operation.

Among the legal limitations that have prevented progress toward greater coverage are exclusion of the member's family, exclusion of the member once pay goes above a predetermined level (entailing the loss even of acquired pension rights), and the express exclusion of government administrative employees and self-employed workers.

Financing of IDSS health and social security programs is based on a percentage of its members' salaries, equivalent to an employer contribution of 7 percent, a worker contribution of 2.5 percent, and, nominally, a state contribution of 2.5 percent. The state has never honored this commitment, however, and hence financing is limited to employer and worker contributions.

The IDSS has another source of funds in work accident insurance; with a contribution that on average is 2.5 percent of total payroll, with no pay ceiling, entirely paid by private sector employers. Since compensations for accidents are rare and amounts are low, 94 percent of revenues under this category are used to subsidize other programs, especially for health.

Funds provided by IDSS contributors are not formally separated, and hence go into a common fund used for health and pension programs, along with general administration of the system. The health program absorbs almost three-fourths of funds.

The health portion of social security covers all risks of illness and dental care, as well as maternity care for the spouse of the insured affiliate and pediatric care for newborns during their first year. It also provides prescription drugs in outpatient visits and during hospital stays.

Industrial Organization of Medical Care Delivery

In 1994, the IDSS had an average of 473,752 members and dependents, as well as the obligation to provide obstetric and pediatric services to spouses and newborn children. For providing medical services it has a network of 200 facilities, including 18 hospitals, 24 polyclinics, and 158 clinics. Management of these services is under a health care office with a manager appointed by the board at the recommendation of the general director. This manager usually changes whenever the director is changed, and like all high-level employees, tends to be a political appointee.

The direct medical care program is divided in principle into four subsidiary programs:

- Specialized medical services performed in hospitals;
- Semispecialized medical services provided through the nine larger polyclinics in Santo Domingo and Santiago;
- Outpatient medical services handled through the other polyclinics set up mainly in medium-sized cities;
- Primary care performed through clinics spread around the country.

Based on these criteria the total sum set aside for providing health services (1994 data) was distributed as shown in Figure 5.1.

FIGURE 5.1. Distribution of the IDSS Health Care Budget, 1994

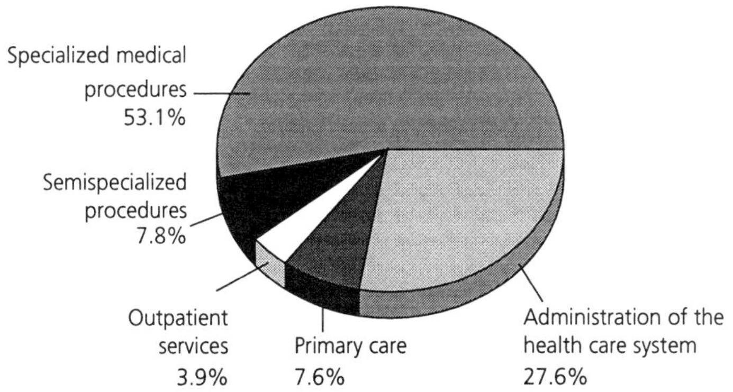

What is most immediately striking about the breakdown of health ser-vice funding shown in Figure 5.1 is the high proportion devoted to special-ized procedures, compared to the low amount for primary and outpatient services. Even more notable is the high cost absorbed by upper-level administration.

This information is deceptive, however, because given the imprecise definitions of service and rational organization of services, many services performed in even the larger and more specialized hospitals are, strictly speak-ing, primary care. As Table 5.1 indicates, a large number of initial consulta-tions, including general medicine, obstetrics and pediatrics, take place in hospitals.

The simplest facility for providing primary care is a clinic, which has a general physician, a nursing assistant, minimal equipment, and a limited supply of medicines. Polyclinics offer more complex outpatient services that include some medical specialties (but do not offer surgical services nor in-patient care), and they have pharmacies and laboratories.

Diagnoses requiring more complex tests, surgery and inpatient care take place as a rule in hospitals. In Santo Domingo, the IDSS has the Dr. Salvador B. Gautier Hospital, the largest and best equipped in the country, with all medical specializations. The hospital consumes 35 percent of the entire IDSS hospital budget and is the point of reference for all cases requir-ing specialized care (except for those that are maternity-related, for which there is a specialized hospital).

Table 5.1. Outpatient Consultations by Specialty, According to Type of IDSS Health Establishment, 1994

	Hospitals	Polyclinics	Offices	Total
Emergencies	153,538	54,112	59,099	266,749
Regular Consultations	664,900	749,549	719,145	2,133,994
Initial	122,401	143,169	138,292	403,862
Subsequent	542,499	606,380	580,853	1,730,132
General Medicine	243,914	477,380	693,670	1,414,964
Initial	45,824	91,696	132,458	269,978
Subsequent	198,090	385,684	561,212	1,144,986
Surgery	12,825	1,827	—	14,652
Initial	2,696	671	—	3,367
Subsequent	10,129	1,156	—	11,285
Pediatrics	49,791	44,921	3,529	98,241
Initial	9,816	9,064	713	19,593
Subsequent	39,975	35,857	2,816	78,648
Obstetrics	57,844	26,558	5,317	89,719
Initial	11,340	4,071	1,116	16,527
Subsequent	46,504	22,487	4,201	73,192
Gynecology	33,393	26,717	11,036	71,146
Initial	5,703	4,857	2,440	13,000
Subsequent	27,690	21,860	8,596	58,146
Orthopedics	24,941	161	—	25,102
Initial	5,236	8	—	5,244
Subsequent	19,705	153	—	19,858
Cardiology	27,779	26,005	—	53,784
Initial	3,877	4,178	—	8,055
Subsequent	23,902	21,827	—	45,729
Dentistry	22,825	42,897	—	65,722
Initial	5,886	9,125	—	15,011
Subsequent	16,939	33,772	—	50,711
Other	191,588	103,083	5,593	300,664
Initial	32,023	19,499	1,565	53,087
Subsequent	159,565	83,584	4,028	247,577
TOTAL	**818,438**	**803,661**	**778,244**	**2,400,743**

Source: Prepared by ECOCARIBE from data in the IDSS Budget Implementation Plan and *Statistical Yearbook*, 1994.

Budgeting for construction, maintenance, equipment, and medicines and medical goods is handled by the IDSS upper administration, which also takes care of hiring, appointment, promotion, removal and remuneration policy for medical and paramedical staff. Because the upper administration reflects party politics or private economic interests,[6] expenditures are often not in keeping with factors suited to the services required. Hence there are great discrepancies between the provision of infrastructure and the number of users; in the provinces, there are some hospitals with fewer than 2,000 affiliated members, in defiance of any reasonable notion of efficiency.

As a rule, the central administration sends supplies to medical facilities with little input from the directors of those facilities. Moreover, each facility, especially those that perform the more complex medical procedures and inpatient services, is allocated an overall sum of money for complementary services. In the case of the Gautier hospital, the overall amount allocated represents a quarter of its budget for direct expenses. This sum is used to buy food for patients, fuel for generating electric power, minor maintenance, and so forth. The head of the hospital is obviously offered a degree of freedom for choosing some productive inputs to improve efficiency.

IDSS health care staff in 1994 included 2,273 physicians, 228 dentists, 188 pharmacists, 473 laboratory technicians, 512 graduate nurses, and 2,068 auxiliary nurses (IDSS *Anuario estadístico,* 1994). These numbers show a marked imbalance in the supply of human resources, reflected in the oversupply of doctors (48 per 10,000 members) as opposed to the support staff. Even so, there remains an oversupply of auxiliary staff (10.8 graduate nurses and 55 nurses overall for every 10,000 members). Those employees work with fixed salaries that are not tied to productivity in any way. The labor contract is shared by all and differs only in the location and the kind of work to be performed, which is by specialization. Hiring takes place by competition, but once it occurs, the regulations assure job stability. The physicians have a strong union, which translates into low governability. Some IDSS officials believe that the medical staff is out of control with regard to fulfilling its labor contracts.

---

[6] In the Dominican Republic, it is common practice, though nothing is written in the law about it, for many officials to collect monetary fees for contracts that they sign or purchases of equipment or supplies that they make.

When labor conflicts lead to a lengthy strike, the administration tends to respond by hiring new staff, who generally go on to join the payroll of permanent physicians. In addition, each new director tends to hire additional staff.[7]

Although the regulations state that a work week for physicians is five six-hour days, in view of the current oversupply of professionals, work days have been set as just three hours per day. Even so, there are no effective ways to assure that limit is heeded.

Productivity Indicators

Although physicians are hired competitively, the promotion system is subject to interference from partisan politics, rather than based on qualifications. As a consequence, there is a loss of commitment and low output. Moreover, there is no ongoing monitoring or supervision, nor do users exert social control over the quality of the supply offered.[8]

Low governability and the lack of mechanisms to create individual competitiveness result in a low quantity and low quality product. Since most physicians also have private practice, their own interests probably prompt them to differentiate the product so as to dissuade users from going to government social security facilities.

Output in 1994 was an average of four visits a day per physician, including the follow-up visits usually made by a patient and emergency care, but not including dental visits. After excluding follow-up visits, which in private practice are not regarded as visits (*Igualas* do not pay for them or make a small symbolic payment), the figure for daily average consultations per physician would be a scant 1.1. In dental service, 1.2 consultations were reported per professional per day, excluding follow-up visits, which numbered only 0.3.

In the IDSS medical practice, an extraordinary number of 4.3 additional patient visits to the physician are associated with each initial visit. By way of comparison, in SESPAS facilities the ratio in 1994 was 0.8 subsequent

---

[7] Even though in 1994 the IDSS had one physician for every 212 inhabitants, an abnormally high proportion, by September 1995 the number of physicians in service had risen to 2,589, that is, by 14 percent.

[8] *Oficina de Coordinación Técnica de la Comisión Nacional de Salud* (1995), p. 44.

Table 5.2. Production and Productivity Indicators of IDSS Medical Services

Year	Medical visits (thous.)	Dental visits (thous.)	Births	Hospital stays	Occupancy (% beds)	Length of stay (days)	Turnover (exits/ bed)	Index of replace- ment[1]
1989	1,503	31	9,624	25,509	40.1	10.9	17.2	12.2
1990	1,496	21	11,573	28,619	37.9	7.3	19.0	12.0
1991	1,500	26	10,569	30,162	37.1	6.4	21.2	10.9
1992	2,092	59	12,022	35,803	45.5	6.5	25.6	7.8
1993	2,361	60	12,409	39,480	42.3	5.7	26.5	8.0
1994	2,335	66	12,292	42,091	53.4	6.8	28.6	7.2

[1] Average number of days that a bed remains unoccupied between the departure of one patient and the arrival of another.

Source: Prepared by ECOCARIBE from data in the IDSS Budget Implementation Plan and *Statistical Yearbook*, 1994.

visits for each initial consultation. In one of the most important private *Igualas*, which makes only a symbolic payment for subsequent consultations amounting to 10 percent of normal visits, the ratio was just 0.05, obviously not including those for which no claim was made.

It may be that this huge difference between the ways of organizing service is affected by definition problems,[9] but the figure is so striking that it must be reflecting some reality. All indications are that this high number of visits that the insured party must make for treatment may reflect chaos in the referral system. Physicians try to get rid of patients as quickly as possible since neither the quantity nor the quality of the product that they offer has any effect on the physicians' income.

Another productivity indicator is the average occupancy of hospital beds, which rose from 37.9 percent in 1990 to 53.4 percent in 1994. This is still abnormally low if the baseline for comparison is that efficient hospital management is considered to have an occupancy level of at least 80 percent.

---

[9] The *Igualas* regard follow-up visits as those made in less than 30 days to examine laboratory tests or to follow up on treatment. The IDSS lists as follow-up visits those that the patient makes to the same physician at his request within a year or to another physician to whom he or she has been referred.

Of the 18 hospital facilities, nine had average occupancies of under 30 percent in 1994, including two under 10 percent.

The most striking indicator is the average hospital stay, which throughout the IDSS system was 6.8 days in 1994. This average includes the low of 1.6 days at the hospital in La Vega to a high of 25.5 days at Gautier. The average stay at this latter hospital is long in all departments, ranging from 19.7 days in general surgery to 38.6 days in orthopedics, in part because the most serious cases go to Gautier.

But the most important reasons have to do with the way service delivery is organized. Patients are often hospitalized for diagnostic purposes before treatment formally begins. Very often surgeries are suspended over a minor conflict or a technical or administrative failure. Patients who have been discharged sometimes remain in the hospital waiting to receive the subsidy check for illness granted them by the law. That happens in the most expensive heath care facility in the Dominican Republic, which takes in over a third of the IDSS budget for hospitals, and 25 percent of direct and indirect spending for medical care.

Costs of Medical Care Delivery

The IDSS is financed with contributions from employers and from those enrolled, plus surpluses from worker compensation insurance. The total contribution comes to 11.85 percent of pay if we take the 1994 obligatory contribution for health and social security programs plus the portion of worker compensation insurance used for such purposes. The average contribution per affiliate is $RD155.55 a month in 1994.

The sums collected ought to be much higher. By way of example, the legal minimum wage in 1994 was $RD1,400 a month, for which the minimum deduction should be $RD165.90. Hence the average contribution should be no lower than this figure; the fact that it is shows that contributors treat the contribution as a tax and seek ways to get around it.

To determine the cost of health insurance for the worker and the employer, and make a viable comparison with what private contractors offer, the portion of the deduction absorbed by expenditures in health had to be calculated and separated from spending on other programs.

Table 5.4 shows that total spending on delivery of medical services was $RD661.5 million in 1994. Hence the cost per month per person insured

Table 5.3. Cost per Member of IDSS Health and Social Security Program, 1994

Items	Amount
Members and dependents	473,752
Employer and employee contributions ($RD millions)	736.9
Surplus from labor accident insurance ($RD millions)	147.4
Total cost of health and social security programs ($RD millions)	884.3
Cost per member ($RD year)	1,866.60
Cost per member ($RD month)	155.55

Source: Prepared by ECOCARIBE from data in the IDSS Budget Implementation Plan and *Statistical Yearbook*, 1994.

was $RD116.35, higher than the average prevailing in the prepaid private *Igualas*.

Why would a health service financed with compulsory contributions but not widely used have a per capita cost higher than another whose members use it intensively?[10] One reason is coverage, because government social security covers all risks and does not limit its use, while private services have a package that excludes serious and chronic illnesses. Likewise, the IDSS covers maternity and pediatric care for the wives and children of its members, and offers medicines at outpatient clinics, services not offered by private insurance.

Even so, there is no doubt that low productivity of the direct factors of production is a major cause of high costs. Likewise, the institute has very high indirect costs, resulting from general administration of the health sys-

---

[10] There is no up-to-date information on the extent to which IDSS is used by its members, but a survey carried out in 1987 indicated that of the IDSS members who went for medical consultations, only 46.5 percent did so at IDSS facilities, while 11 percent did so at SESPAS facilities, and 39 percent went to the private sector. Of those who went into the hospital, only 42 percent did so in IDSS hospitals, while 16 percent were in SESPAS hospitals and 34 percent in private clinics (see Duarte, et al., 1988). A remarkably high percentage of people make obligatory IDSS payments but use private establishments, for which they pay separately. This coincides with information that the ratio between the number of consultations (except for follow-up and emergency) and the number of IDSS enrollees in 1998 was 0.8, while the figure was 2.2. in the two private managed care companies on which information was available.

Table 5.4. Determination of Cost of Health Services in the 1994 IDSS Budget
(In thousands of $RD)

Expense item	IDSS total	Medical care			Upper administration and construction and maintenance of IDSS		Total health cost		
		Upper administration	Direct care	Total	Total	Health portion	Indirect	Direct	Total
Personnel services	464,159	81,917	305,686	387,603	66,232	45,634	127,551	305,686	433,237
Nonpersonnel services	61,667	6,508	3,993	10,501	45,656	31,457	37,965	3,993	41,958
Materials and supplies	83,469	3,178	31,565	34,743	48,585	133,994	13,351	155,386	168,737
Food	10,266		9,297	9,297	969	668	668	9,297	9,965
Medicines	38,178		13,589	13,589	24,589	114,589*		128,178	128,178
Medical equipment	14,083		4,851	4,851	9,232	9,232		14,083	14,083
Other	20,942	3,178	3,828	7,006	13,795	9,505	12,683	3,828	16,511
Current contributions	204,298	510		510	12,167				
Current debt payments	91,071		18,780	18,780	72,291				
Payments to suppliers	85,347*		18,780	18,780	66,567				
Other	5,724				5,724				
Machinery and equipment	9,829	1,764	5,617	7,381	2,390	1,647	3,411	5,617	9,028
Construction and maintenance	8,589				8,589	8,589	1,066	7,523	8,589
Hospital building	1,150				1,150	1,150		1,150	1,150
Expenses—Construction and	0								
Maintenance Department	6,373				6,373	6,373		6,373	6,373
Other	1,066				1,066	1,066	1,066		1,066
Pension fund bank debt	34,000				34,000				
Financial disbursements	3,320				3,320				
TOTAL	960,402	93,877	365,641	459,518	293,230	221,321	183,344	478,205	661,549

*When purchasing medical goods and hospital equipment, IDSS pays its suppliers on a deferred basis. In 1994, $RD85,347,000 in deferred expenses were paid to suppliers, but for purposes of that fiscal year, that amount was not computed as part of that year's expenses. Nevertheless, for 1995, $RD90 million was budgeted for payments to suppliers for debts accumulated in 1994. Accordingly, this figure was included in the 1994 expenses. The budget item for medicines was included as a lump sum, even though this item may have been overvalued, given that a portion of the payments may have gone to suppliers of food, medical equipment and other supplies. But this does not affect the total amount.

tem. For each peso spent directly on medical care delivery, 38 cents was spent on indirect costs in 1994.

The IDSS has over 13,000 employees, in contrast to private services that cover administration with very few employees. In a 1991 study, the Dominican Republic was found to have the highest density of employees per 1,000 people enrolled of all the social security systems in Latin America.[11] The number was 20.5 (the regional average was 8.3) and instead of improving subsequently, it has worsened, reaching 27.5 in 1994.

Another reason for the low productivity is that a portion of spending is absorbed by medical care given to those who are not insured, and who come to the IDSS through political or personal connections. This takes place essentially in instances of costly medical services, for which the IDSS exacts modest recovery fees.

To compare the two types of industrial organization with which this research is concerned, an effort was made through the limited statistics available to determine the unit costs of the main services provided. A previously-used methodology for the Dominican Republic was adopted, translating all medical services into numbers of consultations and patient-days of hospitalization, with the understanding that the intermediate products attained in the process and the actions carried out by the institutions are intended to produce these two results.[12] This implies that the cost of the consultation or of the patient-day calculated includes expenditures for diagnostic procedures and for treatment.

The methodology adopts as a parameter that one patient-day is equivalent to four outpatient consultations. In order to make the data comparable with those from private practice, where follow-up visits are not counted as consultations and are not paid or are paid symbolically, the calculation included only first consultations and emergencies. In any case, to serve as a reference point, the calculation was also carried out including follow-up visits. Given the lack of itemized information on spending, dental visits, which constitute 2.2 percent of the total, are also included. The results can be seen in Table 5.5. In 1994, a consultation at IDSS facilities cost on average $RD363.78 and each hospital stay cost $RD9,292.84. These costs are far higher

---

[11] Mesa-Lago (1991).
[12] Díaz Santana (1993).

Table 5.5. Determination of Cost per Consultation and Hospitalization at IDSS Medical Facilities, 1994
(In $RD)

	Total	Office	Polyclinics	Hospitals
Direct cost	478,205.00	50,198.00	77,279.00	350,728.00
Indirect cost	183,344.00	19,246.00	29,629.00	134,469.00
Total cost	66,549.00	69,444.00	106,908.00	485,197.00
Initial consultant and emergency	670,611.00	197,379.00	197,293.00	275,939.00
Subsequent consultations	1,730,132.00	581,265.00	606,368.00	542,499.00
Days of hospitalization	286,969.00	—	—	286,969.00
Cases of hospitalization	42,091.00	—	—	42,091.00
Total consultations + hospitalization	1,818,537.00	197,379.00	197,293.00	1,423,865.00
Cost/Consultation	363.78	351.83	541.87	340.76
Cost/Discharge	9,292.84	—	—	9,292.84
Cost/Day of hospitalization	1,363.04	—	—	1,363.04
Including subsequent consultations				
Total consultations	2,400,743.00	778,644.00	803,661.00	818,438.00
Total consultations + hospitalization	3,548,619.00	778,644.00	803,661.00	1,966,314.00
Cost/consultation	186.42	89.19	133.03	246.75
Cost/Discharge	6,729.41	—	—	6,729.41
Costs/Day of hospitalization	987.00	—	—	987.00

Source: Prepared by ECOCARIBE from data in the IDSS Budget Implementation Plan and *Statistical Yearbook*, 1994.

than normal costs in the private sector, even where there is direct payment for services.

This is the result of an industrial organization of production of medical service in which the customer has no right to choose, nor any ability to monitor or control the behavior of the actors involved in the production, and remuneration of factors is not linked to the quantity or quality of their product. This is all reflected in low productivity, underutilization of personnel and facilities, administrative deficiencies, and high levels of corruption.

Perception of Users

Normally, workers express their discontent with the quality of the product offered by IDSS by pressuring during collective bargaining to have private health insurance. This gives rise to the widespread phenomenon of double membership and double charging, which entails an extra expense and undermines the competitiveness of the economy.

Interviews were conducted with personnel managers in three large industrial companies. These managers receive complaints from workers on medical services and are responsible for responding. All these companies have contracts with private health insurance companies, even though they make payments to the IDSS. They prefer private health care for a number of reasons. One is how long it takes to reach the doctor in IDSS facilities, due to excessive bureaucracy. It can take a morning simply to locate the patient's medical file, and getting the medications prescribed at the pharmacy entails another workday lost. Often the medications prescribed are not available, and hence several further visits have to be made. There are long lines to see the doctor, and if the patient is referred, delays in getting the referral appointment. Patients cannot choose their physician, and for a single treatment people commonly face successive changes of doctor because of shift changes, staff absences, frequent work stoppages, travel, and so forth. Patients often complain that office hours, particularly of specialists, are not convenient for users. The problems entailing loss of time for the worker also affect the company, translating into lower labor productivity.

The *Igualas Médicas*[13]

Industrial Organization

The *Igualas,* managed care medical plans, are private entities through which prepaid health plans are offered to employees of companies and institutions.

---

[13] For this part of the study the researchers interviewed the President of the Association of Private Medical Managed Care Companies and the presidents of three managed care companies, two in Santo Domingo and one in Santiago. Further information was obtained from two other managed care companies in Santo Domingo. Information was gathered about their organization, service plans, coverage, rates, and some data on costs, and so forth. However, executives were particularly sparing in revealing internal information about financial aspects

Many *Igualas* now have family plans as well. This kind of organization has proven more efficient in prepaid health care coverage than the government health insurance system.

As a rule, these managed care companies are service intermediaries. They buy and sell medical care for a fixed monthly per capita payment *(capitación)*, the cost of which is normally shared between the employee and the employer.[14]

Types of Contractors

Because they are not subject to any government regulation, managed care plans are organized and operate in a variety of ways. Some do not even exist as legal entities, but function as departments of clinics (sometimes called "social plans" or "health plans"). On the basis of this study, at least three types of *Igualas* can be distinguished from among those that are formally organized:

Type I. Model of organization attached to a facility, very similar to health maintenance organizations, in which most of the physicians serving the insured are on the organization payroll.

In this model, which is not very widespread, services are generally provided at a single location owned by the same person or company that owns the *Iguala*. For practical purposes, the hospital and the contractor are the same. On paper, the managed care plan pays a fixed rate to the hospital on a per capita payment basis and has no direct ties to the participating physicians. Instead, the hospital makes contract arrangements with the physicians, so that it is the hospital, rather than the managed care plan, that pays the physicians.

Most of the general physicians are on salary. It is they who refer the patients, acting as a filter to prevent overuse of specialists and the more ex-

---

and the volume of services provided. In order to examine the perception of customers, personnel managers at the three large companies already mentioned were interviewed. Available literature on the matter was also reviewed. An ample description of how the sector is organized can be found in La Forgia (1990).

[14] Díaz Santana (1990).

pensive hospital services. Referrals to these services require authorization from the physician in charge of services.

Physician specialists are hired on a fee-for-service basis, and are either provided work space at the firm's facilities or rent their own space. Specialists are paid according to a fixed rate schedule and contracts can be of several kinds. Depending on the contract, the hospital retains from 10 to 30 percent of the physician's fee for hospital maintenance and for capital reserves. (The percentage reduction depends on whether the physician rents office space or receives it free.)

Type II. A model characterized by individual practice on two levels, affiliated with a single hospital, based on payment for services.

This is the most widespread model for *Igualas*, in which the institutions are less centralized than in the previous model. Even though most physicians work out of the main location of the managed care company, they are paid a fee for service. Because they are not employees of the managed care plan nor of the hospital, they can also see nonaffiliated patients. These patients must nevertheless go to the main site to obtain services or to other clinics with which service contracts have been signed in order to handle the extra inpatients or to reduce the extra patient load at the main site. Referrals are made informally between physicians. The physicians are generally shareholders in the managed care company. However, even those who are not shareholders are often interested in joining on a fee-for-service basis in order to expand their client base.

By contrast with the previous model, these managed care plans (as companies) are not owned by a hospital and the physicians do not receive salaries. Some of the main shareholders are founders of the managed care companies and often owners of the hospital. Even though the hospital is separated from the managed care company organizationally, the shareholders (physicians) exercise a considerable influence on hospital policies and administration. Indeed, the board of directors of the managed care company and that of the hospital are composed mainly of the same members.

The main facility, usually a medium-sized clinic with a large outpatient area, is the primary site for supplying outpatient services, hospitalization, and diagnosis of those enrolled in the managed care plan.

Participating physicians are reimbursed in accordance with a fee-for-service discount plan. Profits, which tend to be modest, are distributed among shareholders annually according to the number of shares held. The physicians, however, are primarily interested in the volume of clients provided by managed care.

Type III. An individual practice model with no affiliation to any hospital based on payment for services.

In this model, the *Igualas* are completely independent of medical facilities, although they are generally owned and managed by physicians. However, they do not directly care for those enrolled, but rather negotiate contracts with a network of services and independent physicians in different facilities, generally in various locations throughout the country.

The *Iguala* negotiates contracts with each facility, specifying responsibilities, limits of service, pre-admission rules, notification requirements, and so forth. Discounted rates are set depending on the category of a particular facility in terms of quality, prestige, location and complete fees. Hence, rates vary widely between member hospitals, even though treatment of patients may be the same.

Participating physicians work in their own offices. They are placed on the provider list of the *Iguala* through a formal selection procedure. It is understood that they accept the plan's policies and rules and a discounted rate as complete payment for their services. Contracting is on a payment-for-services basis. Physicians also tend to receive widely varying fees.

General Aspects

Since their beginnings in the late 1960s, the *Igualas Médicas* have expanded rapidly in terms of the number of companies and in their market share. Their association has 19 members, although for the purposes of this study 24 managed care companies were identified. It is likely, however, that some other clinics have medical insurance plans, and hence there is no exact count of such managed care companies.

Because the clinics came first, the managed care plans often developed primarily to direct a relatively high volume of patients to the establishment and to a limited number of physicians working at their facilities.

Hence, the scope of services offered by managed care is limited by the service capability of these providers, and accordingly some specializations may not be available.

As this sector has grown, however, competition has made it necessary to maintain a relatively broad package of services. In many cases, when membership grew too much the managed care plan had made arrangements with other providers to broaden its ability to respond, especially in terms of hospital services.

Many physicians in private practice accept patients from more than one managed care company and from insurance companies. Others will not accept insurance company payments of any kind, but will join the *Iguala* in order to assure a large volume of patients. The upshot is that the health plan can operate with low administrative costs, a small number of officers and employees, and modest profit margins, because what is important is assuring sufficient revenues for the hospital owners and the physicians. The three companies evaluated here had a total membership of 158,000 and an operating staff of 108 persons. Thus managed care plans offer more extensive coverage in exchange for a lower premium than insurance companies.

Like traditional health insurance, the *Igualas* base their rates on the statistical probability of a claim arising and take into account the costs of anticipated services, administrative costs, and the profit margin. The members, for their part, generally have to pay less for medical treatment within the pre-established limits of use; for more sophisticated services, a copayment is generally necessary, because like traditional indemnity plans, managed care companies set ceilings for payment for various services, and patients must pay the remainder.

Many *Igualas* offer two or three different health care plans so as to reach the desired coverage or in accordance with the wage level of the employee members. Variations in coverage generally do not affect medical attention itself, but rather the amounts covered for hospitalization and complex procedures, after which a copayment is required. Thus, it may happen that a client company has different plans arranged for different levels of employees, and therefore employees who are enrolled in cheaper plans have to use lower-cost hospital rooms or lower ranking hospitals to avoid the copayment.

Coverage and Plans

Regardless of how they are organized, all *Igualas* cover a complete range of outpatient and inpatient services, although they usually exclude people over 65. They also exclude treatment for alcoholism, drug addiction, cancer, AIDS or mental illness. In almost all contracts, the entire nuclear family is covered along with the member, but on a per capita basis.

Exact information on the number of members covered by the *Igualas* is not available. For the purposes of this study, it was estimated that 550,000 persons (7.6 percent of the total population of the country) were covered in 1994, a number that rose to 600,000 in 1995, not including the category of self-managed insurance. The prepaid segment has grown rapidly and surpassed IDSS coverage.

Depending on labor contracts between a company and its workers, employers cover between 50 percent and 100 percent of the monthly premium for employees and their dependents. The remainder is deducted from the employee's pay. The most common arrangement in large companies is that employers cover 75 percent of the cost, although many institutions and some companies cover it entirely. Without this major contribution from employers, few low-wage employees could afford the monthly premiums for their families.

The market for prepaid health services does not appear to be very competitive, since companies make arrangements directly with personnel managers in large companies, normally without the users even being involved. They have very little prior information on the quality of service or on the copayment that must be made, except when the need arises to use them.

Some *Igualas* do not limit the number of outpatient visits, but most establish a maximum of 12 or 15 a year. Emergency services are fully covered in any facility. Except for special contracts, medications prescribed in outpatient treatment are not covered. The main differences between *Igualas* and their plans is in coverage of diagnostic services and hospitalization. As a rule, special diagnostic treatments (through sonograms, MRIs, etc.) require a copayment often as high as 50 percent.

Preventive care is offered only in some cases, and usually through specialists. Routine visits for pregnancy and for healthy babies, vaccinations, and physical examinations are covered, but in pediatric care many *Igualas* set a limit on regular visits for illness. There is also a charge for vaccinations.

In general, hospital stays are not restricted, but some prepaid plans set a maximum number of days and a maximum annual amount to cover hospitalization and diagnostic studies. Many prepaid plans have a waiting period for new members after they join to have access to expensive nonemergency types of surgery.

Productivity in Delivery

There is little quantitative information available to determine the productivity of medical services under the *Igualas*. However, the limited information on costs indicates a productivity level much higher than that of services provided at IDSS facilities.

Because most physicians are paid on a fee-for-service basis, they have a particular interest in raising output at least in quantity. That indicates that output is presumably adequate in terms of the number of consultations per work day. Their interest in quality is not so obvious, except for reasons of personal reputation and because of the monitoring to which they are subjected by patients who have some freedom in choosing their physician.

Since physicians are paid less and with greater delay than in their private practices, it is not uncommon for them to discriminate against the *Igualas'* patients by telling receptionists to send their private patients in first. There is no evidence, however, that this might also be reflected in lower quality care.

Nevertheless, in the Type I prepaid plans described above—that is, where most of the doctors providing care to members are salaried employees of the organization—there is at least one facility (the Alcántara y González Clinic) where there have often been scandals over negligence on the part of medical personnel in treating patients.

As a rule, public and private health care in the Dominican Republic is provided without any control for quality or safety. This reflects the institutional weakness of SESPAS. Given the absence of common treatment standards and of reviews that would make it possible to evaluate the quality of diagnosis and treatment, it is difficult to measure quality of service.[15]

Medical directors of some *Igualas* indicate that unnecessary operations and hospitalizations, and unjustified stays in hospitals, are common

---

[15] La Forgia (1990)

and costly problems. One factor limiting quality and safety has to do with the inability of most hospitals to adequately maintain their facilities and keep equipment in good condition. Rates set at low levels often simply enable the hospital to cover operating costs.

Costs and Monitoring Procedures

Procedures for risk evaluation and control are rudimentary in the *Igualas*, although the risk is reduced by its distribution among large numbers of members, eliminating those over 65, and setting ceilings on use. Some *Iguala* directors interviewed said that they preferred not to negotiate contracts with companies with a high density of blue collar labor, whose illness rate profile raises costs, or with very large companies, which can contest rates and service coverage.

Variability of rates has more to do with variability of fees and amounts of payment stipulated in plans than with differences in benefits. As a rule, the lower-cost prepaid plans are those that limit services to lower-ranking facilities, or that offer care at high-quality clinics but limit patient freedom in choosing facilities.

Because there is no government supervision of the *Igualas*, there are no statistics allowing for quantitative analysis of the costs of their services. Based on the information regarding rates charged to members, it can be inferred that the *Igualas* that operate most inexpensively are those described as Type I, where facilities are contracted on a per person basis, most primary care physicians are on salary, and primary care physicians are responsible for referring patients to more expensive services. The range of their rates is wide, however, and there is also evidence that service is of lower quality.

In Type II *Igualas,* where physicians and facilities are contracted on a payment-for-service basis but are affiliated with a single hospital, and in which there is no formal referral system, costs tend to be somewhat higher than they are for Type I because fees tend to be moderately higher. Physicians (shareholders) have some interest in controlling costs, thus reinforcing efforts in that direction by the company management. However, the physician's personal interest in productivity and quality, and greater freedom of choice for consumers, makes for more efficient service.

Costs are substantially higher in Type III companies with payment-for-services, where there is a complete separation between the *Iguala* and the service providers. This type of prepaid care tends to have higher costs because it requires additional staff for controlling costs and use, since there is no individual interest on the part of the physician or the facility to control them. Consumers have more freedom to choose their physician and hospital, hence rates tend to be considerably higher. Moreover, these companies set a co-pay percentage even for outpatient visits to discourage overuse by patients. In all cases, controls over use, copayment, and spending ceilings for diagnostic tests and hospitalization are the most common cost control procedures. The average rate for five prepaid plans (of all types, since the information available did not allow for them to be studied separately), was $RD110 a month in 1994 and $RD144 in 1995. This is less expensive than the average cost per IDSS member, even though coverage is more limited (but the degree of utilization is greater).

A more effective indicator of costs is obtained by calculating the mean cost per visit and per hospital stay. By utilizing a calculation method to bring the data in line with that used for IDSS calculations, an estimate was made for two prepaid plans for 1994. The result showed a mean cost per physician visit of $RD151.80 in outpatient care and a cost per hospital stay of $RD2,833.98. These costs are much lower than those at IDSS hospitals. This method includes the mean cost not only of physician fees but also of indirect expenses and intermediate products. However, visits and hospital stays handled by the *Igualas* are less complex than those arriving at IDSS facilities, because of the adverse selection risks which are explained below.

Perception of Users

Users do not have significant complaints about the quality of service in the *Igualas*, which they regard as better than IDSS service. Hence, in labor negotiations workers ask for membership in *Igualas*, and those belonging to both systems use the health care provided in IDSS facilities only in cases not covered by the *Iguala*, or when treatments requiring major expenditures for medications are needed.

Although they prefer private service for medical care, customers of *Igualas* often complain that they are treated worse than customers who are not in prepaid plans. In some instances, there have been complaints that the physician charges a copayment even though it is not in the contract.

There are no major complaints about spending limits set by intermediaries, since those belonging to the more inexpensive plans know that to avoid going beyond the limits they cannot use the more expensive facilities or hospital rooms.

Efficiency and Costs of IDSS Medical Care Compared to the *Igualas*

Table 5.6 combines a series of indicators for comparing the efficiency and costs of both types of industrial organization for delivering health care services. In the case of the *Igualas*, these are averages that conceal the wide range that exists between different types of organization. However, the three models of prepaid health care cannot be studied separately on the basis of the data gathered.

The data show the excessive administrative staff maintained by IDSS as compared to the prepay companies, although the indicators are not completely comparable because the administrative employees of direct providers who participate are not necessarily included in the *Igualas'* statistics. The number of visits per 1,000 members, which is very low at IDSS as compared with the prepaid plans, reflects the fact that those who are insured do not use the government social security system because its care is regarded as poor.

The number of surgeries per 10,000 members (including caesarian sections) is also quite low in the IDSS as compared with the *Igualas*. This may indicate low utilization by social security customers and an overuse of prepaid plan services (physician-induced demand) caused by the asymmetric information in the physician-patient relationship.

Productivity in terms of daily consultations per doctor and hospital occupancy is remarkably low in social security facilities, although the figure may be an underestimation because follow-up visits are included in the calculation, many of which in private practice would be classified as visits requiring payment.

The mean stay in IDSS hospitals is too long, possibly reflecting the problems of adverse selection that occur because of cases of more complex illness, but also because of serious management problems.

Average cost per member is slightly less in *Igualas*, although IDSS coverage is greater because it includes risks of chronic diseases with unlimited treatment. On the other hand, social security institute members generally make little use of its services, while customers of the *Igualas* use their services intensively. This is reflected in the figure for visits per 1,000 members. The data for the IDSS is even lower than reported because many of the consultations registered are not really for members but for other persons.

The average cost of a visit is 2.4 times higher in IDSS facilities. Even if

Table 5.6. Efficiency and Cost Indicators in Medical Care Delivery of IDSS Compared to the *Igualas Médicas*, 1994

Efficiency indicators	IDSS	*Igualas Médicas*
1. Administrative staff per 1,000 members	15.24	0.68[a]
2. Consultations per 1,000 members[b]	837	2,248
3. Surgeries per 1,000 members	54.5	156.8
4. Consultations per doctor per day	1.2	n.a.[c]
5. Hospital occupancy (%)	53.4	n.a.
6. Mean hospital stay	6.8	2.9[a]

Cost indicators (in $RD)	IDSS	*Igualas Médicas*
1. Monthly cost per member	113.35	110.00[d]
2. Cost per consultation[e]	363.78	151.80
3. Cost per patient day in hospital [e]	1,363.04	952.77
4. Cost per hospital stay[e]	9,292.84	2,833.98
5. Cost per consultation[f]	186.42	—
6. Cost per patient day in hospital[f]	887.00	—
7. Cost per hospital stay[f]	6,729.41	—

[a] Average of three *Igualas Médicas*.

[b] Does not include follow-up visits, or emergencies.

[c] n.a. means not applicable, because neither the doctor nor the hospital works only for the *Iguala*.

[d] Average of five *Igualas*. All other information in this column is from the average of two *Igualas*.

[e] Does not include subsequent visits as consultations.

[f] Includes follow-up visits as consultations.

Source: Prepared by ECOCARIBE based on information from IDSS and interviews with managed care companies.

follow-up visits are included as visits and given the same value, the cost remains higher than in the prepaid companies. Certainly this may be influenced by the fact that IDSS covers medications for outpatient care, and prepaid companies do not. But when the cost of a hospital stay is compared, where both types of organization offer the same service, the result is even more pronounced because each hospitalization case costs IDSS 3.3 times what it costs the *Igualas*, especially because the stay is longer.

Again, a part of the difference may be explained by problems of adverse selection, because a portion of the average of cases treated by the IDSS consists of chronic diseases not treated by prepaid companies. The differences are so striking and large, however, that they cannot conceal the huge deficiencies in public health care.

These results indicate that the type of industrial organization for health care delivery used by the *Igualas* is much more efficient in cost terms than that used by the IDSS.

Conclusions and Recommendations

Health care delivery through the IDSS is characterized by serious deficiencies in the way production is organized. In the social security institute's hospital network, in which the income of those agents responsible for its delivery has no relationship to their commitment and performance, levels of productivity are astonishingly low. Moreover, in comparison with similar services provided by private companies with prepaid plans, unit costs and costs per member are high, even though many members pay because it is obligatory and do not even make use of the social security institute services. This last point represents an additional social cost for the Dominican Republic in macroeconomic terms because the (effectively) doubled payroll tax makes the economy less competitive.

The Dominican Republic certainly has a serious health care coverage problem. With the way production is currently organized, the IDSS could not deal with a sudden major rise in the demand for medical care that would occur if coverage were to be extended to family members and dependents, let alone what would happen with universal health care, which would entail incorporating successively more sectors of the population, such as government employees, higher-income private sector employees, and workers in the informal sector.

However, because the country has enough installed productive capacity in health care to cover the needs of the population that contributes toward paying for health care expenses, the question arises whether it would be a good idea to offer private services to complement social security facilities. That would make it possible to introduce an element of competition in medical care delivery, allow the user freedom of choice, and improve the quality and lower the average cost of government health care.

The ability of *Iguala* plans to provide better quality health care services at a lower cost than the IDSS is not solely because of the enormous inefficiency of public institutions. The *Igualas* have been operating in the most complete laissez-faire context, without transparent competitive mechanisms, and that has also enabled them to develop without having proper means for controlling cost and quality. Moreover, they have in practice set up methods for screening customers that result in adverse selection, inasmuch as they do not normally accept the elderly or cover illnesses requiring very costly treatment.

In a reformed health care delivery organization, based on obligatory contributions by all workers and where members have the opportunity to choose their preferred provider, the prepaid medical service companies would see their market expand a great deal. However, it would be necessary to establish procedures for supervising and regulating contracts.

Arranging a health plan could take place under the terms of a public contract. Membership should take place by groups in order to discourage potential discrimination mechanisms in the selection process, and health care providers should be obliged to offer the basic plan as defined to any user requesting it.

From a distributional standpoint, all those insured should keep making their obligatory contribution, defined as a particular proportion of their income, with no upper limit for any income level. However, an upper limit on contributions could be set, defined as a parameter based on the minimum wage or some other unit of measurement. This would reduce redistribution, but also reduce the incentive for evasion.

The agency guiding the system, however, would also retain revenue and financing functions and would sign contracts with providers chosen by the members based on capitated payments, as the *Igualas* currently do.

In this case, the need to compete would force *Igualas* to reorganize industrially. Type I companies would probably find it difficult to meet the conditions of fully covering the contract or competing adequately unless they found ways to improve the quality of their services. At the other extreme, Type III *Igualas* would probably not be able to compete in costs, when a common rate for the basic defined health plan was established. This seems to indicate that the system would have to gradually converge toward a Type II style, where such entities come to agreements with direct medical care providers through fees for services. This method is administratively simple;

it induces the service provider to minimize the cost of treatment and gives the customer influence through free choice.

This would still not resolve the health care requirements for a large segment of the population that is unable to make contributions, and hence would have to continue to be financed by the state with regular funds from its budget. The state will have to allocate substantial resources to cover the needs of the unemployed and of the informal sector, who are at the lowest levels of poverty, and hence it would have to rely upon procedures for assistance that are not contribution-based.

References

Barknum, H., J. Kutzin, and H. Saxenian. 1995. *Incentives and Providers Payment Methods.* Human Resources Development Working Paper No. 51, World Bank, Washington, D.C.

Comisión Nacional de Salud. 1991. Situación del sistema público de salud. Comisión Nacional de Salud, Santo Domingo. Mimeo.

Díaz Santana, A. 1990. Articulación de los seguros médicos privados en el desarrollo de la seguridad social y la República Dominicana. Comisión Nacional de Salud, Santo Domingo. Mimeo.

Díaz Santana, A. 1993. Sistema de financiamiento del sector salud. PNUD, Comisión Nacional de Salud, Santo Domingo. Mimeo.

Duarte, I., C. Gómez, G. La Forgia, and M. Molina. 1988. Los servicios de salud del Distrito Nacional por sectores, 1987: organización, cobertura, financiamiento y utilización. Publicación de la Asociación Dominicana Pro Bienestar de la Familia, Estudio No. 22, Instituto de Estudios de Población y Desarrollo, Santo Domingo. Mimeo.

Evans, R.G. 1981. Incomplete Vertical Integration: The Distinctive Structure of the Health-care Industry. In *Health, Economics, and Health Economics,* J. van der Gaag and M. Pearlman. North-Holland Publishing Company.

Fundación Siglo 21. 1995. *Seguridad Social; el proceso de reforma en el área de salud.* Santo Domingo: Siglo. 21.

Gaynorm M. 1994. *Issues in the Industrial Organization of the Market for Physician Services.* NBER Working Paper No. 4695. National Bureau of Economic Research, Cambridge, MA.

Infante, T. Mate, and A. Sancho. 1992. Reforma de los sistemas de prestación de servicios sociales en América Latina. Inter-American Development Bank, Washington, D.C. Mimeo.

Instituto Dominicano de Seguros Sociales. Various years. *Anuario estadístico*. Santo Domingo: IDSS.

Instituto Dominicano de Estudios de Población y Desarrollo. 1991. Informe de la encuesta demográfica y de salud. IEPD, Santo Domingo. Mimeo.

Instituto Dominicano de Estudios de Población y Desarrollo. 1993. Encuesta demográfica y de salud, 1991: Resultados generales cuestionario de hogar ampliado. IEPD, Santo Domingo. Mimeo.

La Forgia, G. 1990. Health Services for Low-income Families: Extending Coverage Through Prepayment Plans in the Dominican Republic. HFS Technical Report No. 2, U.S. Agency for International Development, Washington, D.C.

Lewis, M., M. Sulvetta, and G. La Forgia. 1992. *Public Hospital Costs and Quality in the Dominican Republic.* Working Paper 934, World Bank, Washington, D.C.

Mesa-Lago, C. 1991. La seguridad social en América Latina. In *Progreso económico y social de América Latina.* Washington, D.C.: Inter-American Development Bank.

Oficina de Coordinación Técnica de la Comisión Nacional de Salud. 1995. Salud, una visión del futuro. Santo Domingo. Mimeo.

Programa de las Naciones Unidas para el Desarrollo. Various issues. *Desarrollo humano.* Bogotá, Tercer Mundo Editores.

Santana, I., and M. Rathe. 1992. *El impacto distributivo de la gestión fiscal en la República Dominicana.* Santo Domingo: Fundación Siglo 21.

Santana, I. and M. Rathe. 1993. *Reforma social: una agenda para combatir la pobreza.* Santo Domingo: Fundación Siglo 21.

CHAPTER 6

Competition, Vertical Integration and Performance in Chile's Public and Private Health Services

Ernesto Miranda R. and Ricardo D. Paredes Molina[1]

Among the unique features of the Chilean health system is the mandate that obligates workers, whether active or retired, to contribute 7 percent of their income for health insurance for themselves and their dependents. This obligatory enrollment can be in the government system, which is organized along traditional collective social security lines, or into a private system, which offers health insurance set up to suit the individual. Workers can choose which system they want, but the particular features of the insurance offered and the cost of access have the effect of segmenting the market. People who have higher incomes and are less at risk tend to affiliate with the private sector ISAPREs (*Instituciones de Salud Previsional* or Health Insurance Institutions), while those with lower incomes and greater health risks are handled through the public system.

The reforms of the 1980s and the introduction of the private insurance system led to the creation of organizations with varying features in terms of financing, management, ownership and integration. Such a range of institutions, with limited regulation and state intervention, can be interpreted as the efficient response of a system adapting to the different requirements of its customers. It can also be considered the consequence of a legal

---

[1] Ernesto Miranda R. is General Manager of AFP Aporta. Ricardo D. Paredes Molina teaches in the Economics Department of the University of Chile.

framework that artificially segments institutions and users, thereby producing inefficiencies and inequities.

This chapter analyzes the organization of health insurance by examining the relationship between the different structures of existing markets and their effects on the performance of institutions. To this end, the structure and behavior of health insurance institutions are examined, as well as the coexistence between the public and private systems, and within the latter, the various organizational forms that have emerged over time. In this connection, a typology of these entities has been developed to answer questions related to industrial organization. The chapter also examines the industrial organization of the pharmaceutical and laboratory sectors, which constitute an important stage in the chain of production.

The chapter first summarizes the institutional evolution of the Chilean health care system. Aspects of competition and product differentiation in the private health insurance market are then examined. The third section compares the performance of the various private health care insurance organizations. Bottlenecks in the production and distribution stages of pharmaceuticals are then evaluated.

Evolution of the Chilean Health System

The Chilean health system has been at the forefront of social development that began in the 1920s, when the Obligatory Workers Insurance Fund was set up to offer health and pension guarantees to certain groups of workers. The National Medical Service for Employees (SERMENA), established in 1942, was intended to help white collar employees and their families maintain and recover their health. The National Health Care Service was created in 1952 as the means by which health care coverage was extended to most of the working class population.[2]

In the 1950s, protection and health care were extended into the area of occupational hazards with the creation of Mutual Funds for Work Accidents, a system that was completed in 1968 through the Law for Labor Accidents and Occupational Diseases. It was also in the 1950s that health benefits were extended through the formation of the Pension Funds, which provided social security in the area of pensions and related benefits.

---

[2] See Miranda and Vergara (1993).

By the late 1970s, the Chilean health care system covered about 80 percent of the population, but there were a number of problems hindering its performance,[3] most notably major differences between benefits for blue and white collar workers; the fact that a significant portion of the beneficiary population made no regular contributions to finance health care; and an overly centralized, hierarchical and bureaucratic system. These factors generated poor administration and weak capacity to respond to people's needs. It is widely believed that such problems were rooted in the failures of the traditional government style of financing, managing and delivering health care. The most obvious sign of crisis was the rising cost of social security, which placed a burden of 35 percent on payroll, its main funding source.

Based on this diagnosis, a set of reforms to restructure and decentralize the public system was set in motion in the 1980s. Most primary care visits were transferred to municipal management, and people were given the option of handling pension and welfare by enrolling in private health insurance plans.

Changes in health care, as in the other social sectors, were part of a broad range of reforms based on a more open economy, the state playing a subsidiary role, the primacy of the market for allocating resources, and wide-ranging deregulation of domestic markets.[4] The first round of reforms along these lines had been carried out in the mid-1970s with macroeconomic and sector matters. The second phase was aimed at social sectors, and brought about structural change in the operation of such services as education, pensions, housing and health care.

The institutional framework of the early 1980s remains in place today, with some minor modifications. In May 1995, the ISAPRE law was reformed to provide greater transparency and information in the system. Methods of paying providers have been reformed in the public system with the introduction, in pilot project form, of diagnostic related payments for hospitals (known in Chile by the acronym DRS) and a system of per capita payments for primary care. "Performance commitments" have also been initiated to introduce greater accountability on the part of government health care providers.

---

[3] See Oyarzo (1991 and 1992) and Miranda, Scarpaci and Irarrázaval (1995).
[4] See Edwards and Edwards (1987).

Subsidiary Health Systems

The 1981 health care reform made it possible for a person's obligatory payroll deduction to be directed to the public system (*Fondo Nacional de Salud*, the National Health Fund known by its acronym FONASA), which is organized through a traditional collective social security model, or through private administrators (ISAPREs) that offer health insurance oriented toward serving enrolled individuals. Members in the public system receive preferential access to health care in the government hospital system and at primary care centers run by municipalities; in either case, the supply of providers reflects a bureaucratic organizational model with centralized financing. Little attention is given to demand. Those enrolled in private systems, on the other hand, have access to private providers through free choice, with systems of reimbursement for services provided.

Thus, the Chilean health care system is composed of these two large subsidiary systems. Funding comes from obligatory health care payments, augmented by government contributions for the state system and with additional voluntary deductions for the private system. All employed workers and pensioners have to contribute 7 percent of their taxable income, with a monthly ceiling of 60 UF (indexed units whose unit value is approximately $33). People with no income and indigents are served by the public health system without a payroll deduction or any other type of payment.

In the government system, the obligatory deduction gives access to homogeneous health care. By contrast, ISAPREs offer many different health care plans at different prices, and hence the obligatory deduction may or may not be sufficient. Should members wish to obtain a more complete—and therefore more expensive—health plan than the one allowed by their obligatory contribution, they must pay extra.

State System

FONASA, the agency that administers the state system, receives its revenues (payroll deductions and fiscal contribution) and allocates them to providers in the sector. The productive base of the state system is composed of 26 health services, autonomous bodies with their own legal standing and their own assets. They are responsible for secondary and tertiary health services offered through a network of 200 hospital facilities with different levels of complexity, and centers for outpatient care (attached to hospitals). Also part of the primary health care network are 376 clinics, 1,102 rural health posts and 720 medical stations, most administered by the municipalities of the respective districts.

Two modes of care exist for delivering health care in the state system: institutional and free choice. In the institutional type, people come to primary care clinics, which offer technically simple curative services on an open basis, carry out preventive and health promotion activities, and refer patients when necessary to hospital facilities that provide more complex services. Treatment in primary care clinics is free for those enrolled in the public system, while hospital care requires a copayment, which varies with the type of service provided and in proportion to the contributor's income level. However, this system suffers from major evasion problems due to the lack of an adequate information system.

The free choice mode complements the institutional one, and is open only to those making payments and their dependent family members (thus not to indigents). This mode cofinances access to a set of private providers who agree to offer services at prices preestablished by FONASA. The copayment that the person makes is organized into three rate levels and depends on the kind of provider to which one goes, not on the customer's income level.

The public hospitals are quite vertically integrated. What they offer ranges from consultations to clinical examinations and major surgery. The fact that a major portion of the less complex services are provided in hospitals reflects a certain degree of inefficiency resulting from the lack of coordination among levels providing primary care. It also reflects shortcomings in the management capability of municipalities that have to be remedied at higher levels in the system.

Historically, health service providers in the public sector have been paid in a centralized and bureaucratic manner. Allocation of resources has been made on the basis of historic budgets, qualified by criteria negotiated with some discretion. Payments to professional and nonprofessional employees have been linked basically to variables related to classifications that have no relationship to the productivity of the work done. However, since the 1990s, a set of procedures for payment has been designed based on estimates of anticipated use that consider the population enrolled (in the case of municipal clinics) and the type of services provided in hospital care. These procedures introduce greater rationality and accountability into the supply of services in the public sector. Thus far their effectiveness has not been evaluated.

Private System

The ISAPRE system operates as an individual private insurance scheme in which the benefits offered vary according to the premium and the level of medical risk of those insured. However, the obligation to pay 7 percent of one's income confers a particular feature on the Chilean ISAPRE system. In accordance with the amount of the deduction and medical risk of those insured, the ISAPRE offers a health care plan that relates anticipated expenditure to the premiums that are charged. In economic terminology, the amount of services (i.e., the benefits package) is the endogenous variable, which adjusts to the premium (i.e., the price) that is set exogenously.[5]

The insurance plans offered by ISAPREs specify the percentages of reimbursement on rates charged by health care providers for treatment and related services (examinations, hospital stays, etc.), and ceilings on the fee to be reimbursed. In general terms, contracts establish that the percentages of reimbursements and ceilings increase with the premium paid by the health plan.

The private provider system is composed of clinics, hospitals and independent professionals who treat both those insured in ISAPREs and those who pay into the public system through the free choice method. In some cases, ISAPREs offer health care directly by vertically integrating insurance activities and production of services.

Payment to private providers operates mainly through reimbursements for services rendered, a modality that reduces the financial risk for health service providers to a minimum. This arrangement also offers the consumer population great freedom of choice. There are also alternatives which limit access to a group of providers—the result being less freedom of choice in exchange for lower prices of treatment. This may happen through lists of providers who have an agreement with the particular ISAPRE, where the payment system continues to be on a fee-for-service basis, or through a type of "closed care" in the case of some ISAPREs that maintain their own medical service facilities.

---

[5] An exception to this practice results from the possibility of purchasing additional insurance plans in exchange for a payment of over 7 percent of income.

The ISAPREs constitute the financial center and establish how the various productive stages operate. Among the ISAPREs, two types can be distinguished: closed and open. Closed ISAPREs are private associations that emerged from companies that already had health care agreements with their workers and set aside funds to finance them prior to the creation of the present system. When the current law allowed the health deduction to be directed to private administrators, these companies set up what are called closed ISAPREs in order to use employee payments to finance their health care benefits. Thus these entities are characterized by the fact that entry is limited to people working in the company and by a significant volume of additional payments made by the companies. Prominent among these closed ISAPREs are those of the large mining companies, whose behavior is different by reason of the size and nature of the industry in which they operate.[6]

Thus, closed ISAPREs have a very captive market that isolates them from competition in the health insurance market. This market niche for closed ISAPREs is ultimately rooted in the extra contributions made by the main company, which are lost should the worker cease being a member. In this sense, the benefits obtained or obtainable by members of a closed ISAPRE are better than most of them would be able to get in the market.

Open ISAPREs, on the other hand, are independent private companies that resemble insurance companies. Even though they do not have market niches in the same sense as closed ISAPREs, they practice a great deal of product differentiation under current legislation and incentives. That differentiation may be consistent with providing services adapted to the needs of different consumers. Nevertheless, the existence of a large number of hard-to-compare plans may lead to profit margins higher than those in a competitive market where the product is homogeneous.[7]

In terms of integration, some ISAPREs are owned by private clinics and others have established outpatient care clinics on their own premises ("direct care"). However, most health care is provided through service agree-

---

[6] Contrary to what happens in other ISAPREs, the operation of copper company ISAPREs depends on decisions made by the "mother" company and in fact its staff and executives are part of their staff.

[7] That, for example, may be the consequence of information costs, which have entailed a significant number of claims to anti-monopoly commissions over fraud allegedly practiced not only by ISAPREs but by clinics as well.

FIGURE 6.1. Structure of the Health Care System in Chile

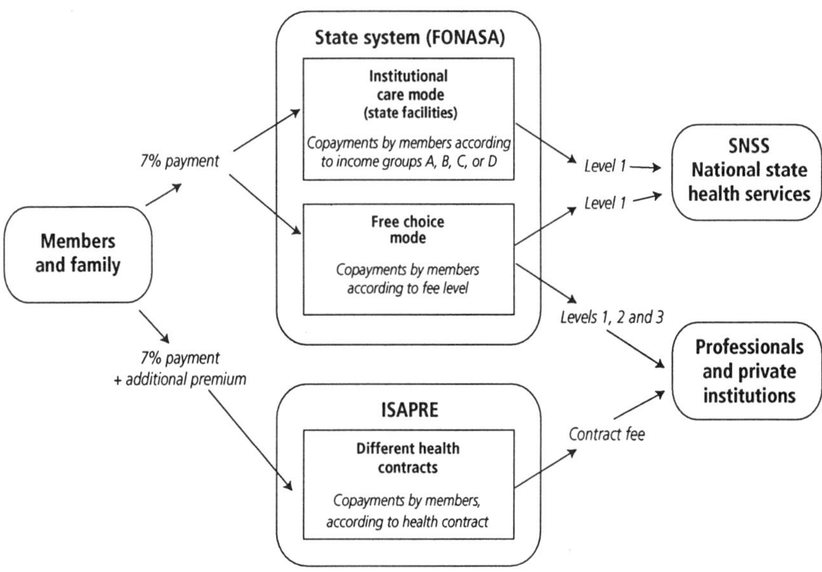

ments with providers, which may provide care either on their own premises or in those of outside suppliers. Closed ISAPREs likewise offer both direct care and complete free choice (see Figure 6.1).

Financing

Table 6.1 presents the financing structures of the public and private health systems as of 1995. The main sources of revenue for the public system were member payments to FONASA (33 percent of spending in the sector) and the contribution from the fiscal budget (48 percent). The copayment for having access to health care in the public sector, that is, free choice of FONASA services, represented revenues amounting to 19 percent of spending in this sector.

The ISAPREs, for their part, received the equivalent of 44 percent of total health care spending in 1995. Payments by those insured represented 82 percent of spending in the sector, followed by the copayments at the moment of treatment (14 percent). The remaining 4 percent came from fiscal contributions for paying maternity leaves and a subsidy for low-income contributors so that they could have access to private insurance.

Table 6.1. Financing of Health Systems in 1995

	Private ISAPRE	Public FONASA (1)
Total in millions of US$	1,118.2 (44%)	1,039.9 (56%)
Sources (%)		
Fiscal contribution	4	48
Premiums	82	33
Copayment	14	19
Spending per beneficiary (US$)	297	205
Average premium (US$)	646	121

Source: Larrañaga (1996).

The Model Underlying Comparison of the Systems

The comparative description of open and closed ISAPREs is of interest insofar as they are motivated differently and hence they can be expected to behave differently. There are also differences between these entities and the public system. The impact of institutional design on the performance of institutions can accordingly be studied.

In each system or subsystem there is a contract between a "principal" (in this case, the user who makes payments and who delegates care for health to a private or public institution) and an "agent." This agent has incentives that are not always in line with those of the principal. Moreover, some objectives, such as that of lowering operating costs, clearly place the parties at odds.

In the case of the public system, the service providers (e.g., the government, doctors and officials) or "agents" do not have contracts that would make their incentives compatible with those of the user, the "principal." In fact, the health benefits are of a conveniently ambiguous nature. The users are not clear on what their rights and powers are. Such a feature is functional in a system that rations according to different price variables, such as waiting lines and discriminatory treatment. The lack of explicit contracts makes monitoring relatively expensive and raises incentives to deviate from the principal's objectives.

In closed ISAPREs, the objectives of the principal with regard to health care alone are restricted to the framework imposed by collective bargaining. The budgetary restriction is somewhat less operative, which may improve services but raise costs excessively. Finally, in open ISAPREs, the budgetary restrictions are more operative, efficiency requirements are greater, and contracts are more efficient.

Regulation

The Chilean health system is regulated fundamentally in two realms: delivery and insurance. With regard to the former, the Chilean Institute of Public Health (ISP) is the health authority responsible throughout the country for authorizing and registering pharmaceutical products and foods for medical and cosmetic use and for assuring quality control.

Legislation sets requirements for accuracy and requirements on the delivery of information on all collateral and secondary effects and the dangers and limitations in the use of medicines. There is also a series of regulations intended to give access to clinical records, whose basic purpose is to allow for prompt communication of knowledge and of the clinical records of patients, a function which is also under ISP supervision. There are also provisions for nondiscrimination against customers, but not under any specific legislation in the health industry. Rather, this falls under the general legal framework, and hence it is the anti-monopoly institutions that are responsible for assuring compliance with such principles.

Health authorities are also responsible for supervising health care providers. In theory, they monitor the quality of care and health outcomes of services, but in practice that does not happen. Currently, the only measurements of performance in the government system involve maintaining records of discharges, visits and days in the hospital. This is carried out through various accounting forms for monthly payments—the *rendición mensual de cobro*—and the estimate of costs per day by patient and procedure (SIGMO or *Sistema de Información y Monitoreo*).

Private providers are regulated by the health service to which they belong (authorized to operate and granted structural accreditation). The authorities require information on services provided, discharges, and illnesses that require notification, but have no information on the quality and outcomes of services provided. Even though health authorities require private providers to send them periodic information on the services they deliver, they are not empowered by the law to enforce such requests. The law enables them to inspect facilities and in doing so to look at records of services provided. In any case, health authorities do not currently make systematic use of the information they gather, except for hospital discharges, which are incorporated into national statistics on hospitalizations.

However, in its policies and programs for guiding providers, the Ministry of Health does not use procedures for regulating the quality and effectiveness of health care. What actually regulates quality and effectiveness in the system is a self-monitoring procedure by medical professionals (peer control, prestige and professional ethics).

Regulation of the operation of ISAPREs during the first few years was generally permissive and refrained from intervention.[8] In fact, at the creation of the system in 1981, the purpose of ISAPREs was set forth very broadly: provide health care delivery, whether directly or by financing, to people with whom a contract is signed.

Initially, ISAPREs were under the oversight of FONASA. As this agency gradually came to operate in the public sector like ISAPREs, administering contributions and financing the delivery of services, it became necessary to create a body to regulate private institutions.

In 1990, the Superintendency of ISAPREs was established exclusively to regulate and monitor this sector. Since then, and especially since 1995, regulation has come into play more forcefully. Contracts are no longer restricted solely to the will of the parties, but incorporate the superintendency as arbiter of last resort. A series of restrictions has been established to make the relationship between ISAPREs and customers more transparent and protecting the latter in the event of abuses.

Today, ISAPREs have a contract relationship with customers who can appeal and seek mediation from the Superintendency of ISAPREs and make a claim in the ordinary courts. The claim may be based on two grounds: nonfulfillment of contract (coverage, copayments) or dissatisfaction with the quality of service received. Claims before the justice system are relatively infrequent (estimated to be 2 percent of beneficiaries) and in most cases have to do with nonfulfillment of contract.

However, contracts between ISAPREs and the insured population are

---

[8] For a critical analysis of the issue of ISAPRE regulation, see Gandolfo (1995).

basically governed by the will of the parties. There are no restrictions on the modes of payment used in treating health service providers. Legislation does not place major entry barriers, except for demonstrating minimum assets, which in 1996 amounted to $160,000.

Notwithstanding the establishment of the superintendency and regulations in the areas of exclusions, price and contract periods, the market is still only minimally regulated. Indeed, existing regulation does not limit but encourages market entry and competition.

Comparative Overview of Public and Private Insurance Systems

From 1981–95, the private sector has continually expanded its coverage (Table 6.2). Thus, the share held by ISAPREs, which was close to 10 percent of users in 1987, had reached 30 percent 10 years later. Annual growth of the ISAPRE system has been around 20 percent on average over the past eight years. The expansion of the system is even greater if one limits consideration to those making contributions, and in particular to those who are active in the labor force. Currently, there are more people contributing to the private than to the public health sector. On the other hand, practically all pensioners are paying into the public system, which reflects the duality of the insurance system.

Expansion of private sector coverage has grown far faster than the increase of the labor force and real pay. That suggests that the ISAPRE system has expanded toward the lower income strata. The private system has been advancing for two reasons. First, the ISAPRE sector has been quite innovative in offering plans attractive for new market segments. The challenge for these institutions is to offer health plans that can be financed with the 7 percent payment from people's incomes, that represent a better product than the one offered by the public system (which has additional sums from the treasury), and that are profitable.

The expansion of the ISAPRE market is obviously constrained by public insurance, which offers health benefit coverage regardless of the level of payment. The health plan that the ISAPREs can offer becomes less attractive as the user's income level (and payment) drops, or as the medical risk rises. Thus there is a level of income and medical risk that makes it rational to prefer the public over the private system. That sets a natural limit to the growth of the ISAPRE system.

Table 6.2. Overall Indicators of Activity by System

Years	Beneficiaries (thousands)		Employees contributing	Average monthly income per contributor (thousands of 1994 pesos)	Annual per capita spending (thousands of 1994 pesos)	
	Public	ISAPRE	ISAPRE (%)	ISAPRE	Public	ISAPRE
1981	9,851.5	61.7	42.8	n.a.	n.a.	n.a.
1984	10,017.6	291.9	35.9	330.0	29.6	145.3
1987	9,980.1	1,087.7	37.2	284.6	28.2	112.5
1990	9,907.6	1,929.7	40.6	292.9	33.8	132.2
1992	9,385.1	2,795.2	41.9	273.2	48.5	124.8
1995	9,009.3	4,400.0	43.2	277.3	61.3	124.6

Sources: SNS and Superintendency of ISAPREs.

Note: In 1994, the exchange rate was 420.1 Chilean pesos to the U.S. dollar.

One of the private system's most expeditious approaches to extending its coverage to lower income levels has been through the use of group contract agreements with such organizations as unions and companies. ISAPRE offers the group member a better health plan than he or she would have access to individually. ISAPRE can offer the group agreement because of the convenience for the insurer represented by larger sales volume, and the lower risk associated with selling insurance to a large portfolio of clients. Moreover, the group mode does not mean that the insurance plans offered by the ISAPREs deviate from the rationale of individual affiliation and pricing. The collective agreements for a group of people (associated with a company, for example) still distinguish benefit levels in accordance with the income level and the risks of the different subgroups comprising it.[9]

The second reason behind the growth of the ISAPRE sector is the fact that its product is more attractive than the one offered in the public system. The private system offers free choice of providers and different treatment to members within the same ISAPRE and in professional care. By contrast, the

---

[9] There are no official figures on the coverage of group agreements, although it is estimated that around 60 percent of users are under some kind of group agreement.

public system, which is thoroughly bureaucratic and fundamentally supply-driven, is hard pressed to offer a product sufficiently differentiated and appealing to consumers.

The limitations of the organizational structure of the public system are clear. During the period of military government, the public system was confronted with a sharp drop in funding, which led to problems with infrastructure, lack of supplies, and departure of staff. In the late 1980s, democratic institutions were established, and the recovery of the public health system became a priority. There was a plentiful injection of funds into the sector, making it possible to practically double per capita spending over the course of the past six years. Nevertheless, opinion surveys of consumers and experts alike point out that these changes have had little impact on the care ultimately received by consumers in this sector.[10]

Another indicator that reflects the supply of health services and infrastructure is the availability of beds in health care systems, which rose from 4,088 in 1980 to 10,600 in 1992 in the private sector, while falling in the public sector from 33,879 to 32,279. These figures suggest that introduction of the ISAPRE system generated vigorous expansion of the private health industry, which today represents around half of total spending in the sector. This is a "hard parameter" of the Chilean system that must be kept in mind, above and beyond problems and shortcomings related to fairness and efficiency.

Dual Nature of the Health Systems

The insurance structure represented by the public and private health sectors is rooted in a dual system that splits the population into two groups. Thus, the logic of an insurance system that operates on an individual and private basis is to select those insured by income and medical risk. By contrast, the logic of solidarity in insurance represented by FONASA is associated with a mechanism of adverse selection, because high income and low medical risk people have an incentive to leave the collective system. Thus both systems encourage the rise of a dual structure that concentrates high income and

---

[10] Nevertheless, in recent years the slowing of the growth of the ISAPRE sector could be related to the strengthening of the public sector. An alternative interpretation would be that the ISAPRE sector is approaching its "natural" size.

Table 6.3. Affiliation by Income Stratum in Each Sector (percent)

Age groups	Income quintiles									
	I		II		III		IV		V	
	Public insurance	ISAPRE	Public insurance	ISAPRE	Public insurance	ISAPRE	Public insurance	ISAPRE	Public insurance	ISAPRE
0–20	93	7	82	18	69	31	51	49	30	70
21–50	92	8	82	18	69	31	53	47	34	66
51–64	97	3	94	6	88	12	81	19	51	49
65 +	99	1	98	2	97	3	94	6	77	23
Total	93	7	84	16	74	26	60	40	39	61

Source: Larrañaga (1996).

low risk people in the ISAPRE system and low income, high risk people in FONASA, an institution that acts as an insurer of last resort and ultimately makes the dual health insurance system viable. Table 6.3 shows that coverage of the ISAPRE system declines with people's income and with their medical risk, as represented by the variable of age.

On the other hand, one result of the competitive nature of the ISAPRE insurance market, which encourages free choice and switching ISAPREs in search of better health alternatives, is transitory insurance that provides coverage parceled out over time and that undermines the establishment of long-term commitments between the ISAPRE and its member. The two main inefficiencies that result are that not enough is done in the way of health education and prevention, and older people are left unprotected. In any case, this dual structure is a rational response of economic agents to the institutional framework and incentives existing in this sector.

Competition and Differentiation Between Plans in the ISAPRE Market

This section examines whether the Chilean health insurance system has moved in a direction that enhances competition and thus increases its ability to serve consumers, or whether it has become segmented and less competitive.

Horizontal Structure in Insurance

The danger of collusion or monopoly in private health insurance is ever present, inasmuch as enrollment (consumption) is obligatory and the public system offers a standard product aimed only at low-income sectors. Nevertheless, the information available points away from collusion: the number and concentration of insurance companies have increased over time, the degree of concentration has fallen, and institutions in this industry have not been brought before the anti-monopoly commissions (Table 6.4).

Even so, return on assets in ISAPREs has been over 20 percent over the history of the system, and in 1995 the figure was 23 percent. Some analysts thus argue that the system must be operating overall in a monopolistic manner, but this argument is mistaken. ISAPREs are companies in which knowledge and human capital are more important than physical assets, and hence profits as compared to physical assets or net wealth are not a true indicator of profitability. Similarly, in an industry in which innovation and risk are substantial, estimates of returns tend to be distorted by measurements as simple as return on assets. Returns vary a great deal among ISAPREs, and some even have negative returns, a fact that does not fit with a traditional model of collusion.

In statistical terms, estimates made from the past five years of the ISAPRE system indicate that the age of the particular ISAPRE is the only variable that explains returns on assets.[11] Neither the number of payers nor the mean income of payers can explain differences in profitability. This suggests that there are no significant economies of scale, which is also apparent from the fact that ISAPREs function in various sizes. The mean income of contributors does not seem to explain returns to fixed assets either. Even though tilting the portfolio toward younger and higher income individuals increases ISAPRE income—because such individuals can pay more and imply lower risk in the government system—those individuals must also be demanding better (and more costly) services. Thus, the fact that only the age of the ISAPRE is a significant and economically relevant variable for

---

[11] The regression, estimated by Ordinary Least Squares and that has an R^2 of 0.54, used data for all ISAPREs between 1990 and 1995. The estimation yielded: Profits/Assets = − 33.1 + 1.47 E-05 number of contributors − 0.0003 mean revenue + 3.65* years (significant at 1 percent).

Table 6.4. Number, Concentration and Profitability of ISAPREs

	Number of ISAPREs			Concentration and profitability		
Year	Open	Closed	Total	C2	C5	Profit/Assets
1981	6	0	6	90	99	. . .
1985	10	7	17	34	69	22.8
1988	20	11	31	37	70	17.3
1990	21	14	35	36	68	26.8
1993	21	14	35	36	73	24.3
1995	21	14	35	39	74	23.0

Source: Superintendency of ISAPREs.

determining return on assets seems to confirm that a more appropriate measure of profitability is needed. In this industry, return on assets must be overestimating true economic yields.

Differentiation of Plans

Various authors (Diamond, 1994; Fuchs and Kramer, 1973) question the virtues of the allocation of market resources in the health system, given the problems faced by consumers in making informed choices conducive to their own welfare. That criticism has been leveled particularly at the unevenness of information between health care providers and customers, but it can also apply to health insurance.

The Chilean case illustrates the difficulties people face when they have to choose private health insurance. Indeed, consumers are confronted with a wide variety of health plans offered by ISAPREs, and they lack the information necessary to adequately distinguish between them. Even if they could, it is not clear that such a variety of plans produces the gains in welfare that are usually associated with having a wider range of alternatives from which to choose.

In 1995, there were around 8,800 different health insurance plans offered by ISAPREs. Such variety partly reflects the range of existing "prices" set exogenously by the obligatory payment of 7 percent of income. As has been described, the market produces a continuous range of insurance plans to respond to the parallel range of premiums that emerge from this financing structure. Within each income category, however, the ISAPRE market offers a range of alternative plans whose value is questionable. Thus, for example, the percentages of reimbursement for treatment of a heart attack vary widely in a sample of maximum and minimum insurance offered by different ISAPREs. That variation does not reflect a logic of efficiency. Health needs must be distinguished from preferences in the area of risk aversion, accommodations and other general features. There could potentially be welfare gains if the variety of insurance plans were to respond to a wide range of preferences over these matters. However, when the plans are differentiated by the kind of services covered, uncertainty enters that can also lead to adverse selection by consumers.

The information problems said to characterize the ISAPRE insurance market increase when one takes into account that each institution operates with a specific fee structure by which copayments for services are determined. A fee system can include several thousand fees varying by type of service, and a customer must go to ISAPRE's offices to review the fee schedule. Under such conditions, it is next to impossible for consumers to rationally evaluate the merits of choosing one health insurance plan over another.

Vertical Integration in Insurance

One of the more controversial issues in the area of industrial performance is that of the practices and behavior of control and vertical integration. The debate in this area has been especially relevant in public utility industries that have natural monopoly features—electricity, gas, telecommunications and water—and similarly applies in industries such as aeronautics and health.[12]

Vertical integration must of necessity take as its reference point the theory of Coase (1937) on the origin and nature of the firm. This now classic analysis of the firm places a very positive value on processes of vertical integration. In simple terms, the analysis establishes that in certain circumstances, the use of the market to allocate resources can be costly, and thus it

---

[12] For a conceptual and practical discussion of the problem of vertical integration in Chile, see Paredes Molina (1997).

may be appropriate to replace it with a more efficient mechanism or institution.

Obviously, firms will not always integrate and there is no operative rule that would indicate when vertical integration is more efficient. Full contracts are a substitute for integration and they will be written when it is feasible to write them. On the other hand, trust between people doing business, the repetitive nature of negotiations, and the ability to change suppliers are some of the many factors having a bearing on such a decision. In any case, vertical integration is a way of reducing transaction costs and therefore constitutes an organizational alternative that can be the most efficient.

Specifically with regard to the health market and its relationship with vertical integration, providing insurance entails several efficiency problems associated with inability of insurance companies to control activities as a result of asymmetric information (e.g., those insured know more about their own health condition than the ISAPRE) and overuse of health services (e.g., members receive a price below cost for these services). Delivery of health services requires investments that differ in terms of their specificity, and hence investors are also exposed to different degrees of expropriation, and so they require different degrees of monitoring. Thus, on both levels there are problems of agency that can be reduced through vertical integration.

Problems That Can Be Handled Through Integration

In order to evaluate the role of vertical integration, the main specific problems in the sector that can in some manner be resolved through some type of vertical integration are indicated below.

Asymmetric Information Between Payer and ISAPRE: The Role of Closed (ISAPRE) Plans

A first problem typical in the insurance industry is that of asymmetric information between the ISAPRE and the payer. The payer may know his or her risk better than the ISAPRE and may to some extent hide it and not take all the measures that would be efficient (that is, a situation of moral hazard). On the other hand, the ISAPRE may be in a better position than the member to be familiar with certain aspects of the overall risk of the population and trends, procedures and alternative plans.

In a voluntary insurance market, the first problem with asymmetric information leads to moral hazard, namely the trend for only high risk people to insure themselves. The second problem is adverse selection, whereby suppliers try to choose low risk people while using discriminatory practices against higher health risks.

In Chile, membership in health plans is obligatory, and ISAPREs cannot exclude from their portfolio those persons who represent higher costs of health care. Nevertheless, the fact that there is public insurance with the features of a collective system introduces adverse selection and moral hazard into the industry. As already described, the private sector tends to concentrate on healthier persons, while the public sector assumes the role of "funder of last resort" for cases of higher risk and lower ability to pay. Likewise, the private sector can induce its higher risk individuals to withdraw by raising the cost of the health plan (after offering an alternative plan to the rest of its portfolio).

Solutions can be promoted through regulations that would restrict termination of contracts. However, such regulation has been avoided because it generates costs by restricting competition and reducing the mobility of clients between different suppliers. Moreover, there are private solutions that to some degree constitute a kind of integration and allow for diversification of risks among consumers. That is in fact what happens with the sale of closed plans to groups of people, whether through what are known as closed ISAPREs, or through the sale of group agreements by open ISAPREs to unions, companies and other groups of workers.

Group plans and self-insurance practices allow for diversification in undertaking insurance, and reduce the problems associated with asymmetric information. However, because voluntary separation is an inalienable right, the operation of this system must involve a net benefit for individuals to remain in the plan. Group plans therefore have to include differentiated benefits for people with different income levels (managers vs. administrators, office vs. manual workers, etc.).

Excess Usage Through Induced Demand: the Role of Vertical Integration

One of the most striking features of the health industry is the fact it is not patients (consumers) who determine their demand but rather physicians who largely determine it for them (Poterba, 1994, and Musgrove, 1996). When arrangements for paying providers are fee-for-service, the provider bears no financial risk. Instead, this risk is absorbed entirely by the consumers (through health insurance companies). Therefore, the provider has no incentives to contain system costs. To the contrary, costs are likely to rise as a consequence of pursuing objectives whose benefits can be internalized by the provider, such as reducing the risk of health care treatments to a minimum, satisfying the consumer in the presence of a third-party payer, and using new technologies without much concern for their cost-effectiveness.

For these reasons, retrospective payment for services provided is a mode only rarely used by health systems. On the other hand, systems that pass on part of the risk to the provider — prospective capitated payments, diagnostic related payments, global budgets, and others — are preferable insofar as they make it possible to address cost containment. In a system that reimburses services, the cost containment goal is restricted to the realm of demand tools (copayments and the like), which can lead to an excessive limitation on access to health services and undermine the objective of health security that such systems ought to provide to their populations (Ellis and McGuire, 1993).

One arrangement that reduces this problem is integration between the ISAPRE and the service provider. Integration between the physician and the ISAPRE ought to lower the cost of medical services incurred in the health system. An especially relevant area is that constituted by the granting of sick leave when workers are temporarily ill. Such leaves allow for payment equivalent to the worker's pay (up to a particular limit) and replaces the company's regular payment while the illness lasts. The problem is that neither providers (physicians) nor consumers (workers) of leaves bear these costs, which must be paid by the insurer. Thus, integration between the ISAPRE and physicians ought to diminish the agency problem and externality that arises in this relationship, besides making monitoring easier.

Characterization of ISAPREs

Various types of industrial organization exist in the Chilean private health insurance system. First, there is the already mentioned division into open and closed ISAPREs. Likewise, there are various types of integration. For this analysis, a typology was constructed by grouping the various agents by their ownership and degree of vertical integration. Two kinds of ISAPREs are identified here: those that have acquired or developed infrastructure for outpatient care, which we call "outpatient,"[13] and those that have acquired or developed hospital infrastructure, which we call "hospital." These latter ISAPREs own or are associated with clinics and hospitals of a secondary or tertiary level of complexity, and even though they design special plans, any person can seek treatment in them.[14] It is expected that the various agency relationships vary specifically for each type of organization, and that over time the more efficient will prevail.

The following analysis of structure and performance in health insurance is subject to certain qualifications. First, there is no information on the coverage that each ISAPRE has group agreements, and hence the analysis that can be made in the area of structure and performance is limited. Second, the benefit level offered by the closed ISAPREs is affected by considerations specific to labor negotiation and other types of relationships between labor and firms. Third, ISAPREs may be aimed at different market segments. Since payment for health care varies by the premium received, the average spending level will vary in accordance with the ISAPRE's customer portfolio. In this sense, it is more important to study trends in revenues and spending than their amounts.[15]

Performance by Levels of Vertical Integration

Evaluation of Competitive Pressure on Costs

A first hypothesis to explore is that competitive pressure would prompt the various agents to improve service to customers and reduce costs in each organization. On the grounds that open ISAPREs are substantially more exposed to competition than closed ones, it is likely that open ISAPREs will offer a high level of service and contain costs.

---

[13] Integration of the outpatient stage has become especially noteworthy since 1987-88. The precursors of this type of integration were the ISAPREs Consalud, Promepar and Compensación, which in this manner are quite similar to health maintenance organizations (HMOs) in the United States.

[14] More detailed classifications offered nothing further by way of interesting results.

[15] Analyzing expenditure figures in relation to the average income of the contributor of each ISAPRE does not change the conclusions reached in the rest of the section.

Different indicators of service and performance were used to verify the effects of competitive pressure on the market. More important than the behavior of any specific indicator, however, is the consistency of different indicators of service and efficiency.

Costs: spending per beneficiary and administration and marketing costs. One of the most typical problems health systems have experienced in more developed countries in recent years has been the explosion of expenditures per beneficiary, a crucial determinant of system costs (Hoffmeyer and McCarthy, 1994). That phenomenon has been especially acute in the United States, where experts believe that the private health care mode has been a factor aggravating that cost explosion (Weisbrod, 1991).

Something similar is true in Chile, given the relative importance of private insurance in financing the industry. Available information can be only partially helpful, since information on copayments made directly to health care providers is not available. Thus, revenue figures include the obligatory 7 percent deduction and any extra voluntary payment. The sum of these revenues determines the level of spending made by ISAPREs, but data on the copayment component is unavailable.

Spending per beneficiary in the private sector rose by 14.3 percent over 1984–94, which can be disaggregated into a 65 percent growth rate for closed ISAPREs and only a moderate spending increase in the open ISAPRE sector (Table 6.5). This suggests that the private system contains costs quite differently, depending on the degree of competition. Indeed, the explosive spending increases in the closed system reached the point in 1994 where the average cost of health care was double the level of the open ISAPREs.

However, spending per beneficiary is only a reflection of the cost of health care, which can rise for a number of reasons: efficiency problems, higher costs for supplies, increases in demand, and so forth. Thus, a better indicator for measuring efficiency is expenditures for administration and marketing.

Productive efficiency is more faithfully reflected in expenditures on administration and marketing per beneficiary. As can be seen in Table 6.5, for the 1984–94 period, this indicator shows a quite systematic and significant decline (30 percent) for ISAPREs as a whole. That decline is related to the pressure to control costs and to the fact that in the early days of the system, ISAPREs made major efforts to position themselves in the market.

Once again, the strong differences between the evolution of indicators

Table 6.5. Spending of ISAPREs per Beneficiary
(thousands of 1995 Pesos)

Year	Medical expenditures			Administration and marketing expenditures		
	1985	1990	1994	1985	1990	1994
Open	131.4	138.2	150.3	73.2	51.9	48.6
Outpatient	70.9	108.2	119.2	45.0	41.2	40.0
Hospital	195.7	169.6	199.9	82.4	55.7	54.0
Closed	166.9	257.4	314.3	33.5	77.1	98.4
Total	139.4	150.3	159.2	64.0	54.6	51.3

Source: On the basis of statistics from the ISAPRE Superintendency.

for open and closed ISAPREs stand out. Thus, by 1994 costs of administration and marketing per beneficiary were substantially higher in closed ISAPREs. Inasmuch as the closed ISAPREs do not have substantial marketing costs—since they are oriented toward the internal market of particular firms—it is clear that administrative costs are strongly influenced by the competitive pressures faced by open ISAPREs (and by their absence in those that are closed).

Only partial information is available on the impact of vertical integration on spending in the system, but it supports the proposed hypothesis. There is evidence of a relationship with spending on sick leaves, which rose to 14.2 percent of the total of ISAPRE system revenues in 1993.[16]

Consalud is the most important ISAPRE of the "outpatient" variety. This ISAPRE provides institutional care at its own facilities, where physicians' earnings are tied to the bottom line of the health center where they work. Thus physicians internalize the ISAPRE's costs for any excessive use of leaves (and other costs). Consequently, in 1993 the average length of leave issued under this mode of health care was 38 percent less than that granted in the free choice mode within the same ISAPRE (6.62 vs. 9.13 days), thus supporting the hypothesis of the impact of the incentive structure on system costs.

---

[16] This information comes from Larrañaga (1995).

The more general hypothesis on the problems of moral hazard associated with health insurance receives further support in the case of sick leaves for high income people. Such people lose income when they make use of sick leave, because there is a ceiling on the payment.[17] An econometric regression for the entire group of open ISAPREs between spending per contributor on sick leaves and average income of the contributor shows a quadratic relationship; that is, spending on sick leaves increases at a declining rate with respect to the payer's income level, thereby demonstrating the relevance of incentives in the spending structure of the system.

Referral and overuse. Referrals and overuse may figure among the main costs of the health care system. It is difficult to analyze them, however, because of the lack of direct information (often not available), and hence it is necessary to use indirect indicators.

Clinical laboratory and imaging services (e.g., scanners, X-rays, and sonograms) provide indirect evidence of a problem in this area, inasmuch as they are especially sensitive to the efficiency of the referral and counter-referral process. Table 6.6 makes it clear that in the case of laboratory tests, frequency of use by closed ISAPREs rose 65 percent in the period, reaching a level double that of open ISAPREs in 1994.[18]

Viewed as a whole, in closed ISAPREs expenditure per beneficiary rose more than the increase in the frequency of use per beneficiary, thereby implying that the average cost of services increased. Insofar as such spending has remained practically constant in open ISAPREs, it can be deduced that the greater cost containment there applies to both the number of services and cost per treatment.

Services: Return on Premiums and Revealed Preferences

Return on premiums. Increased administrative efficiency is a force that should follow competitive pressure. Such pressure, however, is exercised basically in the demand for better services. A good indicator of service is return on premiums, which is defined as the percentage of total revenues (legal deduction

---

[17] This is maximum income that can be charged (approximately US$1,800 a month).

[18] It should be pointed out that in 1994 the state system had caught up with or surpassed the open ISAPRE sector in the frequency of such services, whose rate of use here depends on the underlying model, which makes contracts less efficient in the public sector.

Table 6.6. Health Services Provided: Annual Use per 1,000 Members

Service provided	Year	State system	Open ISAPREs	Closed ISAPREs
Medical visits	1986	2,486.9	3,948.8	5,695.8
	1990	2,603.2	3,460.4	4,507.6
	1994	2,893.3	3,259.0	5,562.8
Laboratory tests	1986	1,781.0	3,024.4	2,957.5
	1990	2,248.8	2,376.0	4,298.8
	1994	3,220.0	2,509.3	4,886.7
Imaging	1986	168.4	1,028.2	682.1
	1990	105.3	557.1	783.9
	1994	95.6	566.8	968.6
Surgeries	1986	91.1	n.a.	n.a.
	1990	105.3	54.6	89.2
	1994	95.6	65.9	175.7
Births by caesarian[1]	1986	5.9	18.8	3.2
	1990	7.2	15.1	7.2
	1994	7.1	13.9	11.0
Vaginal births[1]	1986	17.4	15.0	4.6
	1990	19.3	14.0	45.2
	1994	16.2	9.6	8.3

Source: Ministry of Health.

[1] It was impossible to control for the sex of members and hence the indicator for births is somewhat less reliable. This is particularly important for closed ISAPREs, which are primarily associated with the mining sector.

plus additional payments) that goes into financing health benefits. A greater return thus means that a greater portion of the payer's contribution is returned through services, and that a smaller fraction goes to finance administrative expenses or to profits.

A certain increase in return on premiums can be noted, rising from 71 percent in 1985 to almost 75 percent in 1994 (see Table 6.7). Again a clear differentiation among ISAPREs is apparent. While open ISAPREs increased their return yield by almost 10 points, that of closed ISAPREs declined, indicating that cost containment in open ISAPREs has been associated with greater benefits to consumers, but not for closed ISAPREs.

Table 6.7. Indicators of Services in ISAPREs

ISAPRE	% of return on payments			% of additional payments			Membership (thousands)		
	1985	1990	1994	1985	1990	1994	1985	1990	1994
Open	65.9	70.4	74.0	11.5	12.5	16.7	417.7	1,878.2	3,468.2
Outpatient	65.1	71.8	72.9	14.3	8.3	9.4	193.6	883.8	1,482.6
Hospital	75.4	71.0	75.6	6.7	15.8	23.9	90.1	421.5	746.0
Closed	89.2	81.5	80.3	32.1	36.0	38.3	119.0	208.0	190.5
Total	71.1	72.2	74.6	16.1	16.0	18.9	536.7	2,086.3	3,658.8

Source: Superintendency of ISAPREs

With regard to a more detailed comparison of integrated and nonintegrated ISAPREs, no major differences can be seen. If anything has occurred, it has been a convergence between various types of ISAPREs in terms of this return.[19]

Revealed Preferences: membership, additional premiums and grievances. Even though it is clear that membership in the private system has grown in recent years, studies of declared preferences indicate that dissatisfaction with the system is relatively high.[20] These studies, however, do not necessarily reflect the clients' true willingness to pay, and hence satisfaction. Indicators of revealed preferences are therefore more reliable and trustworthy, and three are particularly revealing:

- *Membership.* As has already been emphasized, affiliation with the private system has been very high and persistent, despite the declining gap in spending per beneficiary between the private and public system in recent years. Of the open ISAPREs, those that are integrated into outpatient infrastructure, and to a lesser extent those integrated into the hospital infrastructure, are the ones whose membership has grown most. That would reflect the success of these

---

[19] These results are robust when we correct the values for average income per beneficiary, which are in proportion to their contributions, and hence with their requirements.

[20] See CEP (1993).

schemes in attracting a larger share of demand in a highly competitive market (see Table 6.7).

Closed ISAPREs are increasing their coverage only to a lesser extent, which suggests that their continuance depends on the negotiation of health plans as part of collective bargaining and of "acquired rights." Thus, even though they are not efficient, they may continue to survive without ever becoming predominant in the market.[21]

- *Additional premiums.* Premiums beyond the required payroll deduction constitute an even better indicator of preferences for open ISAPREs than for closed ones. In the former, they are primarily additional voluntary payments that reflect a willingness to pay, while in the latter they are employer contributions that result from union and labor negotiations.

  The magnitude of the extra contributions made by employers is significant. In 1994, such contributions represented 38 percent of total income in closed ISAPREs, as opposed to 16.7 percent in open ones (see Table 6.7). In both cases, they represent a significant increase over the levels in effect in 1985, a possible indicator of cost pressures or of a high income elasticity of the demand for health insurance.

- *Complaints to the Superintendency.* This indicator, calculated per number of affiliates and by period, is available starting in 1991. It shows that the number of consultations and complaints rose from 1,475 in 1991 to 11,270 in 1994. The number of grievances for all open ISAPREs in 1994 was 127.7 per million beneficiaries. This figure was 43.8 per million for ISAPREs with integrated outpatient facilities, which were those that received fewest complaints. That fact could be reflecting both greater satisfaction and less assertiveness on the part of users (who represent lower income sectors in the ISAPRE system).

---

[21] These ISAPREs have additional financing provided by the company.

Structure of the Pharmaceutical Market

While it is true that the analysis of the financing structure in the health sector is currently the most relevant in Chile, the organizational structure of other levels of the input-product chain is also basic for determining performance. Two input markets can be critical—the market for physicians and the supply and distribution of pharmaceuticals—because they constitute focal points of market power that are not readily constrained by greater competitive pressures.

Analysis of the structure of the pharmaceutical market can shed light on variables such as prices and availability of medicines. It is best to analyze the structure of this segment around 1990, when revised legislation made it possible to patent medicines. That development understandably gave rise to the widely circulating hypothesis that the market has become more concentrated and less competitive since that time. Specifically, if there has been greater market concentration, has there been a tendency toward greater collusion in the pharmaceutical market? The existence of collusion at this stage would raise health care costs, particularly in the private sector, which does not have the purchasing power to offset the power of suppliers. Two levels are analyzed here: wholesale production, examined in terms of laboratories, and retail distribution, examined in terms of pharmacies.

Laboratories

Transactions on the pharmaceutical market are estimated to be around $600 million a year, representing around 1.3 percent of Chile's gross domestic product. Of that total, 63 percent is sold by laboratories and 37 percent by the institutional market (the public sector through the State Central Office for Supply, Hospitals and Clinics).

Over the past 30 years, the number of registered laboratories has gradually increased from 64 in 1979 to 82 in 1990, and to 97 in 1994. The share of Chilean laboratories in total sales rose from 17.1 percent over 1967–69 to 31.4 percent over 1982–84, and to 54.4 percent over 1990–93.

In terms of volume, annual growth in units was 3.5 percent during 1977–93. Since 1985, average growth in sale of units has been more vigorous, reaching 6.8 percent annually. Sales expressed in national currency have grown by 7.5 percent and 10 percent in real terms during those same periods.

One of the concerns triggered by these figures is that despite the larger number of laboratories, mean prices (sales/units) increased from a 3.4 percent annual rate in 1985–93 to 7.8 percent between 1990 and 1993. While this indicator may suggest that the sector's competitiveness is declining, its relevance is also questionable, since it is apparently influenced by improvements in quality, product substitution, and the incorporation of patented products. Consequently, this claim must be analyzed in light of trends in other aspects of the structure in order to determine how well it stands up.

A number of studies of the Chilean pharmaceutical industry conclude that the overall concentration of laboratories is no higher than the average of other industries, and that concentration for a market such as Chile's is relatively low when compared with Argentina and Brazil.[22] In order to analyze the problem of concentration adequately, it also important to break down the market into therapeutical categories. Concentration at the level of therapeutical categories has not increased over time.

Table 6.8 shows changes in the concentration indices for sales of the five and 10 largest participants in the industry, as shown in columns C5 and C10. As is apparent both for the market as a whole and for the prescription and over-the-counter markets, the degrees of concentration as measured by C5 and C10 sales are not very high. Nor have they increased over time. Furthermore, the ranking of companies makes it clear that each of the most important companies holds a relatively small share, and that this ranking has been varying significantly over time (Paredes Molina and Vatter, 1996). For example, while Syney-Ross was in first place and Recalcine was in fifth from 1967–69, by 1991–93 Syney-Ross no longer existed and Recalcine was in second place. Moreover, between the 1982–84 and 1991–93 periods, three new companies had entered the 10 largest, and the Laboratorio Chile share dropped from 12.2 percent to 10.4 percent. That suggests considerable fluctuation, as is typical of industries subject to strong competition.

In addition, indices of concentration by therapeutic category have fallen. Thus, whereas in 1984 the average of the C5 concentration index for the various therapeutic categories was 68.5 percent, in 1993 that average was 63 percent. Likewise, the respective numbers for the C10 index were 82 percent and 83.1 percent.

---

[22] See Gómez and Joffre (1987), Fraser and Olcese (1988), and Paredes Molina and Vatter (1996).

Table 6.8. Concentration of Sales of the Five and 10 Largest Companies

	Prescription market		Over-the-counter market		Total	
	C5	C10	C5	C10	C5	C10
1982	30.3	46.1	79.7	95.4	28.2	43.1
1985	23.7	48.0	67.4	85.1	30.2	45.5
1988	30.7	46.4	70.5	88.4	28.7	44.0
1989	31.5	47.3	73.8	90.8	29.7	44.9
1990	29.9	44.6	77.2	93.2	27.8	42.1
1991	32.9	46.2	76.5	94.2	30.7	44.3
1992	33.4	46.3	75.5	94.5	31.2	44.5
1993	31.1	44.3	76.5	94.7	28.9	41.8

Source: International Marketing Services, Geneva, Switzerland (1994).

The grounds for analyzing the therapeutic subcategory level may be that not all products belonging to the same category have to do with the same pathology, and hence findings range from very close substitutes to products that are complementary in their therapeutic effects. This is the most important level to study because it is where most of the products that are truly substitutes for use against particular pathologies would be concentrated. For a group of 31 therapeutic subcategories chosen with regard to their relative importance for the years 1984, 1990 and 1993, once more a pattern toward decentralization of the market was discovered (Paredes Molina, and Vatter, 1996). Finally, the evolution of market concentration by active ingredients, that is, the portion of medications that produce therapeutic effects, has also declined. Thus it can be said that concentration has not increased in the past ten years, since patents were introduced. On the contrary, concentration has fallen in comparison to the level in effect before patents were introduced into the industry and also in comparison to the time when Laboratorios Chile, the largest laboratory in the country, was state property. There has only been one complaint of collusive behavior among laboratories to the antimonopoly commissions. Even so, in this case, which involved Laboratorio Chile (now private) and Recalcine, the other laboratories violated the alleged agreement, so that even if there had been collusion, it was far from successful and was actually self-defeating.[23]

---

[23] See Paredes Molina (1996)

Pharmacies

The other link in the pharmacy chain is distribution, which can be divided into an institutional category and a retail pharmacy category. The former includes purchases made by both public and private health care delivery institutions, which absorb around 21 percent of the supply. The latter encompasses the distribution chain, which leads to sales to final consumers by small and chain pharmacies, which account for the remaining 79 percent.

Within the institutional sector, public sector demand, made up of direct demand for health care services and that of the Central Supply Center, comprises over two-thirds of this segment, but a mere 14 percent of total supply. The private sector, made up of clinics and other hospitalization facilities, represent the remainder, with only 6.5 percent of total supply.

Demand in the pharmaceutical sector is split into medium-size and small pharmacies, which order directly from laboratories and have around 40 percent of the sector; large pharmaceutical chains, with 29 percent of the sector; and distributors, who are middlemen between the laboratories and the pharmacies, with 31 percent of the sector. The latter two do not sell directly at retail, but rather to large drugstore chains and small and medium-sized pharmacies.

As with laboratories, there has been an ongoing struggle in distribution between pharmacy chains, small pharmacies, and some laboratories, and that is where the largest number of complaints to the anti-monopoly commissions have been concentrated. Such complaints may even suggest that there is a great deal of competition at the distribution level. Indeed, most complaints have to do with fact that the pharmacy chains charge low prices and that they demand large discounts from the laboratories. In no complaint is it alleged that there is collusion between chains or any other practice that could really be harmful to the welfare of consumers.

Conclusions

A number of lessons can be drawn from analyzing health care in Chile. The country's current dual system preserves the characteristic virtues and vices of the public and private modes comprising it. Thus, the ISAPRE sector is subject to the problems usually affecting individual insurance plans (adverse selection, short-term coverage, high administration and sales costs), while the vices of the public system are concentrated on the problems of serving users that are typical to bureaucratically organized schemes where financing is supply-driven. The private system has been developing admittedly imperfect structures that have nonetheless made it more efficient over time, especially in comparison to what the state sector delivers.

Indeed, even though the obligation to deduct a fixed percentage of income makes it predictable that membership in the private sector will grow — given the quality of care in the public health care sector — the shift of members from the public to the private sector has far surpassed what would be expected on the basis of income and population growth alone. This demonstrates that the private health care arrangement is a viable and sustainable alternative for a growing proportion of the population. Even so, there is significant room for improving equity within the state system and in the health care system as a whole.

Analysis of the private system suggests that companies in the sector that have been subjected to the disciplinary effects of competition and the market have developed greater administrative efficiency and improved the service they provide their customers, in contrast to companies in the sector that are not subject to competition. This is especially interesting inasmuch as one criticism of the way the health care system operates in Chile (also applicable to the social security system) is that companies spend too much on attracting customers, which would be a simple zero-sum game.

In light of the results, it would seem that distortions from information problems typical of the health care sector do not mean that the use of the market is inefficient. In other words, even though competition imposes transaction costs, ultimately it is beneficial because it disciplines the action of companies and helps contain costs. Nevertheless, the private sector in Chile appears to be successful in containing costs because of the presence of the state sector, which takes in individuals who are more at risk. A definitive conclusion also requires that information on trends in copayments be available.

The evidence suggests that the ISAPREs that are vertically integrated are more efficient than those that are not. In particular, integration toward the outpatient service level seems to be an efficient way to contain costs caused by excessive referrals and especially for abuse of sick leave.

Greater transparency must be encouraged and users must be provided more information. The fact that there is a large number of health plans that are difficult to compare reduces the advantages of competition. Even though rising income in Chile will mean growing private sector coverage, the safety-net role that the public sector has assumed for higher risks and poorer people must be clarified. Otherwise, the system will perpetuate the undesirable features of adverse selection and hazard that characterize it today.

Finally, this chapter analyzed the structure and performance of pharmacies, another link in the production and distribution chain in the health care sector. No collusion or monopoly behavior was found there, nor were there signs of entry barriers that might constitute a bottleneck to future development of the system.

References

Arrow, K. 1963. Uncertainty and the Welfare Economics of Medical Care. *American Economic Review* 52(5): 941–69.

CEP. 1993. Estudio social y de opinión pública No. 20, July 1993. Temas especiales: percepciones y opiniones de la salud en Chile y la evaluación de la gestión del Presidente Aylwin: un modelo explicativo. Documento de Trabajo no. 200, August. Centro de Estudios Públicos, Santiago.

Cheyre, H. 1988. La previsión en Chile, ayer y hoy. Centro de Estudios Públicos, Santiago.

Coase, R. 1987. The Nature of the Firm. *Economica* 4: 386–405.

Diamond, P. 1994. Privatization of Social Security: Lessons from Chile. *Revista de Análisis Económico* 9(1) June: 1–43.

Edwards, S., and A. Edwards. 1987. *Monetarism and Liberalization: The Chilean Experience.* Cambridge, MA: Harper and Row, Ballinger.

Ellis, R., and T. McGuire. 1993. Supply-Side and Demand-Side Cost Sharing in Health Care. *Journal of Economic Perspectives* 7(4): 135–51.

Fisher, R., and J. Gutiérrez. 1992. Análisis económico del rol de la superintendencia de ISAPRE. Superintendencia de ISAPRE, Santiago. Mimeo.

Fisher, R., P. Romaguera, and A. Mizala. 1995. Alternativas de solución para el financiamiento de la salud en la tercera edad en el sistema de ISAPRE. Departamento de Ingeniería Industrial Universidad de Chile, Santiago. Mimeo.

Fraser, W., and R. Olcese. 1988. Análisis de la concentración en el mercado de la industria farmacéutica chilena. In *Sinergia, estudios de administración, economía y ciencias de comportamiento humano,* Vol. 6. Valparaíso, Chile: Universidad Católica de Valparaíso, pp. 1–34.

Fuchs, V., and M. Kramer. 1973. Determinants of Expenditures for Physicians: Services in the U.S. NBER Occasional Paper No. 116.

Gandolfo. 1995. Legislación relacionada con el Sistema Isapre, Anexo Legal. In "Hacia la modernidad en salud." Superintendencia de ISAPRES, Santiago. Mimeo.

Gómez, A., and E. Jofre. 1987. Análisis estratégico de la industria farmacéutica y recomendaciones de política pública. Serie de Estudios CEPAL, Universidad de Chile, Departamento de Ingeniería Industrial. September.

Hasiao, W. 1995. Abnormal Economics in the Health Sector. *Health Policy* 32: 125–39.

Hoffmayer, U., and T. McCarthy. 1994. *Financing Health Care*. Dordrecht, Boston, London: Kluer Academic.

Larrañaga, O. 1995. Los sistemas de salud público y privado en Chile. Inter-American Development Bank, Washington, D.C. Mimeo.

________ . 1996. El sistema de salud dual chileno. Universidad de Chile and CEPAL, Santiago. Mimeo.

Miranda, E., J. Scarpaci, and I. Irarrazaval. 1995. A Decade of HMOs in Chile: Market Behavior, Consumer Choice and the State. *Health and Place* 1(1): 51–59.

Miranda, E., and M. Vergara. 1993. Evolución y estructura del sector salud en Chile. Cuadernos Técnicos 36. Pan American Health Organization, Washington, D.C.

Musgrove, P. 1996. Public and Private Roles in Health: Theory and Financing Patterns. World Bank, Human Development Department, Washington, D.C. Mimeo.

Oyarzo, C. 1991. Análisis crítico de las transformaciones financieras del sector salud en la década de los 80 y propuesta para una reforma. In *Sistemas de salud en transición a la democracia*, ed. J. Jiménez. Santiago: Ministerio de Salud de Chile, pp. 23–42.

————. 1992. Financiamiento del sector de salud en una situación de crisis: el caso chileno. Serie de Investigación 1–58. ILADES/Georgetown University, Programa Post-Grado de Economía, Santiago. November.

Paredes Molina, R. 1996. Autonomía de las instituciones antimonopolio en Chile. Departamento de Economía, Universidad de Chile, Santiago. Mimeo.

————. 1997. Integración vertical: teoría e implicancias de política pública. *Estudios Públicos* (Summer), Centro de Estudios Públicos, Santiago, pp. 189–214.

Paredes Molina, R., and Vatter, J. 1996. Patentes, NAFTA y el mercado farmacéutico en Chile. Ministerio de Relaciones Exteriores, Santiago. Mimeo.

Pauly, M. 1968. The Economics of Moral Hazard: Comments. *American Economic Review* 58(3): 312–15.

Poterba, J. 1994. Government Intervention in the Markets for Education and Health Care: How and Why. Working document No. 4916, MANBER, Cambridge.

Superintendencia de Instituciones de Salud Previsional. 1994. Factores que inciden en la rentabilidad de las ISAPRE abiertas. *Estudios de Circulación Interna* (July): 1–63.

Superintendencia de Seguridad Social. 1994. *Estadísticas de Seguridad Social 1994*, Santiago: SSS.

Valdés, S., C. Díaz, R. Gazitúa, and A. Torche. 1996. Cobertura catastrófica para los cotizantes del sistema ISAPRES. Instituto de Economía, Universidad Católica. Mimeo.

Weisbrod, B. 1991. The Health Care Quadrilemma: An Essay on Technological Change, Insurance, Quality and Cost Containment. *Journal of Economic Literature* 29(2): 30–79.

CHAPTER 7

Regulation and Performance of Health Cooperatives in Uruguay

Gastón J. Labadie[1]

As in many other countries in Latin America, the Uruguayan health system consists of public and private providers. The public sector comprises hospitals and clinics of the ASSE, an agency of the Ministry of Health that provides health services directly and covers from 25 to 30 percent of the population; police and military hospitals and sanitoriums that cover another 10 percent to 15 percent; and other government institutions, like the hospital of the *Banco de Seguros*, which covers specific groups. Although social security subsidizes demand by covering a monthly health payment for those employed in the private sector, it does not directly provide services. Instead, social security transfers a monthly amount to IAMCs (Collective Medical Assistance Institutions - *Instituciones de Asistencia Médica Colectiva*), prepaid health services which make up the most important part of the private institutional sector and provide services covering 52 percent of the population.

In contrast to the rest of the private health sector, these institutions are heavily regulated, at least formally, by the Ministries of Health, Labor and the Economy. They are organized along various lines from the standpoint of property rights—many are physician cooperatives and others are consumer cooperatives called mutual aid societies—and their resources and services

---

[1] Gastón J. Labadie is director at the School of Management and International Studies, Universidad ORT Uruguay.

are vertically integrated to varying degrees. They also operate in markets that are radically different from the standpoint of alternative supply of providers, of the monopsony they face, and of the monopoly or oligopoly power that they maintain vis-à-vis those seeking services. The degree of monopoly power tends to vary according to the department where they are located, given that the capital is different from the rest of Uruguay. The Uruguayan case therefore offers an interesting opportunity to examine the effects of a single regulatory framework applied to two markets that are quite different from each other; to evaluate the consequences of such regulation; and to observe the economic performance of the IAMCs, bearing in mind the incentives offered by their forms of institutional property and governance and the different ways in which compensation of physicians is organized.

This chapter compares the performance and behavior of the two subsidiary systems in terms of the different types of institutions within each subsidiary system, and the different ways in which delivery of services is organized within a particular type of institution.

The first section examines the context of the markets of Montevideo and the rest of the country, along with their regulatory framework. Certain analytical concepts about IAMCs are introduced that make it possible to examine empirically the effects of that regulatory framework and of other organizational aspects that affect the decision made by the insured to join one IAMC or another. The inquiry considers whether there really are two different models; what effects different regulations have had; and whether the different kinds of organization that have operated in Uruguay have displayed differences in terms of the mobility of their members. In particular, the effects found in price regulation make possible a series of reflections on the market aspects that ought to be regulated in Uruguay.

The next section examines the incentives offered by the various types of organizations, particularly in terms of the structure of "property rights" and the governance of the institution, and whether they are owners or employees of health services. Predictions are made based on the premise that imperfect information in health care markets,[2] when associated with the incentives faced by physicians when they operate institutions and have the

------

[2] See Evans, 1974; Pauly, 1980, 1988b; Dranove and White, 1987; Blomqvist, 1991; and Newhouse, 1992.

right to the economic surplus from the organizations in question, produces different collective behavior in terms of investments, relative spending on health care and pay, and other aspects of economic performance and welfare.[3]

Finally, the chapter looks at some forms of governance and organization of medical work within a single type of organization. There is also a case study of the largest IAMC in the country, with a preliminary examination of the effects of the various kinds of organizations and compensation for medical services within it.

Montevideo and the Interior: Regulation and its Effects

Definition of IAMCs (Collective Medical Assistance Institutions)

An IAMC is a prepaid health insurance institution, at least partly run by physicians, that agrees to provide an accessible, broad and comprehensive set of health services. These services are provided by the IAMC's own doctors or by a group of doctors under contract. The services may be provided either at the IAMC's own facilities or in facilities maintained by a contracted group of doctors, but always administered by the institution.

Since the early 1980s, the IAMCs have been differentiated most from other assistance institutions, such as those called partial insurers, by their provision of comprehensive coverage. IAMCs were obliged to offer certain services, only a few of which were excluded by the Ministry of Public Health (MSP). Since 1989, however, these organizations have not been obliged to offer certain high-technology or high-cost services, unless the Ministry indicates otherwise, and since February 1992 they have been permitted to exclude medications. Beyond traditional factors characteristic of institutions, it was this broad and homogenous range of services that differentiated IAMCs, at least theoretically, from other types of organizations, and that made it possible for the IAMCs, after being qualified by the MSP, to accept the regulatory framework intended for them. Finally, the obligatory participation of physicians in running IAMCs is another factor that has set them apart since they were first established by legislation in 1943 (Labadie, et al., 1994).

---

[3] See Sloan, 1988; and Phelps, 1992.

Differences Between the Two Subsidiary Systems

The IAMC market in Montevideo differs substantially from the market in the interior of Uruguay. First, provider institutions have very different scales in terms of the number of those insured and risk profile, the number of physicians, installed capacity, and the reliability of services provided. They also differ with regard to lists and waiting lines and other similar transaction costs. The Montevideo market is very competitive, with 19 IAMCs providing services to the 1.5 million inhabitants concentrated there. It is relatively uniform in terms of the time and distance to services, but IAMCs differ significantly in size, ranging from 7,000 to 270,000 members. The market of inputs into these institutions is characterized by a large supply of physicians (71 physicians for every 10,000 inhabitants in 1990), a concentrated supply of high technology, and a significant private supply in the areas of hospitalization and health care support (see Labadie and Sánchez, 1993).

The subsidiary system of IAMCs in the interior of the country is characterized by relatively oligopolistic markets. In each capital city, only one institution, typically a medical cooperative, provides services in conjunction with the Ministry of Health hospital, the main provider of certain hospital services, which are sometimes contracted by the IAMC. From 1981 to 1990, there was only one IAMC in 15 of the 18 cities in the interior. Hence these IAMCs are characteristically monopolistic and monopsonistic.

In terms of inputs, markets in the interior have a lower supply of physicians (12 for every 10,000 inhabitants in 1990) and other resources, and they offer less freedom of choice to consumers of their services, including those on social security, which subsidizes the demand of private sector employees. On the other hand, this more restricted supply means that they can be monitored informally, and it places more information within reach of a market plagued with imperfections. Both quality and reputation become especially relevant when users must choose an institution.[4]

Differences between the markets of Montevideo and the interior also have to do with the form and degree of relationship between IAMCs, which are organized along different lines, with different degrees of connection

---

[4] See McGuire, 1983; Getzen, 1984; Satterthwaite, 1983; and Haas-Wilson, 1990.

through contracts and ownership that limit competition. The situation gives rise to different negotiations between providers and customers of services, and between providers and customers and the state (which indeed acts as a regulator), professional associations of physicians, and laboratories supplying medicines.

Growth Trend of the Markets

Coverage, Financing and Structure of the Market. The numbers of persons affiliated with IAMCs in Montevideo and the interior has varied. In 1983, IAMCs covered 1.26 million persons, only 300,000 of whom were from the interior (Labadie et al., 1997). Ten years later the system covered 1.5 million and almost 520,000 were from the interior, thereby accounting for almost the entire growth of coverage in this sector. A good portion of the increase of members has been due to increased social security coverage, which covers actively employed people as a third party private sector payer.

    Switching. There is a great deal of switching back and forth between IAMCs, since no restrictions oblige people to remain in them for a minimum period. Even though regulations prohibit "marketing," in practice there are people working on commission who promote membership to consumers, especially those financed by social security. In 1993, 292,000 persons left their IAMCs, and in 1984, 364,000 left, possibly as a consequence of regulatory changes introduced at that time. Since the system was stabilized in 1989, over 305,000 people a year, more than 20 percent of total affiliation, have left their IAMCs. Nevertheless, total membership has increased and remained stable. Thus, people who withdraw from one IAMC appear to join another.

Regulatory Framework of Collective Medical Assistance Institutions[5]

The differences between the markets of Montevideo and the interior are not a response to different regulatory frameworks, since at least in theory both subsidiary systems are under similar regulation for price setting (premiums and copayments); "basket" of services offered; acceptance of members and

---

[5] This section updates studies previously carried out by Labadie, Ramos and Sánchez (1994) and Gherardi, Labadie and Sánchez (1992).

Table 7.1. Timeline of Regulations in Price Control, Movement of Members and Organizational Structure of IAMCs, 1968 to 1992

Year	
1968	• COPRIN: Price controls
1969	• Coordinating Group for Collective Assistance • Categories of prices (1 to 3) • Definition of nonprofit: no remuneration to board members
1975	• ASSE-DISSE: Immediate unlimited entry for private sector employees
1981	• IAMCs provide basic care
1983	• Price controls partly lifted: general ceiling • Definition of basic comprehensive care • Minimum size for IAMC • Automatic incorporation of members of IAMCs that close without examination or extra payment • Complete acceptance 90 days after medical examination: 12 months for operations; 24 months for medical condition. Emergency and surgery at rates set by the MSP
1984	• Prices liberalized (with powers from DINACOPRIN for price deviations) • Ceilings for copayments regardless of premiums
1985	• Price controls reintroduced (after being raised) • Copayments fixed
1986	• Board membership can be "leased" • Requirement on minimum size eliminated
1988	• Limiting age of those entering permitted • Limiting medications permitted • Rights of pregnant women in effect only after 300 days • Rights dependent on results of medical examination for people who switch
1989	• Ceiling for investment contributions • Ceiling for copayments
1990	• Price controls partly lifted: ceiling for premiums and copayments
1992	• Controls on regular payment and copayment entirely lifted • Nominal value of DISSE payment fixed administratively • Monitoring of prices by categories reestablished • DISSE members may be completely rejected • IAMCs allowed to provide "partial" services (without medications)

affiliates; labor relations and pay; structure and internal organization; systems of information and accounting; and tax exemptions associated with their nonprofit institutional status. When some of these regulations began to be developed in 1984, however, the changes were marginally different in terms of dates and other aspects. That makes it possible to utilize the data base available for the 1983-93 period to study the different reactions to some changes in the regulatory framework. Examples are two brief periods in the mid-1980s and early 1990s, when prices were lifted on premiums of mutual aid societies. Such changes were no doubt reflected in differences in membership mobility and a redistribution of surplus in pay or investments.

Table 7.1 summarizes changes over time from 1968 to 1992 of some aspects of the regulatory framework. It shows that the price controls continued until 1983, when a ceiling was established (but subsequently dropped in July 1985). That gave rise to the first complete liberalization of premiums, a process that halted in October 1985 when prices began to be controlled again through the National Office of Costs, Prices and Incomes.

This system was changed once more in late 1990, when controls on premiums were partially lifted. The system changed again in February 1992, when authorization for a complete liberalization of such payments was given, but then changed three months later when price controls were reintroduced. This last control is exercised "informally" and its rules are not clearly established.

The first liberalization of the 1980s was accompanied by changes intended to allow members greater mobility. That was necessary to adjust the system, since minimum limits had been set on the size of institutions between 1983 and 1986. The measure also made it obligatory for the institutions to accept all those who transferred from one institution to another. It established that after 90 days, new members would have full access to all benefits once they had been examined by a physician.

This increased mobility ended in 1988. IAMCs were allowed to select their members on the basis of age limits for entry and risks covered, and the requirement for coverage of medications was eliminated. Authorization was also granted to allow differential rates for pregnant women. The requirement from 1975 that the IAMCs had to automatically accept any person whose payment was financed by social security was modified in 1992, when a nominal payment for those enrolled in the DISSE (Department of Social

Security for Illness) was fixed and institutions were given the right to reject some of their members.

The more recent lifting of price controls was not accompanied by authorizations that would allow adequate mobility for consumers. Had that been the case, the resulting transfers might have forced institutions to adjust their premiums to changes in demand. Neither of the two price liberalizations allowed enough time for this market adjustment to take place: the first lasted 13 months and the second a mere three. Indeed, controls were immediately reestablished after an initial jump in premiums.

IAMCs have also been heavily regulated in other aspects (Table 1.2 in Labadie, Cassoni and Jorcín, 1997). In relatively few areas can business decisions be made freely, particularly with regard to the basket of services and prices, and hence potential strategies for differentiating institutions are curtailed.

If the numerous changes in regulation that have occurred in this sector are also considered, it comes as no surprise that a qualified body of professional managers has not developed, except in handling inflation as a source of financing.[6] In fact, traditionally in the industry board members were not allowed to be remunerated; it is still illegal to hire so-called "promoters" for the various IAMC services (but that has not resolved the problem of those affiliated in DISSE switching, as was noted in the previous section), and it is established that the technical director (by law a physician) is the one ultimately responsible for the performance of the institution, even when he or she is not its owner or co-owner. Organizational objectives are not delineated and hence there are no clear incentives for striving to make IAMCs efficient and effective.

---

[6] Inflation gains have been common in this sector, whose monetary liabilities have traditionally exceeded its assets, leading to a net negative balance of monetary assets and hence an enormous positive exposure to inflation. This feature has enabled the industry to earn no less than 9 percent of its net worth under this heading. The greatest inflation gain occurred in the 1983-84 fiscal year, when the gain was 51 percent of net worth. The system has operated differently in Montevideo, where IAMCs have gained more from inflation than in the interior, which had inflation losses in 1987 and 1988, and at the beginning of the period under consideration (Labadie, Ramos and Sánchez, 1994).

Despite meticulous regulation in many aspects, it is striking that regulation neither assures the quality of services nor even that services are actually provided. The problem of the quality of care is made worse by the limited mobility of members in the interior, where there is little competition between institutions. Quality becomes especially important in organizational forms such as physician cooperatives, where there are certain incentives to minimize costs other than physicians' salaries. Consequently, in a structure so regulated that costs have to be adjusted, it is surprising that more attention has not been given to the quality issue, ever apparent in the variations between delays and waiting lines, and in levels of use[7]

Effects of Regulation[8]

The Decision to Join or Leave an IAMC. Among the regulatory changes during 1983-93, lifting controls on monthly premiums in 1984 and 1985 and in the 1990s, as well as liberalization of copayments in 1989, stand out as the most important in relation to the decisionmaking power of individuals.

Other changes also placed restrictions on institutions, which then reacted by changing conditions for individual clients during the period. This must have been the case in 1984, when institutions had to reach a minimum size in a relatively short time period, and many smaller institutions were absorbed by larger ones. Some small institutions grew fast enough to reach the required size before the time limit imposed by the regulations, while others closed down. Thus, some suddenly lost members, while others expanded by absorbing another institution.

Matters also changed quickly in the interior during those years, particularly up to 1988. IAMCs were created or expanded and FEMI (*Federación Médica del Interior* or Medical Federation of the Interior), which connects physicians associations in each local area, was strengthened. Growth in the interior was related to the already mentioned expansion of social security coverage (extended in 1985 to cover agricultural workers), rising employ-

---

[7] See Labadie, Ramos and Sánchez, 1994.
[8] This section was prepared with A. Cassoni as coauthor. It is based on prior studies up to 1990 (Cassoni and Labadie, 1994). C. Grau also helped with economic work.

ment, and the consolidation of FEMI, which promoted group health agreements with many government institutions (besides social security). In Montevideo, the relative composition of the market changed, as the number of mutual aid institutions fell and the number of medical cooperatives increased. To study the effects of these regulatory changes, and particularly the lifting of price controls, an econometric model was calculated to explain movement by members.[9]

The individual's decision to join or withdraw from an IAMC depends basically on two elements: the individual's perception of the quality and quantity of services offered by the institution, and the price in terms of monthly premiums and copayments. Because quality cannot be observed in advance and consumers do not have statistical information readily available, each consumer has to consider the variables that can be observed as proxies for relevant features in order to evaluate how an institution performs and provides services. Those outside the institution probably have less access to information than those who already belong to it. It is also plausible that they may consider other variables or they consider the same ones but use different indicators.

Economic Specification. Decisions to join or withdraw from an IAMC should be analyzed separately. The initial specification of models includes the same set of explanatory variables and assumes that there is a single market in the country from 1983-93. Thus a panel model with 586 observations is estimated. Although we have chosen not to follow the alternative of estimating a fixed effects model by institution because our specific interest is to examine the impact of some dichotomous variables, a random effects model can be estimated.[10]

The set of data examined includes price variables (premiums and copayments); the size of the institution; attributes associated with scale (net worth, availability of beds and other hospitalization services) and risk level

---

[9] The movement of members entering and leaving an IAMC can be quantified through a migration model that takes into account factors determining the decision to belong to an institution or withdraw from it. Other models cannot be applied because price regulation had been in effect during the period.

[10] It has been possible to calculate a family of models and their results are compatible with those presented here.

(percentage of those enrolled over 65); characteristics of organizational structure (union, nonunion, and mutual aid cooperatives); and dichotomous variables that seek to capture the possible impact of regulatory changes having to do with price setting, minimum size and social security financing. Finally, given the existence of multiple regional markets, the effect on price elasticity of the degree of monopoly power enjoyed by an institution was analyzed.

Finally, the regulatory changes already described refer to two elements: size of the institution and prices. In the case of the former, it will be necessary to define dichotomous variables that capture one-time effects. For example, an exceptional number of entries (or exits) of members for an IAMC may have resulted from the absorption of or merger with another less viable institution as a consequence of changes in regulations. Also, there may be different behavior during certain years as a consequence of not meeting certain new requirements. With regard to price policy, it will be necessary to distinguish the independent effect that these changes could produce in the decision to join the institution or leave it, and its possible impact on price elasticity.

In view of certain previous analyses in which the existence of two markets was established, both subsamples were analyzed separately.[11] While the starting point is a common general specification, it is gradually modified through the imposition of restrictions of exclusion, which allow for a better adjustment of the model. The final result of that process is presented next.

Results: the Decision to Join an IAMC. The decision to join is clearly related to some of the variables proposed, and differs by geographical region, the market being considered, and expected benefit. Table 7.2 presents separately the entries into IAMCs in Montevideo and the interior.

The effect of the number of members is significant because of the importance that the number itself has to the expected flow of entries, owing,

---

[11] A first hypothesis is that there is only one market, as opposed to the hypothesis that there are multiple regional markets. To that end, the general model was calculated first and a Chow test was performed to verify the hypothesis, which was rejected (see Labadie, Cassoni and Jorcín, 1997, Annex 3.3, Section 3.3.1).

Table 7.2. Entries to Collective Medical Assistance Institutions

	Montevideo		Interior	
	Coefficient	Elasticity	Coefficient	Elasticity
Number of members	0.12	0.63	0.28	0.86
Absorptions	2640.09	—	—	—
Premium	0.64	0.2	–0.17	–0.11
Free copayments	–2.78	–0.09	—	—
Nonunion cooperative	2665.46	—	773.70	—
CTIDAYS	—	—	0.95	0.04
YR83	–2821.20	—	—	—
YR95	—	—	2233.75	—
R^2	0.88		0.84	

Source: Labadie, et al. (1997).

among other things, to the natural growth of the member population itself, which is consistently a little higher in the interior. Nevertheless, the scale of the IAMC, which serves to replace the variable of installed capacity, does not turn out to be significant when entries are evaluated. Nor does the number of bed-days in an intensive care unit (ICI) for every thousand members of the IAMC, a variable used as a proxy for the intensity of technology used in the institution's services, turn out to be significant in Montevideo, although it is significant in the interior.

The level of payment, on the other hand, has a distinct effect on inflows of new memberships, depending on the market where the IAMC is located. While people who join in Montevideo see the payment as an indicator of quality—that is, the higher the payment the more people enter— prices in the interior for nonmonopoly institutions have a "price" effect, thereby lowering average income for institutions with higher premiums per member.[12]

---

[12] Even though they are regulated, both monthly premiums and revenues from copayments (*tickets*, or moderating premiums) show significant variations from one institution to another (see Labadie, Cassoni and Jorcín, 1994, Annex 14).

This difference is consistent with the characteristics of the markets, because it is easier to obtain information in small markets like those in the interior than in Montevideo, where there is a more competitive market and less knowledge of the personal characteristics of physicians. This explains the fact that prices act more as "signals." The effect did not vary during periods of liberalization. Nor did copayments have verifiable effects throughout the period in Montevideo or in the interior, although they do have a normal inverse effect on inflows during the more recent liberalization in the 1990s in Montevideo. This did not happen in the interior, however, because it is more monopolistic.

The type of organization also has an effect. In both Montevideo and the interior, nonunion cooperatives had greater inflows of members. This could be because they are more dynamic IAMCs or simply because they are at a different stage of development, since historically they are more recent organizational forms (all after 1960).

Some changes in the regulatory environment were significant, as was expected, although only in Montevideo. As has been noted, of all the price changes, only the more recent liberalization of copayments seems to have affected inflows of members. Some institutions also had an increase at a single moment resulting from their absorption of smaller institutions. In 1983, the figure for inflow was negative in Montevideo, while in 1985 there was an exceptional influx into IAMCs in the interior. The decline in 1983 is not surprising, since that was the most recessionary year of the decade. In addition, people knew that a reform was underway, and it finally took shape in the decrees issued in early 1984. The upswing in 1985 fits perfectly with a change in coverage of social security financing, when DISSE took responsibility for making the monthly payment of rural workers.

Results: the Decision to Withdraw from an IAMC. The decision to withdraw from an institution is not based on the same variables as the decision to join it; particularly important is the effect of the size of the IAMC. The results of the economic estimate of people leaving are presented in Table 7.3.

A larger number of members implies that when people withdraw, other family members or dependents go along with them. This effect is especially great in institutions in the interior, where the larger-size institutions lose fewer people. In Montevideo, on the other hand, the larger IAMCs lose more people—perhaps as a result of reactions to crowding, which is more common in larger institutions. In the interior, professional associa-

Table 7.3. Withdrawals from Collective Medical Assistance Institutions

	Montevideo		Interior	
	Coefficient	Elasticity	Coefficient	Elasticity
Number of members	0.10	0.55	0.36	1.34
Premium	−0.49	−0.17	−0.23	−0.17
Liberalized premiums	752.92	—	362.89	—
Copayments	−4.13	−0.12	3.06	0.13
Size	1739.31	—	−1120.5	—
PARTNCOO	—	—	672.48	—
YR85	—	—	619.89	—
R^2	0.91	—	0.91	

Source: Labadie, et al. (1997).

tion-based cooperatives lose more people. Even so, the net result continues to be positive.

People in IAMCs in Montevideo, whose premiums and copayments are higher, do not leave them so frequently. This situation further supports the idea that premiums are perceived as quality indicators by those who are outside of institutions and have to choose which IAMC to enter. It is taken for granted that those who are in an IAMC have more knowledge about the other attributes of the institution, which are surely correlated with levels of care. In the interior, on the other hand, only premiums seem to have such an effect, because the IAMCs with larger copayments tend to lose more people as a result of the expected price effect.

Lifting controls on premiums in 1984 and 1985 increased the number of withdrawals in both Montevideo and the interior. The effects were again somewhat greater in the more competitive Montevideo market, where they caused an increase in the average number of departures of around 9 percent. The 1992 liberalization, by contrast, had no effect on departures, nor did the liberalization of copayments. These latter liberaiizations, however, lasted only three months and were not associated with measures that would make it easy for members to transfer.

Differences Between Types of Institutions[13]

IAMCs take three characteristic forms: two types of "producer cooperatives" (physicians) and "consumer cooperatives" (users or members), which are usually called *mutualistas*.[14] The first type of physicians cooperatives is those connected to the local physicians' association (the largest IAMC is located in Montevideo and is called CASMU—Aid Center of the Physicians League of Uruguay or *Centre de Asistencia del Sindicato Médico del Uruguay*, and in the interior the original monopolistic cooperatives).[15] The second is medical cooperatives, properly speaking, in which there is a group of associated physicians who hire medical staff to work for them. Although there have been changes more recently, traditionally and for legal reasons that have been in effect since IAMCs were declared nonprofit institutions in 1943, a cooperative physician generally does not earn profits, although he may receive a salary. That presumably gives rise to a number of incentives for members because, besides being on the board, they are service providers. They themselves receive whatever income there is through their earnings as physicians. On the one hand, this creates conflicting incentives in terms of use of services, through physician referrals. On the other hand, an incentive could be generated to increase the proportion of costs destined for medical payments, possibly reducing the amount set aside for investments or other costs. This also leads the current members to raise the cost of joining for new physicians, blocking entry and increasing conflicts with their own professional association, which is sometimes the owner and whose members press for access to employment.

---

[13] This section was coauthored with G. Jorcín and updates the findings of Ramos, Glejberman and Jorcín (1992) and Glejberman and Jorcín (1993).

[14] The distinction was introduced by Labadie and Sánchez (1993). Solari (1992) goes further into the typology.

[15] All physicians' association cooperatives were originally linked to the local physicians' association. Due to legal requirements, they had to become legally distinct. In the interior, this led to the emergence of the Medical Federation of the Interior, which is complex in structure. That also happened with CASMU, which operates as the Montevideo association for such purposes.

The third category of IAMCs is mutual aid society cooperatives, the oldest system in Uruguay, having begun with ethnic groups in 1853. Their governing structure is similar to that of a consumer cooperative whose board members are elected by the members. Besides being obliged to be part of the board (by 1943 legislation), physicians are hired and paid on salary. They provide services, but do not decide which services the institution operates or buys. Hence the degree of vertical integration of services could be very different in such institutions.

Effects of Various Kinds of Organization

Given that health care providers both own and administer services in physician cooperatives, their economic incentives are likely to lead to different behavior than that found in mutual aid societies in various ways. This is particularly so with regard to accounting and financial performance and investment rates; to vertical integration of services (to what extent services are bought externally or produced within the IAMC); and to a larger wage share in total costs, favoring the distribution of earnings among cooperative members. Behavior will vary with regard to usage levels because one way to generate savings and surplus is to reduce the use of services if one is the owner, or to increase usage by inducing greater demand when one is the supplier.

Bottom Line, Investment and Surpluses or Profits. Given the incentives proper to physician cooperatives in particular, profits or surpluses of institutions ought to tend toward zero, regardless of the operating situation, since by law the residual surplus cannot be distributed. In any case, such operating surpluses are only necessary when further investments, above and beyond the existing investment surcharge, are advisable.

As Table 7.4 indicates, the expected differences are borne out empirically. Mutual aid societies generally have greater net income with respect to revenues, and systematically less investment over the period, even when they do not contract hospitalization services or intensive care.

Table 7.4. Net Income and Investment, 1984-93
(In percent)

Year	Mutual aid societies		Nonprofessional associations		CASMU		Professional associations		Total for country	
	Net Income/ Revenues	Investment	Net Income/ Revenues	Investment	Net Income/ Revenues	Investment	Net Income/ Revenues	Investment	Net Income/ Revenues	Investment
1984	19.48	1.63	0.87	4.17	3.49	5.57	5.20	5.74	10.02	3.76
1985	10.08	2.38	18.11	2.14	−0.14	2.98	4.51	4.18	7.88	2.90
1986	8.59	1.93	0.68	1.71	2.65	2.55	5.47	5.15	5.27	2.82
1987	6.71	2.54	4.64	2.04	−16.81	2.72	2.51	4.10	0.19	2.88
1988	−2.08	2.30	−1.14	2.88	3.19	4.25	−2.52	5.35	−0.93	3.56
1989	1.41	2.21	4.48	10.91	8.03	2.45	5.72	5.58	4.43	4.70
1990	5.00	3.13	1.97	3.48	3.21	5.21	2.54	6.46	3.43	4.53
1991	8.24	4.89	9.26	6.45	11.36	3.93	9.99	5.31	9.54	5.20
1992	0.21	4.51	−1.79	6.16	1.72	4.95	2.08	6.85	0.58	5.68
1993	8.81	4.97	4.66	5.55	4.25	5.70	3.72	5.25	5.49	5.33
Mean	6.65	3.05	4.17	4.55	2.09	4.03	3.92	5.40	4.59	4.14

Table 7.5. Annual Expenditures in Services per Member, 1991–93
(In thousands of 1990 pesos)

Year	Total	Mutual aid societies	Nonprofessional associations	CASMU	Professional societies
Expenditures in contracted services per member					
1991	50.60	39.21	77.20	51.96	40.62
1992	61.23	40.90	101.86	58.00	51.68
1993	74.10	42.85	126.75	71.64	65.01
Expenditures in contracting hospitalization services per member					
1991	15.70	6.03	28.58	22.76	10.75
1992	20.52	7.30	40.14	28.39	13.64
1993	25.47	4.03	51.78	37.65	18.61
Expenditures in contracting adult ICU per member					
1991	2.81	1.70	5.75	1.36	2.47
1992	3.63	0.87	8.49	1.80	3.54
1993	4.84	1.31	12.30	2.86	3.67
Expenditures in contracting child ICU per member					
1991	1.54	1.34	1.23	1.84	1.75
1992	1.57	0.89	1.76	1.84	1.85
1993	1.84	1.89	2.42	0.92	1.88
Expenditures in contracted services/member (excluding simple hospitalization and ICU)					
1991	30.55	30.14	41.64	26.00	25.66
1992	35.50	31.84	51.47	25.96	32.65
1993	41.95	35.62	60.25	30.21	40.85

Note: In 1990, the exchange rate was 1.150 Uruguayan pesos per U.S. dollar.

Vertical Integration and Hiring of Services

As can be seen in Table 7.5, those institutions that are cooperatives (except mutual aid societies) are the ones that spend more in hiring services. This spending is especially high for hospitalization and outpatient clinical services. Part of this hiring may be due to reasons of scale, given that the numbers of members in nonprofessional association cooperatives in Montevideo may not justify having all services vertically integrated.

Table 7.6 shows the expenditure structure of the various types of institutions. The highest proportion of services hired is found in cooperative institutions not based on professional associations, and next in other kinds of cooperatives. In nonprofessional association cooperatives, however, salaries do not constitute an especially high proportion of spending (between 13 percent and 15 percent), while in professional association-based cooperatives, especially those in the interior, the salary proportion is significantly higher (between 28 percent and 30 percent).

Impact of Remuneration and Distribution of Profits on Other Spending

Because of the property rights structure in institutions, surpluses are likely to be distributed through salaries, especially in medical cooperatives connected with a professional association. That ought to be reflected particularly in higher physician salaries, perhaps at the expense of administrative pay and other categories of spending in the institution.

By calculating the amount spent per member on fixed salaries, service payments, and externally contracted clinical services (radiology, sonograms and others), further evidence emerges consistent with predictions, as presented in Table 7.7.

In 1993, the IAMCs that spent more on salaries and clinical services per member (not in proportional terms, because that was already considered) are, first, professional association cooperatives from the interior, followed by CASMU, nonassociation-based cooperatives, and, finally, mutual aid societies. This same order is applicable to payment-per-service, as was also to be expected, given the incentives of professional association cooperatives not to integrate services vertically. Nevertheless, fixed salaries for physicians follow a somewhat different order because the wage bill per affiliate is significantly lower in cooperatives that are not based on professional associations.

Except for 1993, in no years did the order follow the same structure, because CASMU offers fixed salaries per member that are low in comparison to association and mutual aid cooperatives. The result is that total CASMU spending on medical pay and services is comparable to that of mutual aid societies (but their spending on payment per treatment is more than double).

The fact that nonassociation cooperatives spend so little could be due to size. The number of affiliates might make it economically infeasible to

Table 7.6. Total Expenditures for Goods and Services, 1991 to 1993

(In percent)

Year	Total personnel	Remuneration				Other expenditures			
		Total of support personnel	Physicians with fixed remuneration	Physicians with remuneration per treatment	Medications	Services contract outside	Hospitalizations outside	Hospitalization of adults outside	Hospitalization of children outside
			Support personnel						
Mutual aid societies									
1991	50.7	39.5	14.0	3.1	17.0	11.0	1.7	0.5	0.4
1992	52.4	40.8	14.7	3.2	17.2	9.8	1.7	0.2	0.2
1993	54.4	43.3	15.7	3.3	16.2	9.2	0.9	0.3	0.4
Nonprofessional associations									
1991	42.8	30.7	10.3	5.0	13.4	22.4	8.3	1.7	0.4
1992	42.8	30.7	10.4	5.1	13.1	23.9	9.4	2.0	0.4
1993	42.4	30.2	9.0	5.5	12.1	24.2	9.9	2.4	0.5
CASMU									
1991	50.3	43.0	10.9	7.5	19.5	14.8	6.5	0.4	0.5
1992	51.0	42.8	11.6	8.0	18.7	14.3	7.0	0.4	0.5
1993	52.5	45.5	15.0	7.1	16.9	14.5	7.6	0.6	0.2
Professional associations									
1991	54.1	44.6	20.1	8.3	14.0	14.7	3.9	0.9	0.6
1992	54.7	45.3	21.0	9.1	14.3	15.1	4.0	1.0	0.5
1993	53.7	44.5	19.3	9.8	14.1	15.6	4.5	0.9	45.0

Table 7.7. Expenditures in Remunerations per Member, 1991 to 1993
(Thousands of 1990 pesos)

Year	Mutual aid societies	Nonprofessional associations	CASMU	Professional associations
Expenditures in fixed remuneration				
1991	49.67	35.30	38.29	55.50
1992	61.29	44.51	47.05	72.20
1993	73.59	46.90	74.41	80.64
Expenditures in remuneration per treatment				
1991	10.95	17.31	26.31	22.99
1992	13.39	21.71	32.33	31.13
1993	15.63	28.82	35.11	40.99
Expenditures in medical remuneration				
1991	60.62	52.61	64.60	78.48
1992	74.68	66.22	79.37	103.33
1993	89.22	75.72	109.52	121.64
Expenditures in remuneration and contracted clinic services				
1991	90.76	94.25	90.60	104.14
1992	106.52	117.69	105.33	135.98
1993	124.84	135.97	139.73	162.49

Note: In 1990, the exchange rate was 1.151 Uruguayan pesos per U.S. dollar.

establish contracts with certain kinds of medical specialists. CASMU, by contrast, has over 250,000 members, and hence it could integrate services vertically as is done by mutual aid societies with even fewer members.

Hence, the explanation that CASMU and nonprofessional association physician cooperatives spend little on salaries or fixed remuneration cannot be based on the same considerations. CASMU has relatively low fixed spending, offset by relatively high spending per treatment. This latter is comparable only to spending of other association-based cooperatives (which moreover have higher fixed expenditures, as one would expect). Cooperatives not based on associations, by contrast, spend a low proportion on service reimbursals in comparison to fixed salaries, and their low fixed expenditure could be due to the smaller number of physicians per person enrolled, which must be lower than in other institutions. This interpretation is consistent with the much lower number of nonemergency medical visits observable in this type of IAMC, a factor which may affect the quality of care. However, as long as there are no statistics on physicians per member, it is difficult to draw completely valid conclusions.

The increase in remuneration and the proportion of spending that it represents do not seem to have had any effect on annual investment per member. Investment seems to have a force of its own, perhaps related more to the so-called investment surcharge — an extra payment that is charged to members with the permission of the health authorities, who decide on the merits of the proposed investment. In this case, the additional charges must be used solely for the proposed investment. Therefore this regulation may be resolving the problem of potential incentives to underinvestment. Capital funds seem to be associated with the average size of IAMCs in each category. By contrast, spending on medication (goods consumed) per member has evolved as shown in Table 7.8, with mutual aid societies taking the lead over CASMU in spending (they were even in 1993).

Spending by these two types of institutions is much greater than that of the nonprofessional association cooperatives in Montevideo, and still greater than professional association cooperatives in the interior. Remuneration of physicians in the interior is a much higher proportion of spending, even though the gap that used to separate these institutions has gradually been closing. The incentives of mutual aid societies and CASMU must be different, despite their similar expenditures on medications relative to the lower levels of spending in the other cooperatives. It may be that some aspects of CASMU's internal organization favor over-prescription by physicians (Kraft and van der Schulenberg, 1986).

The Care Center of the Physicians Union of Uruguay: a Case Study

The governing structures of CASMU are heavily dependent on medical service providers, since CASMU is owned by the medical association as a whole. By reason of this power the physicians enjoy in running the institution and serving on its board, treatment services that a private doctor can provide

Table 7.8. Expense in Consumables per Member, 1983-1993
(Thousands of 1990 pesos)

Year	Total	Mutual aid societies	Nonprofessional associations	CASMU	Professional associations
1983	55.73	62.52	44.62	71.62	38.25
1984	53.76	59.02	41.04	73.66	38.13
1985	58.35	59.91	50.51	84.52	41.30
1986	60.39	71.08	45.58	78.97	43.97
1987	58.55	72.11	42.22	68.88	44.17
1988	57.23	73.14	45.36	68.68	41.94
1989	56.97	73.84	44.83	70.21	41.46
1990	54.23	75.96	33.61	68.23	40.82
1991	66.97	82.51	62.24	81.27	49.98
1992	78.67	96.42	73.37	89.89	61.67
1993	87.41	99.24	82.92	100.70	73.55

Note: In 1990, the exchange rate was 1.151 Uruguayan pesos per U.S. dollar.

tend to be decentralized. This peculiar feature is made obvious in the prominence of fee-for-service arrangements in the total sum of physician payments made by CASMU, a point mentioned previously. Consequently, we can do some preliminary tests of whether these systems affect the levels of usage and the rate of excessive prescriptions as a result of these delivery arrangements, which are in turn connected to particular forms of medical remuneration.

Types of Organization and Remuneration

For medical services provided in clinics, CASMU works in two different ways. In the centralized scheme, physicians work in the institution's clinics, while in the decentralized scheme, physicians provide care in clinics that do not belong to CASMU. General surgery and all surgical specializations except for gynecology and otorhinolaryngology are centralized, while general medicine, pediatrics and all medical specializations, except for physical therapy and internal medicine, are decentralized.

    Centralized Physicians and Surgery. Until 1992, a centralized surgeon charged only an hourly wage for work at the clinic, but since 1993 the per hour price has been supplemented with an extra payment per patient served. The physician must handle no more than six patients per hour in clinic work.

With regard to surgical work, CASMU organizes its surgical services in departments and pays for the various functions that the surgical specialist performs: consultation, team and emergency surgeries, and emergency life support.

Decentralized Physicians. Medical services that are decentralized (or by zone) have always been particularly significant for CASMU. CASMU is a service organization under a professional association, whose purpose is to provide employment opportunities for all its members. The traditional policy has been to allow all professionals who were members of the Medical Union of Uruguay (SMU) to appear on CASMU's medical listing. Consumers retained free choice, and individual services were reimbursed. Faced with an explosive growth in the number of physicians, which tripled over the previous 30 years, entry of further decentralized physicians was halted under the military government until 1984. In response to pressure from young doctors, the SMU in 1987 decided to open the listing, and a large number of new physicians was admitted. Until February 1992, consultations and nonemergency house calls of decentralized physicians were charged on a per service basis. In almost all specialties, the physician is limited to seeing no more than six patients per hour at the clinic, except for psychiatrists, neurologists and physical therapists, who can see no more than four. In February 1992, as CASMU was financially strapped, two steps were taken with regard to decentralized physicians: professionals with fewer than 10 orders a month were put on administrative leave, and the payment system for the rest was changed. The fee-for-service system was replaced by a fixed salary that was equivalent to the average orders performed the previous year. If professionals on administrative leave are left aside, on September 15, 1992, there were 1,656 decentralized physicians active in CASMU, including 794 general practitioners, 213 pediatricians, 616 specialists, and 33 consulting physicians.

Empirical Evidence of Levels of Usage

As can be seen in Table 7.9, which shows the number of nonemergency visits per thousand people enrolled in the various types of organization, CASMU is used much more than other types of IAMCs in general medicine and in pediatrics, both in Montevideo and the interior. Both specializations show a

Table 7.9. Nonemergency Visits per 1,000 Persons, by Type of IAMC, 1983–89

	Mutual aid societies	Nonprofessional association cooperatives	CASMU	Professional association cooperatives	Mutual aid societies	Nonprofessional association cooperatives	CASMU	Professional association cooperatives
	1983				**1984**			
Outpatient clinic	3,189	3,159	5,610	3,229	3,081	2,971	5,347	3,336
Surgery	835	749	590	800	779	729	472	787
Gyn. & ob.	353	341	359	391	337	328	344	463
Pediatrics	545	474	830	664	505	440	765	607
Other	1	5		25	0			8
Total	4,923	4,728	7,388	5,108	4,703	4,468	6,928	5,201
	1985				**1986**			
Outpatient clinic	3,069	3,000	5,846	3,927	3,285	2,998	5,487	3,680
Surgery	747	719	372	844	851	729	610	833
Gyn. & ob.	336	347	354	559	375	361	638	575
Pediatrics	476	435	788	676	555	436	752	614
Other	1			8				10
Total	4,629	4,500	7,359	6,014	5,066	4,524	7,487	5,711
	1988				**1989**			
Outpatient clinic	3,192	2,795	5,847	3,748	3,093	2,639	6,045	3,402
Surgery	855	724	541	795	807	716	564	767
Gyn. & ob.	369	378	342	515	378	423	343	585
Pediatrics	569	498	597	601	566	499	677	585
Other		4		15	1	12		14
Total	4,985	4,399	7,327	5,674	4,845	4,289	7,629	5,353
	1990				**1991**			
Outpatient clinic	3,128	2,343	5,654	3,244	3,293	2,592	6,900	3,415
Surgery	830	646	658	746	907	704	786	750
Gyn. & ob.	373	353	373	586	406	404	404	453
Pediatrics	567	448	628	566	582	454	738	505
Other	1	14		12	1	6		12
Total	4,899	3,804	7,313	5,154	5,189	4,160	8,828	5,135
	1992				**1993**			
Outpatient clinic	3,244	2,493	5,842	3,578	3,084	2,283	6,715	3,623
Surgery	893	700	764	780	686	596	775	812
Gyn. & ob.	393	399	369	454	312	341	339	487
Pediatrics	546	442	573	501	518	395	590	536
Other	1	1		16	1	2775		18
Total	5,077	4,035	7,548	5,329	4,601	3,620	8,419	5,476

Note: Totals do not agree due to rounding.

similar pattern in remuneration and usage. Indeed, usage levels jumped in 1985 when physicians rejoined the institution after the military government intervention ended. Usage jumped again between 1986 and 1988, when the lists were opened to bring in 700 more physicians. The rising usage rates that ensued until 1989 fell in 1990, continued to fall in 1991, and fell again when another 700 physicians were removed from the lists. Figures for 1993 may reflect new forms of remuneration for each medical service, although the data do not permit definitive conclusions. On the other hand, levels of use of surgery and gynecology were lower than those of other institutions in both Montevideo and the interior.

The evidence plainly shows a significant difference between utilization rates prompted by centralized or decentralized organizational practices, and by payment on a fixed salary or fee-for-service basis.

Conclusions

Econometric analysis of the effects of regulation on the two subsidiary systems studied, in Montevideo and in the interior of Uruguay, indicates that they have reacted differently to changes in regulations. In Montevideo, premiums are perceived as an indicator of quality by those who enroll as members and also by those who leave IAMCs. In the interior, on the other hand, payments charged by nonmonopoly institutions tend to dissuade entry of new members, but they are indicators of quality for those who leave. Nevertheless, this dissuasive effect cannot be seen when the payment of monopolistic IAMCs in the interior is examined.

In Montevideo, copayments, like premiums, are associated with quality and have a negative effect on numbers of people leaving. Lifting price controls did not have effects on inflows in Montevideo or the interior, but did increase exits in the mid-1980s, to a somewhat greater extent in Montevideo.

The more recent lifting of controls on copayments in the 1990s had a price effect because it lowered inflows in Montevideo, but not in the interior, which is more monopolistic. Nor did these liberalizations affect the number of people leaving. The regulatory changes in the area of prices had no effect on people entering, in the absence of rules that would have facilitated mobility between institutions, or because mobility was not possible because of the monopolistic character of the market.

In this sense, empirical evidence indicates that consumers are sensitive to price variation and that the mechanisms of supply and demand seem to operate if allowed by the market structure. In the case of Montevideo, price regulation would not be justified if it were associated with other types of regulation that could assure a certain quantity and quality of health services. Hence, mechanisms that can increase market competitiveness and prevent adverse risk selection or passing off of risks seem to be especially important for efficiency of markets by producing and publicizing reliable information about quality of care (Enthoven and Singer, 1995). Thus the price signal content ought to decrease.

Such information and regulation with regard to quality of care ought to be more efficient than what now exists in Uruguay, where regulation presumably standardizes benefits. However, in practice, when this standardization operates in conjunction with price regulation, it actually only introduces "noise" into the system. The existence of such regulations enables IAMCs to claim that they are providing the same services, when actually this is only a "formal" appearance. In practice, institutions offer very different packages, and individuals ought to know how to distinguish one from the other through the signal content of their premiums, among other things. The importance of social security as a central actor in the current IAMC system ought to make it easier to introduce policies along these lines.

Besides the effects of regulation, this chapter has examined the effects of the property and governance structure of IAMCs. Although evidence is not conclusive, because a multivariate analysis was not carried out, it was found that professional association cooperatives subcontract more outside clinical services. Those connected to professional associations subcontract somewhat less, and devote the highest proportion of total spending to physicians' salaries.

The high wage share paid to physicians, a likely consequence of the way professional association cooperatives distribute their "surplus," seems to have effects on other expenditures of the institution. Although spending on medications per member in those IAMCs that are professional association cooperatives has increased in the past decade, it remains the lowest in absolute terms. Cooperatives not tied to professional associations are next in terms of spending on medications per member, and this figure was was highest in mutual aid societies and in CASMU.

It is surprising that spending should be so high at CASMU, since it is a professional association cooperative. However, it may be that the use of medications in this IAMC is related more to its system of compensation and the way it is organized, which seem to favor overprescribing and thereby lead to greater demand for such inputs. Indeed, in the case study of CASMU, it is found that the range of schemes and physician compensation mechanisms encourage greater demand for what are called "decentralized" services (pediatrics and gynecology), which are paid primarily on a fee-for-service basis.

Investment, on the other hand, does not seem to be associated with the organizational characteristics of the IAMC. Existing regulations oblige institutions to propose investment plans to the Ministry of Health, and, if they are regarded as worthwhile, additional financing through an investment "surcharge" is authorized. It may be that through such a monthly "surcharge" beyond the IAMC premium, compensation is being made for the effect of incentives to underinvest by cooperatives whether related to professional organizations or not. That explains the absence of the expected pattern across institutions, and would speak in favor of such regulation.

References

Blomqvist, A. 1991. The Doctor as Double Agent: Information Asymmetry, Health Insurance and Medical Care. Journal of Health Economics 10 (4):411–32.

Bonus, H. 1986. The Cooperative Association as a Business Enterprise: A Study in the Economics of Transactions. *Journal of Institutional and Theoretical Economics* 142: 310–39.

Cassoni, A., L. DeBrock, and G. Labadie. 1993. Utilization in Uruguayan HMOs: An Econometric Study. GEOPS. Mimeo.

Cassoni, A., and G. Labadie. 1994. The Decision to Join or Leave a IAMC: An Econometric Study. GEOPS. Mimeo.

Cook, K., S. Shortell, D. Conrad, and M. Morrisey. 1983. A Theory of Organizational Response to Regulation: The Case of Hospitals. *Academy of Management Review* 8(2): 193–205.

Dranove, D., and A. Satterthwaite. 1992. Monopolistic Competition When Price and Quality are Not Perfectly Observable. *Rand Journal of Economics* 23(4): 517–34.

Dranove, D., and W. White. 1987. Agency and the Organization of Health Care Delivery. *Inquiry* 24(4): 405–15.

Ellis, R., and T. McGuire. 1993. Supply-Side and Demand-Side Cost Sharing in Health Care. *Journal of Economic Perspectives* 7(4):135–51.

———. 1990. Optimal Payment Systems for Health Services. *Journal of Health Economics* 9(4): 375–96.

Enthoven, A., and S. Singer. 1995. Market-Based Reform: What to Regulate and by Whom. *Health Affairs* (Spring): 105–19.

Evans, R., 1974. Supplier-Induced Demand: Some Empirical Evidence and Implications. In *The Economics of Health and Medical Care*, ed. Mark Perlman. London: Macmillan, pp. 66–77.

Felman, R., and J. Begun. 1978. The Effects of Advertising Restrictions: Lessons from Optometry. *Journal of Human Resources* 13 (supplement): 247–62.

Folland, S., A. Goodman, and M. Stano. 1993. *The Economics of Health and Health Care*. New York: Macmillan.

Frech, H.E., III. 1986. Preferred Provider Organizations and Health Care Competitions. In *Private and Public Health Insurance: Research and Policy*, ed. H.E. Frech, III. Cambridge, MA: Ballinger Publishing Co., pp. 24.

Gaynor, M. 1989. Competition Within the Firm: Theory Plus Some Evidence from Medical Group Practice. *Rand Journal of Economics* 29(1): 59–76.

Gaynor, M., and M.V. Pauly. 1990. Compensation and Productivity in Partnerships: Evidence from Medical Group Practice. *Journal of Political Economy* 90.

Getzen, T.E. 1984. A Brand Name Theory of Medical Group Practice. *Journal of Industrial Economics* 33: 199–215.

Gherardi, A., G. Labadie, and D. Sánchez. 1992. La asistencia médica colectiva en el Uruguay: algunos aspectos históricos. *Revista Noticias* 56: 16–18.

Glejberman, D., and G. Jorcín. 1993. Inversiones en la IAMC. GEOPS. Mimeo.

Greenwood, M.J. 1976. Research on Internal Migration in the United States: A Survey. *Journal of Economic Literature* 14: 397–433.

Haas-Wilson, D. 1990. Consumer Information and Providers' Reputations. *Journal of Health Economics* 999(3): 321–33.

Hansmann, H. 1985. The Organization of Insurance Companies: Mutual versus Stock. *Journal of Law, Economics and Organizations* 1(1).

Held, P., and U. Reinhardt. 1979. Analysis of Economic Performance in Medical Group Practices. Report on project 79–05, Mathematica Policy Research, Inc., Princeton.

Kraft, K., J. van der Schulenberg, and M. Graf. 1986. Co-insurance and Supplier-induced Demand in Medical Care: What Do We Have to Expect as the Physician's Response to Increased Out-of-Pocket Payments? *Journal of Institutional and Theoretical Economics* 142: 360–79.

Kralewski, J., L. Pitt, and D. Shatin. 1985. Structural Characteristics of Medical Group Practices. *Administrative Science Quarterly* 30: 34–45.

Labadie, G., A. Cassoni, and G. Jorcín. 1997. Regulación y desempeño comparado de dos subsistemas privados de salud en el Uruguay. Serie de Documentos de Trabajo, R-307, Oficina del Economista Jefe. Inter-American Development Bank, Washington, D.C. July.

Labadie, G., and D. Sánchez. 1993. El Sector Salud en el Uruguay. In *Estructura y comportamiento del sector salud en la Argentina, Chile y el Uruguay*. Cuaderno Técnico 36, Pan American Health Organization, Washington, D.C.

Labadie, G., A. Ramos, and D. Sánchez. 1994. Instituciones de asistencia médica colectiva en el Uruguay: regulación y desempeño. In Serie Políticas Sociales, No. 6, Comisión Económica para América Latina y el Caribe, Washington, D.C., p. 49.

McGuire, T. 1983. Patients' Trust and the Quality of Physicians. *Economic Inquiry* 21: 203–222.

McGuire, T., and M. Pauly. 1991. Physician Response to Fee Changes with Multiple Payers. *Journal of Health Economics* 10(4): 385–410.

Newhouse, J.P. 1992. Pricing and Imperfections in the Medical Care Marketplace. In *Health Economics Worldwide*, eds. P. Zweifel and H. Frech. Norwell MA and Dordrecht: Kluwer Academic, pp. 3–22.

————. 1978. The Structure of Health Insurance and the Erosion of Competition in the Medical Marketplace. In *Competition in the Health Care Sector: Past, Present, and Future*, eds. Lawrence Goldberg and Warren Greenberg. Washington, D.C.: Federal Trade Commission.

Pauly, M.V. 1988a. A Primer on Competition in Medical Markets. In *Health Care in America: The Political Economy of Hospitals and Health Insurance*, ed. H. Frech. San Francisco: Pacific Research Institute for Public Policy.

————. 1988b. Market and Power, Monopsony, and Health Insurance Markets. *Journal of Health Economics* 7(2): 111–28.

————. 1980. *Doctors and Their Workshops*. Chicago: University of Chicago Press.

Phelps, C. 1992. *Health Economics*. New York: Harper Collins.

Ramos, A., D. Glejberman, and G. Jorcín. 1992. *Situación financiera y patrimonial de las IAMC*. CERES, Montevideo. Mimeo.

Rizzo, J., and R. Zeckhauser. 1990. Advertising and the Price, Quantity, and Quality of Primary Care Physician Services. *Journal of Human Resources* 27(3): 381–421.

Satterthwaite, M. 1985. Competition and Equilibrium as a Driving Force in the Health Services Sector. In *Managing the Service Economy: Prospects and Problems*, ed. R.P. Inman. Cambridge University Press, pp. 239–72.

Sloan, F. 1988. Property Rights in the Hospital Industry. In *Health Care in America: The Political Economy of Hospitals and Health Insurance.* San Francisco: Pacific Research Institute for Public Policy, pp. 103–41.

Solari, A. 1992. Asistencia médica colectiva: formas de organización y marco normativo. In *Descripción e Indices*, No. 10, Centro de Estudios de la Realidad Económica y Social (CERES).

Stiglitz, J. 1987. The Causes and Consequences of the Dependence of Quality on Price. *Journal of Economic Literature* 25: 1–48.

Vanderkamp, J. 1972. Return Migration: Its Significance and Behavior. *Western Economic Journal* 10: 460–65.

Wolinsky, A. 1993. Competition in a Market for Informed Experts. *Rand Journal of Economics* 24(3): 380–98.